THE GARDEN AS A FINE ART

FROM ANTIQUITY TO MODERN TIMES

F. R. COWELL

Houghton Mifflin Company Boston
1978

Dedicated by permission to the
Royal Patrons
and in honour of the Presidents, the Councils,
Fellows and Members of The Royal Horticultural Society,
The National Trust of Great Britain, their staffs,
and of Garden Clubs and Societies who seek
everywhere to preserve and develop
Garden-making as a Fine Art.

ISBN 0-395-27065-0

First Printing

Printed in Great Britain

CONTENTS

The author and publishers would like to thank the following museums, institutions and photographers for permission to reproduce illustrations and for supplying photographs:

Agyptisches Museum, Staatliche Musseen Preussischer Kulturbesitz, Berlin, (photo Jürgen Liepe) 13 below; Heather Angel 91; Ashmolean Museum, Griffith Institute, 13 above, 55; Atheneum Library 10–11, *17* below, 21 below, 22, 23, 26; John Bethell *145*; British Library *17* above, *19*, 36, *37*, 70, 78, 81, 86, *121* above and below, *141*; Peter Coats *177*; Cooper-Bridgeman Library 138; Michael Holford 30, 92, *124* (photo Janet Chapman), *142*; Angelo Hornak *197*; A. F. Kersting 97, 100; William MacQuitty *38*, 60–61, 120, 126, *198*; Mansell Collection 12, 14–15, 21 above, 32–3, 47, 48, 50, 185; 201; Metropolitan Museum of Art, New York, Louisa E. McDurney Gift Fund, 129; Museum of Fine Arts, Boston, 95; National Portrait Gallery 170, 171; Popperfoto 16; J. Powell 34; Kenneth Scowan *200*; Ronald Sheridan *18*, *20*, *25*; Edwin Smith 1, 134–5, *143*, 146, 148, 149 below, 153, 159, 161 above and below, 168–9, 171–2, 182, 207, 219, 223, endpapers; G. Towell 43; Victoria and Albert Museum *39*, *40*, 65, 68, 94, 98, 99, *122–3* (photo Michael Holford), 127 below, 131, 139, 149 above, 165, 167 below, 181; Weidenfeld and Nicolson Archive 2, 4, 28, 29, 41, 51, 54, 55, 57, 59, 62, 73, 74, 75, 76, 83, 89, 97, 102–3, 104, 108, 109, 110, 111, 115, 116, 117, 127 above, 155, 157, 160, 163, 164, 167 above, 174, 175, *180*, 186, 188, 190, 192–3, 195 above and below, 196, 199, 203, 204, 205, 206, 208, 210, 212, 213, 214–15, 217; Jeremy Whittaker *178–9*, 183.

Numbers in italics refer to colour illustrations

Picture research by Juliet Scott

ACKNOWLEDGMENTS

This essay on gardens in their social and cultural setting would have been an even more hazardous venture without the friendly criticism and advice which some of its pages had from Mr Cyril Aldred and Mr Peter Clayton on the early Egyptians; Mrs Joan Oates on Mesopotamian lands; Mr John Hamilton on the Arabs; Mr Basil Gray on the Persians; Professor Sterling Dow on the ancient Greeks; Mlle J. Auboyer on early India; Dr Joseph Needham on China; Dr Hidé Ishiguro on Japan and India; Mr Patrick Synge on Mediterranean lands; Mr Christopher Brickell and Mr P. F. M. Stageman of the Royal Horticultural Society; and Mr G. A. Jellicoe for general criticisms.

I owe a great debt to the publishers, Weidenfeld and Nicolson, for undertaking the book on so generous a scale, and especially to Miss Ann Wilson. She courageously and most expeditiously undertook the invidious task of omitting from the manuscript many sections that could not be included in the necessarily limited space available. She also selected the illustrations from the hundreds I had assembled, in which task she was aided by Miss Juliet Scott, who also substituted one or two others.

Naturally such aid neither frees me from responsibility for what is printed here nor implicates others in its shortcomings. This recognition and gratitude, inadequate though it is, extends also to the many authors and their publishers listed in my brief bibliography. I am grateful for permission to quote from them, and particularly to:

The University of Chicago Press, *Ancient Records of Egypt* by J. H. Breasted;

Oxford University Press, *A Survey of Persian Art* by A. U. Pope;

The Ronald Press, New York, *Gardens of China* and *Gardens of Europe* by O. Siren, and *Garden Flowers of China* by H. L. Li;

The Hunt Botanical Library, Pittsburgh, *Hortulus* of Walahfrid Strabo.

A book on so vast a theme inevitably is subject to the limitations it shares with every other garden history which results from the impossibility of describing the immense variety of the gardens of the world. Many thousand miles of travel in Canada and the USA and opportunities of seeing gardens in South America, Europe, the Near East and India, in addition to the more familiar scenes of the British Isles have yielded vistas and memories of gardens evoking a lasting gratitude to their hospitable owners which cannot be adequately acknowledged here.

INTRODUCTION

Men were artists long before they were gardeners growing food, and very long before anyone thought and wrote about the nature of the pleasure, peace, and aesthetic satisfaction constantly to be had by creating or visiting and re-visiting fine gardens. So late in the annals of humanity was the rise of cultural interests and so slowly did they develop, that it was not until periods of high civilization, and only then, that gardens began to be created, to be relished and appreciated solely for their great aesthetic qualities. In all such early centres of civilization, in early Egypt, China, and Japan, the quest for beauty, peace, contentment and delight, won by continual study, effort, and care, raised gardening above a useful and very necessary craft to become fine art.

When John Ruskin said that 'fine art is that in which the hand, the head and the *heart* of man go together' he emphasized *heart* to make a distinction between 'fine' art and the art or craft of 'manufacture in which the hand of man and his head go together'. His rough and ready distinction points to the difference between the ability of 'hand and head' to raise flowers, fruit and vegetables which all gardeners need, and the touch of inspiration which must be added if they are to be combined to form as artistic and as pleasing a garden as possible.

Gardeners do not normally pose as artists or as pillars of civilization. Neither do historians of gardening so describe them or claim a place of honour for gardens in cultural history, in which they are usually forgotten. Yet there can be no doubt about the essentially aesthetic appeal of a good garden, ephemeral as it so often is destined to be. Nature's magic power is rightly credited with much of that appeal; 'things made perfect by nature are better than those finished by art', said Cicero, a matter-of-fact Roman. But gardens must be shaped, directed and maintained by constant efforts of head, heart, and hand. Those efforts may not succeed; or they may please one or two generations and then lose their appeal. Garden styles of other times or of other lands may arouse small response.

Inasmuch as all gardens arise from the activity of head, heart and hand, their differences can result only from the varying emphasis allowed each of these three elements of all human action, in the same way that all other cultural activities also must arise. When the human heart prompts 'the formation of ideas of things not present to the senses', those ideas and the way of life they inspire can, according to the *Oxford English Dictionary*, be described by the seventeenth-century word 'ideational'. Such a way of life with the cultural values it cherishes has endured for the greater part of human history, during which most people's lives have been governed by 'the ways of our ancestors' embodied in tradition and religion. When the hold of these traditional ideas over the minds of men weakens and vanishes, the work of their hands begins to promote the enjoyment of 'things perceived by the senses'.

Thus, in time, arises, again to quote the *Oxford English Dictionary*, a 'sensate' type of cultural life, 'down-to-earth', matter-of-fact, committed to the pursuit of interests and pleasures of a worldly nature and caring less and less for the other-worldly pursuits of 'ideational' times. Before 'ideational' values are greatly impaired, to be more or less forgotten and later ignored, and before 'sensate' interests exalt individual preferences, desires, hopes and fears, there have been short-lived periods when reason, intellect, 'the head', takes command to produce a blend of imaginative, otherworldly yearnings, with a restrained delight in the pleasures of the senses, both guided and controlled by reason. Then arise those all-too-brief 'idealist' or 'idealistic' periods that have given rise to some of the highest forms of art, literature, thought and action, as in the 'classical' cultures of Athens in the fifth century BC and in the European Renaissance.

Such periods of reasonably well preserved cultural unity are unlikely ever to have been absolutely uniform and the three broad distinctions proposed here must always be a matter of relative emphasis. How far the history of gardening illustrates this general scheme, and how far that scheme can be used to interpret garden history, is the theme of this book. That such a development through the whole of history, though often broken and destroyed, has occurred, to result in very varied styles, is evident in the magnificent gardens of modern times which millions annually flock to visit and which make a supreme contribution to man's heritage of beauty and inspiration.

I

GARDENS IN THE DAWN OF CIVILIZATION

The first human being known to have left a record of his life's work was an Egyptian, Methen or Amten, governor of the northern delta district. He was also the first human being to describe a garden. Around the walls of the tomb in which he was laid to rest in the reign of his master King Sneferu (*c* 2600–2576 BC), the first king of Dynasty IV of the Old Kingdom, he tells his story in hieroglyphics, in a terse, crude style after the manner of early writing, from which it is evident that his garden gave him as great a satisfaction as his distinguished career. It was, he records, '200 cubits [34 metres, 110 yards] long and 200 cubits wide, built and equipped, fine trees were set out, a very large lake was made therein, figs and vines were set out. Very plentiful trees and vines were set out, a great quantity of wine was made therein.' With a house and garden covering two-and-a-half acres, Methen had evidently lived in some style. His garden and vineyard of 1300 acres was more than a mere subsistence plot. His 'fine trees' 'set out' and his 'very large' lake imply a pleasure garden yielding genuine aesthetic satisfaction. Here was a tradition of gardening as an art already established and vigorous nearly 3000 years before the beginning of the Christian era.

The quality prized above all in the gardens of ancient as of modern Egypt and in all countries exposed, as Egypt is, to fierce summer heat was the shelter they provided, allowing an escape from the burning rays of the sun and the glare of a cloudless, brazen sky into a retreat graced by leafy trees throwing a dark shade, by pleasantly scented flowers and above all by a pool of fresh water. In Egypt, in the evening, a refreshing cool breeze from the north restores some of the vitality drained by the heat, toil and burdens of the day. Then the life-giving early morning sun, as in the brief Egyptian winter, is again welcomed as it restores warmth and fertility by its beneficent rays.

In contributing to a sense of well-being in hot climates, gardens arouse pleasant but not necessarily artistic emotions, although those may naturally be more easily

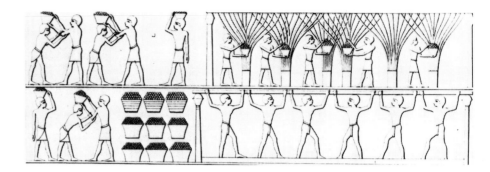

Gathering the grape harvest; from drawings dating from Dynasty VI of the Old Kingdom

stimulated in comfortable physical conditions enjoyed among beautiful garden plants and trees.

Other scraps of evidence suggest that the garden style Methen described was generally adopted by wealthier Egyptians to meet the climatic conditions of the country. Water was the first essential, so myriads of Egyptians down the ages were harnessed every day to the task of keeping fields and gardens alive by finding water, wherever it could not be conducted automatically along irrigation channels. Every year thousands of tons of Nile water had to be raised and carried in pots and jars by human muscles. Some of this back-aching toil was lightened by the *shaduf*, or river-sweep, a long lever with a water scoop at one end and a weight at the other (illustrated on the previous page, below left).

'Kitchen' gardens for vegetables and herbs preceded pleasure gardens. Trees were scarce. The date palm and the sycamore fig were precious possessions, both for their shade and their fruit; so were vines, as Methen recorded. Long after his day the ceilings of rich houses were charmingly decorated with vines and bunches of grapes patterned with great artistry to match the trellised arbours under which rich Egyptians reclined in their gardens. Other native trees were few, the most common being acacia, doum palm, persea, sidder, tamarisk and willow. Shrubs were even fewer. There were never enough trees or shrubs to form a wood or forest. Pomegranates and olives were not grown in Egypt until foreign invaders, the Hyksos kings, had seized power in northern Egypt between about 1640 and 1570 BC. Olives never succeeded widely, apart from a few groves in the Fayum.

Flowers also were few. With their keen colour sense, the Egyptians made full use of what they had. That prized above all others was the blue water-lily, *Nymphaea lotus* L., symbol of the life-giving Nile and sacred flower of Osiris, one of the greater gods of Egypt. Other varieties of the lotus had red and white flowers. Poppies, corn-marigold, *Chrysanthemum coronarium*, sometimes mistranslated as the (Chinese) chrysanthemum, jasmine, delphinium, oleander and convolvulus virtually complete the list of the commoner blooms.

Flowers entered largely into an Egyptian's idea of the good life. They were used as the sources of perfumes, for funeral wreaths, at festivals, and upon religious and ceremonial occasions. Then also, as in many parts of the world today, flowers were made into floral collars, into fillets for the hair and, what is now by no means so usual, they were carried in the hand. They were made up into bouquets and garlands by the garland-makers, who were held in high regard. In those ancient times, as today, flowers were brought into the house to decorate walls and furniture and to serve as table decorations in jars and vases, which might be of glass, faience or bronze. The lotus, queen of flowers then, as the rose has long been in the West, took pride of place at every great occasion in family life

PREVIOUS PAGES The cultivation and watering of plants in ancient Egypt; after tomb paintings, reproduced in *The Monuments of Egypt and Nubia*, 1834

and at feasts, when each honoured guest would be given a bloom.

Floral wreaths in an astonishing state of preservation have been recovered from some royal tombs, that of Tutankh-Amun (1362–1353 BC) being the most famous. The three wreaths discovered in his tomb were made from the leaves of the olive, willow and wild celery, from lotus and cornflower blossoms, berries of the woody nightshade or bitter-sweet and fruits of the mandrake. One other plant has not been identified. So at a high point in the power and glory of Egypt, at a time when a fabulous wealth of gold and treasure could be lavished on the decoration of the tomb of one of its kings, no more than a few flowers of the field could be found to adorn his bier. Hundreds of flowers that are common today, notably countless varieties of rose, were then unknown.

At this very early time in the history of civilization, Egyptian attitudes to nature, to flowers and gardens were swayed by traditional magic, mysticism and religion, as were all aspects of daily life. Over a vast period of time a mystical, deep religious feeling coloured Egyptian attitudes to nature, a feeling which is not shared by people of later time for whom flowers and gardens minister merely to the satisfaction of human senses. Poets, almost alone, have kept vibrant some faint echoes of ancient beliefs about the divine quality of such natural beauty.

An Egyptian text of a hymn to the sun-god Amun or Amun-Re of the second millennium BC has preserved written evidence of this aspect of traditional Egyptian religion, mixed as it was with survivals of primitive cattle cults; with wonder and gratitude at the annually renewed fertility of the land by the miracle of the overflowing Nile; and with worship of the divine king, Amun the incarnate god, living and ruling among men:

> ... Unique One who made
> what exists, who created the fruit-tree,
> who made the green herb and sustaineth the cattle ...

Hymns of praise were also inspired by the divine quality attributed to the Nile:

> ... Praise to thee, O Nile, that issueth
> from the earth and cometh to nourish Egypt ...
> that watereth the gardens; he that Re
> hath created to nourish all cattle.

Delight in flowers was associated with the sun-god, Re: 'I am the pure lily which comes out of the fields of Re.'

Until nearly the end of the third millennium BC the formal, severe culture of the Old Kingdom is believed to have prevailed, maintaining traditional religious customs and beliefs. Methen's brevity about his garden supports the conjecture that Egyptian gardens of that early period were more than mere pleasure resorts ministering predominantly to 'sensate' satisfactions.

About 500 years after Methen's lifetime the apparently stable Egyptian way of life had been shattered by a gigantic outburst of mob violence. A bitter record of those terrible years told how 'serfs have become the masters of serfs ... they that had clothes are now in rags ... squalor is throughout the land ... corn has perished everywhere ... people are stripped of clothing, perfume and oil ... laughter has perished. Grief walks the land.' At such a time of troubles, the fierce sun of Egypt must have burned up many a garden no longer tended and watered every day by the peasants in revolt. After great suffering, peace and security were once more forcibly established by a new elite, the inevitable sequel to destructive revolution throughout history. The Middle Kingdom established around 2060

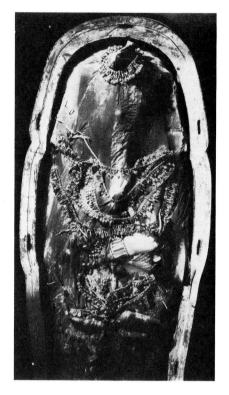

The famous wreath and garlands of flowers found in the second coffin of the VIIIth Dynasty Pharaoh, Tutankh-Amun

Offerings of flowers to a young prince, probably Tutankh-Amun, by one of the daughters of Akhenaten. VIIIth Dynasty

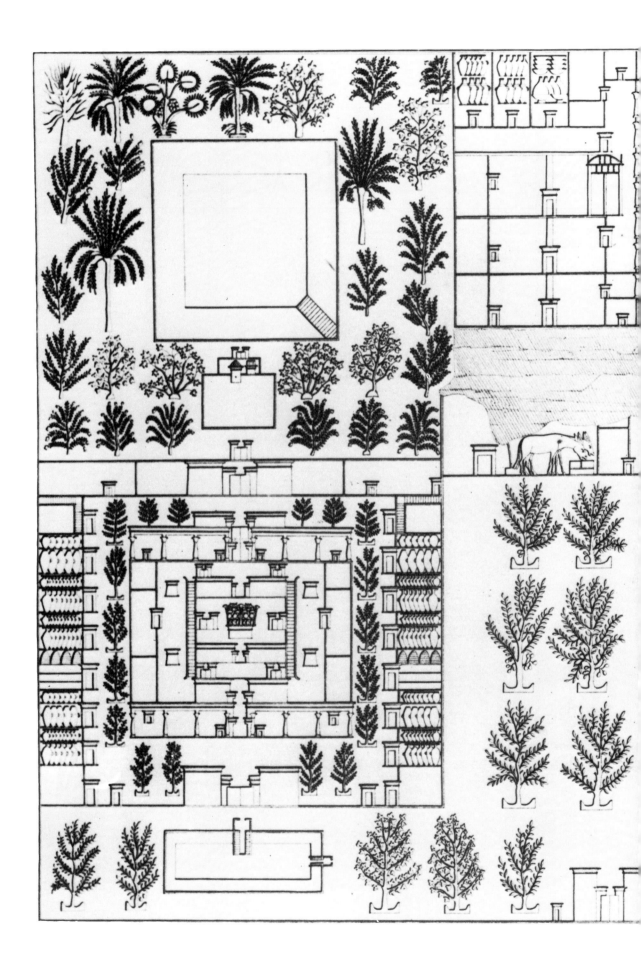

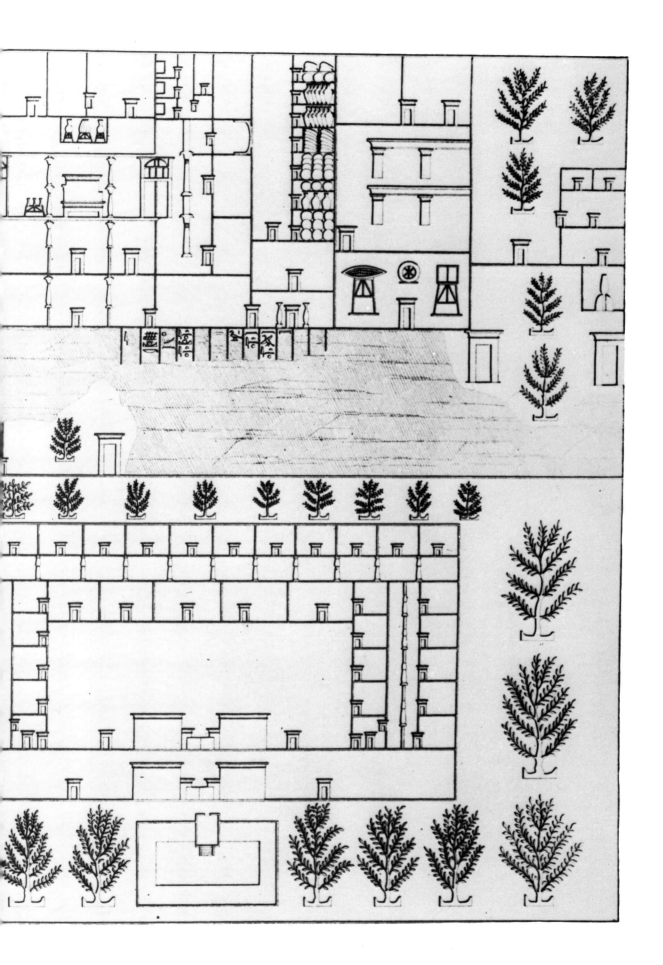

Detail from the splendid painted floor of Akhenaten's summer palace at Tell-el Amarna; a duck rises from a clump of reeds, a papyrus bush is to the right

BC in turn disintegrated, allowing foreign Hyksos from overseas to invade and rule the land. In reaction to this alien domination the restored dynasties of Egyptian kings of the New Kingdom began to rebuild the fortunes and to renew the strength of Egypt.

When Akhenaten (1379–1362 BC), the creator of Tell-el Amarna, came to the throne, Egypt was by far the strongest power in the Eastern Mediterranean. In the resurgence of national activity and the expansion of Egypt evident in the New Kingdom, an idealistic trend can be detected in cultural life. Traditional Egyptian religious sentiment, firmly consolidated over more than 2000 years, was for a time superseded in a striking reformation.

Incarnation of the sun-god Aten though the 'heretic' king Akhenaten claimed to be, he was depicted as a warm-hearted family man in the company of his astonishingly beautiful queen. In his hymn to Aten more positive evidence may be read of the new, idealistic spirit which seems then to have been stirring. It was 'idealistic' in the sense that it sought to integrate loyalties to principle and otherworldly faith with a reasonable concern at the same time for bodily well-being and a restrained satisfaction for the desires of the flesh, without making the claims of either the paramount consideration in life.

Hypothetical although such an interpretation may be, it seems confirmed by the layout of Akhenaten's new capital city of Amarna; in the design of his palace and gardens, of the houses of his principal officials and courtiers, and in the mural paintings of plants and flowers with which some of them at least were adorned. Whereas for centuries Egyptian artists had stylized trees and flowers in conventional designs, some of the splendid plant and flower paintings from Tell-el Amarna have a more naturalistic quality than the traditionally rigid, 'hieratical' forms which had hitherto served to denote lotus, papyrus or vines. When Akhenaten enforced his 'heresy' of the sole worship of the sun-god Aten and closed the temples of other gods, he did nothing to diminish traditional Egyptian reverence for nature's gifts. His remarkable anticipation, in the Bronze Age, of monotheism was short-lived, for after his death the older beliefs resumed their authority.

Rulers of the New Kingdom who reigned from about 1559 to 1085 BC led the Egyptians on the path of imperialist expansion. During their campaigns in Palestine and Syria they sought for new plants to redeem the poverty of their

OPPOSITE ABOVE An ornamental fish-pond in the garden of Nebamun; painting at Thebes, c 1400 BC. Rows of palms bearing heavy clusters of dates, and other fruit-bearing trees, line the pool

OPPOSITE BELOW Egyptian garden with its symmetrical plan, shaded pools and profusion of trees and plants

OVERLEAF LEFT 'Prince of Lilies'; Minoan fresco from Knossos, c 1800 BC

OVERLEAF RIGHT Harvesting olives; clay wine vessel, Athenian, c 520 BC

PREVIOUS PAGES Plan of Akhenaten's palace and gardens, from carvings at Tell-el Amarna, c 1370 BC

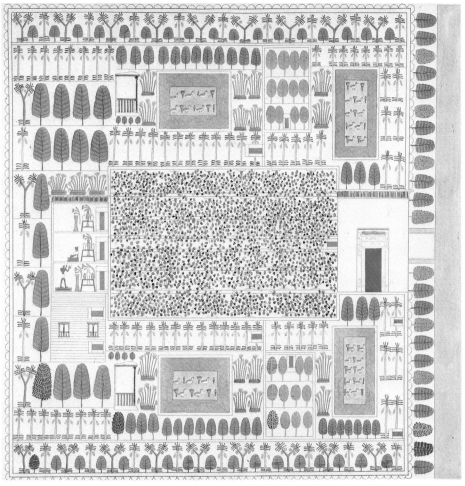

LEFT Carvings at Deir-el-Bahari celebrating the great expedition to Punt commissioned by Queen Hatshepsut, Dynasty XVIII: (top) African village with incense trees; (centre and below) the transportation of plants and trees back to Egypt

OPPOSITE Garden by the sea; fresco at Pompeii

native flora. Many plants and trees collected in this way, and acquired by trade, went to adorn the temples of Amun. There is a famous pictorial record of one such voyage commissioned by the vigorous Queen Hatshepsut of Dynasty XVIII (c 1489–1460 BC), 'for whom all Egypt was made to labour with bowed head', which brought thirty-one frankincense trees from Dhofar, the modern Somalia, known to the Egyptians as Punt. They were 'for the majesty of this god Amun, Lord of Thebes. Never was seen the like since the beginning. Trees were set up in God's land and set in the ground of Egypt,' she boasted. When some 3500 years later the site was excavated, stumps of trees were discovered in the pits in which they had been planted, but they were persea. Later the T-shaped papyrus pools and flower-beds flanking the ramp to the upper terraces of the Queen's temple were uncovered.

The great Queen's co-monarch and supplanter, Tuthmosis III (c 1490–1436 BC), was even more vigorous. From the third of his many expeditions to Syria he returned bringing 'all plants that grow, all flowers that are in God's land'. A long series of reliefs depicting the flora and fauna collected in this campaign was added to the walls of the temple at Karnak. Akhenaten's predecessor from whom he inherited the throne of Egypt, Amenophis III (c 1405–1367 BC), built another temple at Karnak. It was, he said, 'a marvellous thing ... an enclosure ... made to shine with flowers ... it is planted with all flowers; how beautiful is Nun in his pool of Every Season.'

During Dynasty XX, Rameses III (1198–1166 BC) continued the work. The great Harris papyrus in the British Museum records his many gifts to gods and men – flowers in garlands, lotus for the hand, bouquets of papyrus flowers and blossoms of 'garden fragrance'. The temple of Amun of Thebes, of Re at Helio-

Offerings of flowers and fruits; after a painting in the tomb of Thebes, XIXth Dynasty; reproduced from *Histoire de L'Art Egyptien*, 1863

Egyptian stone decorations based on flowers, showing the characteristic preference for the straight and rectangular rather than the circular; after paintings at Thebes reproduced from *Histoire de L'Art Egyptien*, 1863

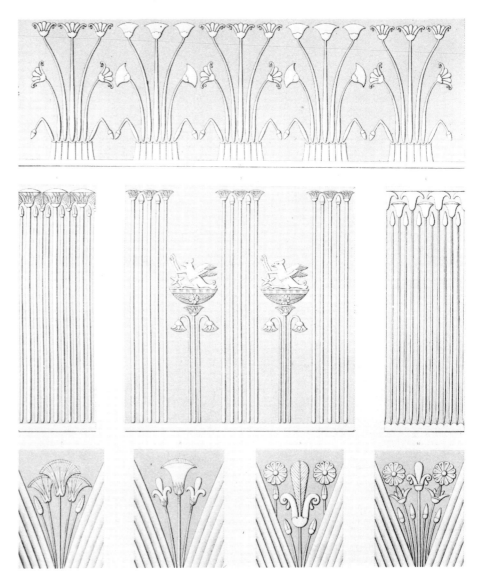

polis, and of Ptah at Memphis were all beneficiaries. At Heliopolis he reminds the God: 'I made for thee groves and arbours containing date trees, lakes supplied with lotus flowers, *isi* flowers, the flowers of every land, *dedmet* flowers, myrrh and sweet and fragrant woods for thy beautiful face.'

Reflective Egyptians such as Akhenaten had already risen to a belief in a single beneficent god or divine power in the second millennium BC, an achievement remarkably in advance of the cruder religious notions of other early peoples. Much later, in the Stone Age of Central America for example, Aztecs and Mayas debased religion into a form of devil worship requiring human sacrifices, an enormity of which the Egyptians were not guilty. They considered flowers, garlands, bouquets and gardens to be the most acceptable, the most precious gifts which they could provide as offerings to their benign divinity. No better evidence is needed of the deep reverence the Egyptians themselves had of such natural beauty. It was a joy the more intense because of its simplicity, the joy of a young child set down in a meadow among buttercups and daisies.

Flowers and gardens clearly had a ritual and religious significance for the Egyptians which both promoted and conditioned their very early development of

Reconstructed plan of part of a palace and garden at Tell-el Amarna, showing the characteristic rectangular shape of the gardens, and the ponds and alleys within them

gardening art. Such influences predisposed them, as the same influences will be seen to have done in much later times, to prefer a formal somewhat austerely obvious arrangement of their gardens. Not until religious beliefs weakened, relatively late in Egyptian history, were there hints of a more relaxed attitude leading to what is commonly regarded as a 'romantic' gardening style. Religion and ritual lie beyond the world of art and culture in which this book seeks to place gardens, so the main question here must be whether it is possible, despite the thousands of years that have elapsed since all the gardens of ancient Egypt perished, to detect the artistic qualities that made them a source of aesthetic satisfaction in those ancient times.

Long before any other people on earth had begun to create works of great artistry, the Egyptians were giving a grace of form to temples, monuments, sculptures, statues, sculptured reliefs, paintings, caskets, furniture and jewellery that has often been described, although not by them, as perfection itself. 'The limits of art cannot be set, and no artist fully possesseth his skill' was the conclusion of that sage counsellor of Egyptian kings of Dynasty v, Ptah-hopet, around 2370 BC, whose wise sayings, repeated down the ages, powerfully guided and moulded the Egyptian way of life. In his day the art and civilization of Egypt's Old Kingdom had already attained such splendour that it was ever afterwards regarded by the Egyptians themselves as their Golden Age.

But gardens receive no attention in the many books that have been devoted to the more striking achievements of the craftsmen of early Egypt. Yet a cultivated early Egyptian, if asked what it was among his possessions that gave him the greatest satisfaction, would probably have chosen his garden. To obtain an opinion about gardening as a form of art would not be easy, because there were no abstract words in the Egyptian language such as 'art' in the sense of 'aesthetics'. 'Beautiful', he would certainly have agreed, for *nefer, neferu*, signifying general approbation – beautiful, good, excellent – was about the hardest-worked word in the Egyptian language. Long centuries of peace seem to have brought a measure of contentment at least to those who could write, whatever may have been the fate of the illiterate masses. Yet the loveliness of many of the finer products of Egyptian craftsmen is such that they could not have been created except by earnest application of hand, head and heart, an intense effort to make things well in the service of some high purpose. It was not 'art for art's sake' or the expression of a conscious search for beauty. Splendid artists worked for thousands of years before philosophers began to discuss the nature and meaning of 'art'.

So gifted a people as the early Egyptians were not likely to falter or fail when they came to plan and maintain gardens. They alone of all the peoples of remote antiquity enjoyed the essential conditions without which garden artistry cannot develop. They had long periods of security from hostile attack, a sufficient and exceedingly fertile soil, water, constant sunshine and warmth, and, for a considerable and fortunate minority, wealth, leisure, and an abundant force of cheap, skilled labour. It is true that desert conditions beyond the narrow valley of the Nile and its annual floods, combined with a relative paucity of native trees, shrubs, flowers and other plants, limited the range and variety of Egyptian gardens; but within those limits everything favoured an open-air life and encouraged those with time and money to create and to develop gardens.

Gardens were not among the interests of Dr Henri Frankfort in his penetrating account of Egyptian art, its special style and qualities. Yet some of his conclusions about Egyptian sculpture and architecture can also be seen to be relevant to them. In striking contrast with the Babylonians, who were influenced by the cylinder

The shady pool and garden of the XVIIIth Dynasty scribe Nakht *c* 1340–1300 BC

as a foundation or matrix for the arrangement of sculptured objects, the Egyptians chose the cube. Egyptian 'cubism', as he called it, is most pronounced in their works in stone, where the composition, even of Egyptian statues in the round, is pronouncedly that of a series of block-forms.

Dr Frankfort observed that the decoration of a circle, the composition of sculpture in the round and wall decoration in rooms were treated in distinctive, different styles in Egypt and Babylon. The Egyptians forced squareness into the circle. The Assyrians forced cylindrical or circular continuity on the cube. The special aesthetic qualities of Egyptian sculpture were summarized by Dr Frankfort as 'self-sufficiency, self-containedness, complete plastic corporeality, independence as an object in space clearly constituted by the emphatic elaboration of its co-ordinates from the block of stone of indeterminate extension'. Substitute the word 'desert' for 'block of stone' and the focus on Egyptian gardens at once becomes sharper.

Egyptian gardens were self-contained. They sometimes swallowed the houses they were made to adorn. Where other countries have houses and gardens, rich Egyptians had gardens with houses in them. Egyptian gardens were sharply marked off as 'blocks' from the vast surrounding deserts. They were filled to capacity because everything grew to profusion in the rich Nile silt, mud and water which with infinite labour was brought up from the flood level and spread on the gardens on higher ground. Rectangular co-ordinates were elaborated within the garden by deliberate design. This rectangular shape of gardens themselves, of the flower-beds, ponds and alleys in them, has been explained as the result of the imperative need for irrigation channels, which, it is assumed, had to be in straight lines. Dr Frankfort's analysis of Egyptian art forms suggests that they were straight and rectangular because Egyptian aesthetic sense preferred them that way. 'The circle,' he said, 'did not provide the Egyptians with a particularly congenial decorative problem to solve.' An irrigation channel could be a curve if the lie of the land and the design of the garden allows. From the rhythmical quality discernible in some other Egyptian art forms it is however possible

25

Flowers made into a fillet for the hair; bas-relief of vith Dynasty

to believe that at some periods at least, circularity was not without influence.

Other marked characteristics of Egyptian art are found by Dr Frankfort in a harmony between material and form in sculptured stone and in a harmonious contrast between organic and inorganic form in the siting of statues against a well-defined background of pillars or walls. Harmony, balance of the elements of the garden, the siting of the house and its pavilions in relation to the trees, vines, flowers and pools; their composition and symmetrical arrangement, are all aesthetic qualities to be seen in the few pictures and plans of Egyptian gardens that have remained or can be reconstructed after 4000 years.

What was grown in the gardens was set out sharply without blurred edges, an example, perhaps, of what Frankfort described as the 'expressive' nature of Egyptian art. It was not 'expressionism' in the modern sense of the use of shapes and colours in order to 'express' the personality of the artist. Besides affording additional evidence of the power of reason and thought which the ancient Egyptians put into their garden design, its well-devised geometrical precision of layout has a pronounced intellectual quality as well as being in conformity with a certain austerity already suggested as a quality of their dominant religious and ritualistic orientation.

Here, as in all writing about the far-distant historical past, any generalizations about 'the Egyptian garden' are hazardous because they are based upon evidence that is very slight in relation to the enormous time-span they cover. Where the evidence seems exceptionally good and detailed, allowance must be made for artistic stylization and for a possible artistic licence which permitted divergence between the picture and reality. Fortunately the sands of Egypt have preserved traces of foundations as well as pictorial representations of ancient gardens so that Egyptologists are able to suggest reconstructions and descriptions of the gardens of Egypt with a greater assurance than archaeologists at work in other lands dare to assume. Egyptian gardens could not have varied very greatly in form and contents, but the manner in which their owners enjoyed them would have varied as Egyptian social and cultural life went through remarkable vicissitudes, possibly more than those of which any record remains.

In the light of such shreds of evidence indicating the possibility of an 'idealistic' or 'integral' interpretation of cultural life in the New Kingdom, it is easier to reconcile apparently conflicting pious and pleasurable Egyptian attitudes to gardens.

Among some more reflective and well-established Egyptians, gardens entered so profoundly into everyday life and religion that they were associated with thoughts about the life after death to which Egyptians looked forward, although often with no very firm faith. A stock petition inscribed on some tombs of Dynasty XVIII is that 'I may each day walk continuously on the banks of my water, that my soul may repose on the branches of the trees that I have planted, that I may refresh myself under the shade of my sycomore'.

Gardens then might be the scene of pleasure of a more worldly sort. The small collection of love songs which has survived from the New Kingdom (1559–1085 BC), a golden age of lyric poetry, brings a fresh feeling for nature and a sense of joy in garden trees and flowers and garden pools. They tell of various flowers, characterized by their more outstanding qualities. Trees were personified in a way indicating some deep symbolic meaning now hard to imagine.

The little sycomore which she hath planted with her hand, it moveth its mouth to speak. The whispering of its leaves is as sweet as refined honey. How charming are its pretty verdant branches. It is laden with *neku*-fruits that are redder than jasper. Its

26

leaves are like unto malachite . . . It draweth them that are not already under it, its shadow is so cool.

It invites the beloved.

Come and pass the time with thy maiden. The garden is in its day. There are bowers and shelters there for thee. My gardeners are glad and rejoice when they see thee. Send thy slaves ahead of thee . . . the servants come and bring beer of every sort and all manner of mixed loaves, and many flowers of yesterday and today and all manner of refreshing fruit. Come and spend the day in merriment, and tomorrow, and the day after, three whole days and sit in my shadow.

Thus was the sycamore fig tree imagined to beckon a young man to enjoyment in an Egyptian love lyric that has lost nothing of its charm and power of evoking an atmosphere of a garden of sensuous delight, to which it seems evident that some Egyptians at that time were not averse to surrender.

Before the dawn of Western civilization, therefore, among people whose ways were not our ways, whose whole background of experience, tradition and sense of values had been formed in the Stone Age and Bronze Age and can now only be conjectured, some evidence is none the less clear. From it may be derived hints at some general ideas about the early development of garden art, beginning with a formal garden style having religious overtones alien to modern habits of thought, then followed by gardens from which more mundane joys were also sought which are by no means foreign to contemporary experience. If, as this brief record suggests, we can have a link with this strange people living in a foreign land over 3000 years ago, it seems probable that garden arts at other times practised by other people may have had a similar development.

A cultural product as obvious and as attractive as a fine garden might seem likely to impress many who would wish to possess something like it themselves. During the greater part of the first millennium BC, Egypt was ruled by foreign conquerors. Nubians from the kingdom of Kush, the modern Sudan, overthrew the Egyptian king in 750 BC. They were less alien to Egyptian ways than the savage Assyrians who swept into the land around 700 BC, to be ejected again some fifty years later. Then came the Persians under Cambyses in 525 BC, to rule for over a century until 404 BC when a movement of liberation to evict them began with Greek aid. They came back again in force in 341 BC, but not for long. After Alexander the Great began the conquest of Persia in 323 BC, Egypt fell to him also. Greek monarchs then ruled Egypt until Queen Cleopatra VII, the last of her line, preferred to die rather than to submit to the Romans under the victorious Octavian in 30 BC. Powerfully aided by looting the treasure of the Pharaohs, he consolidated his one-man rule over the Roman world, including Egypt which he reserved as a private imperial domain. Few Romans were allowed to visit the Nile, apart from Roman administrators. Within two or three hundred years Egypt, despite its fabulous fertility and renown as a principal granary of Rome, was reduced to ruin by Roman greed and maladministration.

No other people in history, except possibly the Chinese, had as long and as undisturbed a cultural life as the Egyptians. In the course of over 3000 years they had developed human intellectual powers in astronomy, geometry, building, and agriculture, and they had created masterpieces of art and architecture which have always ranked high among the wonders of the world. Gardens were among them. When Israelites, Assyrians, Persians, Greeks and Romans lived among them, their splendour was intact, yet the extent to which any of these

Bas-reliefs in the Palace of Sennacherib, Nineveh, showing warriors cutting down date-palm trees, the most common of the Assyrian trees

alien people were able to profit from the age-old creations of Egypt's artists and craftsmen, including gardens, was limited. Apart from natural differences in soil and climate between Egypt and their own homelands, there was, above all, a difference in cultural levels, traditional skills and interests which made them disinclined to copy Egyptian models, even if they had possessed the ability to do so, which many, particularly most of the Romans, certainly had not. Difficult as it is, therefore, to regard Egyptian art and Egyptian gardens as models which were assiduously copied abroad, it remains possible that some at least of those who witnessed them were inspired with a resolution to develop their own cultural life, their art and their gardens in their own way. That, after all, is about as much as any teacher, anywhere, can hope to achieve.

The familiar biblical story of man's first home in a glorious garden 'eastward in Eden' at the source of four rivers, two of which were the Tigris and the Euphrates, successfully locates another beginning of human civilization. Mesopotamia, the land of the two rivers, very early in the annals of humanity sustained a small population of primitive agriculturists scattered in little villages. Even before the Egyptians, they may have made some progress in the arts of civilization. Unlike the Egyptians, however, they had no security. Constantly renewed aggressive assaults by predatory neighbours from the distant hills forced them to seek the refuge of walled towns. Within such fortresses, Sumerians, Babylonians and Assyrians were able for a time to fend off their fierce enemies, and to develop a cultural life far superior to that of all their immediate neighbours in western Asia. Striking although their achievement was, it never developed to become as rich and exquisite as many of the products of Egyptian culture.

Men carrying offerings of flowers, from carvings in the Palace of Sennacherib, Nineveh

Nothing is known about the existence or the nature of gardens in Mesopotamian towns and villages throughout the greater part of their history. Where a town was fortified by double defensive walls, the space between the inner and outer wall would probably have been used for growing foodstuffs. Some may have become pleasure gardens. Wealthier folk with larger houses than the average may perhaps have endeavoured to grow a few plants in pots in their courtyards. Where space allowed, there would probably have been one or more date-palms, that revered tree, named by the Assyrians the 'tree of life' because its fruit was the staff of life in a hot marshy land such as riparian Mesopotamia. Probably also the acutely cramped state of siege under which the townsfolk often had to live and the fierce warlike attitudes which were a condition of survival, combined with the eternal problem of providing sufficient water in their sub-tropical desert, ruled out pleasure gardens. The famous Code of the vigorous monarch Hammurabi of the first Babylonian Dynasty (c 1730–1685 BC) did however distinguish between houses, fields and gardens, but it seems that the plant so often named on Babylonian clay tablets as growing in gardens was the vine.

Late in Mesopotamian history, a clay tablet with a list of the plants in the royal gardens of Merodach Baladan, Babylonian vassal of the King of Assyria (721–710 and 703–702 BC) boasts: 'I brought cedars, boxwood and [?] oak trees the like of which none of the Kings my forefathers ever planted and I planted them in the gardens of my land. I took rare garden fruits not found in my own land and caused them to flourish.' Such a claim seems to show that garden arts had indeed been backward. His palace gardeners raised a variety of herbs and vegetables of which over seventy are mentioned. They were all utilitarian crops and they do not give any clear indication of that gardening for pleasure or delight in which highly-placed Egyptians had long been able to indulge.

Mesopotamian wars, battles and sieges were fierce, bloody and brutal, pushed to the utter extermination of the enemy and the destruction of towns, villages and plantations in scenes of the most revolting cruelty which are depicted and recorded upon stone with evident relish. No wonder therefore that Assyrian art has been described as 'baffling and full of contradictions like so much that pertains to Assyrian culture'.

Few but warrior kings could enjoy in brief periods of their success the security which gardens demand. Sennacherib (705-681 BC) boasted that he had adorned Assyria's capital, Nineveh, with gardens above and below the city. Again there is no mention of flowers. Scenes in Ashurbanipal's royal park in Nineveh, showing musicians, guards and a wild boar in a thicket, were depicted on sculptured reliefs which adorned the royal domain at the height of its development. One shows the King feasting with his Queen in the royal garden.

In 612 BC Babylonians, Medes and savage Scythians banded together in an attack which humbled Nineveh to the dust. Enriched as it had been by the spoils of its neighbours during four centuries and more of bloody strife, and adorned

Sculptured relief of King Ashurbanipal feasting with his Queen in the celebrated royal park in Nineveh, 668–627 BC

with parks glowing with almond blossom in spring, with lilies and cotton plants and by captive lions and other wild animals, Nineveh, in the words of a Babylonian chronicler, was 'turned into ruined mounds'.

The rise and fall of great states such as Assyria, and the yet more primitive and warlike Hittites and Scythians, obscures the fate of lesser kingdoms such as that of Urartu in Armenia, whose capital, 'the garden city of Van', was built out into Lake Van. When it was overcome by the Assyrians in 714 BC, it had enjoyed little more than one hundred years of comparative power and glory. Little is known of the life of its people, but archaeologists are gradually uncovering some of its ancient sites.

The second period of Babylon's renown set in after the destructive revenge its army had taken on the Assyrians under a successful adventurer whose son, Nebuchadnezzar, the Nebuchadnezzar of the Bible, a brilliant commander, established his empire far and wide (605–562 BC).

In restoring the old city of Babylon, he built the so-called Hanging Gardens to please his young wife, who came from the hill country and pined for some cool shade and greenery on the torrid plain of Babylon. Another legend ascribed them to the fabled Queen Semiramis, who was supposed to have ruled over

Assyria and founded Babylon. No description by any ancient writer who had actually seen these gardens exists and the only scrappy details that remain were written by two Greeks some 500 years after Babylon had been captured in 539 BC by the Persian conqueror, Cyrus. These early accounts of the gardens differ and it is impossible to derive any reliable description from them. The adjective 'hanging' is misleading, because they were built on terraces. The description of their waterproof foundation base of layers of reed and asphalt stone slabs, bricks and mortar proves that they must have been roof gardens needing very substantial support and continual water and attention. French archaeologists, working in the area in 1949, believed that they had found the site of the gardens near the royal palace by the Ishtar Gate. They thought that the gardens had rested on four terraces there, one above the other, reaching a total height of some 21 metres (70 feet) so that the tops of trees in the garden would appear above the city walls to amaze caravans arriving at Babylon. The lowest terrace, which was the longest, was estimated to be about 40 metres (130 feet) long, the higher terraces were shorter. If this is correct, the Greeks much exaggerated the dimensions of the gardens, for they said that the garden frontage was over 450 metres (500 yards) long.

Their relatively large size would explain their great renown. Roof gardens imposed the prohibitive toil of hoisting up water every day to keep the plants alive. None but a supreme autocratic ruler could have commanded the slave labour and resources necessary to create and maintain anything as vast as a flourishing green hill on the sun-baked plain of Mesopotamia. However exaggerated the splendour of Babylon's Hanging Gardens may be, it is not difficult to understand how they came to be regarded as one of the Seven Wonders of the Ancient World. There seems to be no evidence to support the idea that trees or plants were grown on the great artificial mounds or ziggurats of which Nebuchadrezzar's Tower of Babel near Babylon, dedicated to the god Marduk, is the most famous. Babylon was not destroyed by the Persians. It gradually fell into decay after the foundation of the new capital Seleucia around 300 BC. The Hanging Gardens would have quickly dried up and perished as soon as constant watering ceased.

Any reference to garden arts in ancient Mesopotamia must be conjectural because very few archaeological remains such as sculptured reliefs or scraps of writing on clay tablets give any indication of Assyrian and Babylonian attitudes to garden development. That it could not have been very generally pursued is understandable in the light of both the military as well as the social and cultural conditions of life, torn, as it so often was, by fierce enmities as Assyrians and Babylonians hacked themselves to pieces when they were not warring against neighbouring peoples. Unlike the Egyptians, they enjoyed security and prosperity only as long as it could be preserved by a strong, warlike king or ruler. His supremacy was symbolized in his royal park which no priest, great official or private person either could or would seek to rival.

One other indication that pleasure gardening would not be much developed can be surmised from the strong, traditional worship of rival gods in the Mesopotamian plain. When human interests, human instinctive urges for the satisfaction of the senses have to be repressed in the service of religion, gardening for pleasure is usually absent.

II

THE CREATORS OF WESTERN CULTURE

reat numbers of splendid flowers grow wild in profusion in Crete as in Greece and they are unlikely to have been fewer 3000 years ago. They abound in the spring and autumn but they vanish in summer when the burning rays of the sun parch the land. Anemones, asphodel, crocus, dianthus, daisies, cistus, oleander, campanula, scarlet lilies, iris, orchids, periwinkle are among the commoner sorts, as well as climbing plants such as convolvulus, honeysuckle, smilax, clematis and ivy.

Richly endowed with the beauty of nature on the Mediterranean island of Crete, lying off Greece to the south-east, a civilization slowly matured from about 3000 BC which attained, before it was suddenly obliterated between 1500 and 1400 BC, a degree of refinement truly extraordinary at so early a time.

Such sources of knowledge about Minoan civilization that exist so far have been well described as 'a picture book without any text'. Three main phases have been distinguished in that civilization, Minoan I, II and III, each showing a development beyond the preceding period in technical and aesthetic skills and competence. Minoan III, which flourished roughly about the time of Egypt's New Kingdom, after around 1500 BC, has also been subdivided into three periods of which the later, more 'modern', is better documented.

Just as Egypt had the protective desert around its borders, so Minoan Crete was protected by the sea. As in Egypt, there were no walled towns. During their long history the Minoans had suffered shattering disasters, but they are thought to have been due to natural causes, notably to violent earthquakes which sufficient Minoans survived to be able fairly rapidly to restore their homes. As in the New Kingdom of Egypt, a civilization of considerable sophistication is evident in many later Minoan remains. Evidence about Minoan religious beliefs is very slight, but beyond indications that a mother goddess, served by priestesses, once reigned supreme, there are also clear signs that trees were worshipped, as later

Detail from a Minoan coffin lid found at Knossos, painted with papyrus plants, birds and fishes

in the sacred groves and gardens of Greeks and Romans. At the same time a high standard of personal comfort is evident in well-built Minoan houses, giving protection against summer heat and wintry cold and provided with a water supply and sanitary drainage system superior to those of many towns in modern times. Splendid also were the mural paintings adorning the walls of living rooms. Using none but primary colours – red, blue and yellow – and ignorant of perspective or relief, Minoan artists yet achieved striking schemes of decoration by depicting on walls and pottery ware flowers and animals drawn from domestic and more exotic sources. Among the flowers are white lilies, wild irises, crocuses, wild roses, violets and lotus. Caution is needed in identifying some of them because there was much restoration in Knossos under the archaeologist, Sir Arthur Evans. Such evidence from building and interior decoration, as well as from many pottery remains, points to a developed sensuous enjoyment of life much more 'modern' in essence than is evident among the Babylonians and Assyrians. Small statuettes or figurines of ladies in sophisticated costumes or half costumes have been found which reveal the female bosom in a way unknown until libertarian times, briefly in early eighteenth-century London and spasmodically in a few 'topless' exhibitions of the 1960s. Minoan ladies seem to have enjoyed an independence that was very unusual in ancient times.

If such partial scraps of evidence do not convincingly indicate a 'sensate' social and cultural life, given over to the enjoyment of the good things of this world, they at least point to such a moderation of any earlier rigid, theocratic, 'ideational' rule as to make it plausible to believe that the later Minoans could have relished flowers and gardens of delight because of their direct, sensuous appeal to pleasure-loving instincts, which were not catered for by more formal garden designs such as those of the earlier Egyptian temples and palaces.

At Knossos, Sir Arthur Evans found large flower pots with holes in the bottom from which he concluded that the Minoans decorated courtyards in their palaces and the light-wells in their larger private houses by growing flowers and shrubs intensively. To do so would make considerable demands upon the working population (free or slave) for water-carrying. But what appear to be irrigation channels have been found below the palace of Phaistos leading from the Geropotamo river to level ground on which kitchen and flower gardens once probably flourished.

Sir Arthur Evans believed that in pots and tubs the Minoans would have grown madonna and pancratium lilies, wild roses, irises, honeysuckle, convolvulus, wild peas or vetches, with myrtles and young palm trees. Outside the house the same flowers and shrubs together with ivy and sacred trees would probably appear also. If so, these would have been the very first gardens of delight graced by cultivated flowers of which there is any evidence in Europe.

Fortunately exciting discoveries are still being made about the highly developed Minoan culture and civilization which came to an extraordinarily sudden, violent end around 1450–1400 BC. Many guesses have been made about the cause of this disaster, such as conquest by Mycenaeans, bubonic plague and the recent and strongly supported theory that the Minoans were literally blown out of existence by a colossal volcanic explosion having the force of an atomic bomb. Its blast obliterated Thera, the island of Santorin nearly a hundred miles from Crete, with flames, red-hot debris and an immense tidal wave, all of which could have thrown down also the palaces, mansions and humbler dwellings of Crete. The usual explanation is that invaders destroyed all such homes instead of living in them themselves, without finding the many treasures since discovered

PREVIOUS PAGES Garden scene painted on the walls of the villa of Livia Augustus, Rome

under some of the ruins.

After the disappearance of great numbers of Minoans, Crete was then occupied by Achaean Greeks or Mycenaeans from their fortress towns of southern Greece. Warriors and hunters, they carried on something of the Minoan culture but they were unable to rival the Minoans in taste or technical skill. They wrote in hieroglyphic style described as Linear B (to distinguish it from the Minoan script labelled Linear A) in a language which has very recently been discovered to be an early form of Greek. If they had conquered the Minoans it might be supposed that they would keep gardens going with Minoan slaves. From what little remains in Linear B that has been deciphered so far, however, it is not possible to glean anything throwing light upon gardens or flowers, although lists have been found of food crops and herbs such as celery, sesame, figs, olives, fennel and coriander. The Minoan Linear A still defies interpretation.

In the twelfth century BC the Mycenaeans went down before hordes of invading, destructive Dorian Greeks, who were almost savages in comparison with the Minoans. History, civilization and culture in Greece and Crete became blank pages for some 400 years.

At length, perhaps in the ninth century BC, legends of vanished heroes of olden time, some of whom may have been Minoan and Mycenaean, which had survived in folk-memory were put together so skilfully by Homer, to be sung or recited to listening groups of warriors, that they became an imperishable part of the human heritage. For centuries the *Iliad* and the *Odyssey* formed the minds of young Greeks and of many young Romans almost in the way that the Authorized Version of the Bible AD 1611 has formed the minds of generation after generation of English-speaking peoples. No educated Greek could hear the word 'garden' without recalling the gardens of Alcinous and of Laertes in the story of Odysseus whose 'locks flowed in curls like unto the hyacinth flower'.

The 'great garden' of King Alcinous 'with a hedge on either side where grew trees, tall and luxuriant', was possibly a dim tradition of the splendour of a royal garden in Crete. At the end of his epic journey, Odysseus went to see his aged father whom he found in old, patched clothes digging in his well-ordered vineyard. No ornamental pleasure gardens these, but well-tended fruit orchards, vineyards with beds of pot-herbs and flavourings, all strictly utilitarian and praised as such, but with an undertone of satisfaction at their pleasant appearance as well. But in those heroic days when men knew and feared hunger and could perish miserably in a famine year, they yearned above all for that miracle of a never-failing supply of the fruits of the earth enjoyed by Alcinous which today is taken for granted wherever there are free markets.

If Alcinous and Laertes grew any flowers, Homer does not mention them, although outside the cave into which Calypso lured Odysseus were 'soft meadows of violets and celery'. Homer, despite his vivid appreciation of natural beauty, does not praise their scent or that of any other flower, but then his epics tell about heroes, not about flowers or gardens, which he mentions as only a background to his stories of human adventure. Trees were scarce in Greece. It was the 'sweet-smelling cypress' outside Calypso's cave that Odysseus relished more than the violets.

So later, when the Greek lyric poet Ibycus of the early sixth century BC sang of a garden, he wrote: 'Tis but in Spring the quince trees of the Maid's holy garden grow green with the watering rills from the river, and the vine-blossoms wax 'neath the mantling sprays of the vines' – words appropriate to the mythical garden where the four Hesperides guarded the golden 'apples' (probably

Winged Eros holds out a wreath to Dionysus, the tree-god, with ivy as his symbol, depicted on this vase as a human-headed bull

quinces), symbols of love and fertility given to the bride of the almighty Zeus.

For the Greeks, as for the Minoans and Egyptians, trees had a mysterious fascination. Religion and piety towards the dead found expression in the planting of trees and shrubs around temples and tombs. Flowers also evoked religious associations. Many of the gods and goddesses whose stories people the imaginative Greek mind were thought to love flowers. Persephone, daughter of Demeter who bestowed on mankind the arts of agriculture, was snatched by Pluto to become his bride in the underworld while she, with other goddesses, was gathering flowers, 'soft crocuses mixed with irises and hyacinths and rose-blooms and lilies marvellous to see and the narcissus ... as yellow as the crocus'.

The beginnings of a small roof garden have been seen in the annual festival of mourning for Adonis beloved of Aphrodite but slain by a wild boar. Plants of lettuce, fennel, wheat and barley were traditionally set out by Greek women in pots on the flat roofs of the houses to spring up, wither and die; symbols of the short life of Adonis. It was as a religious duty and not as a gardening exercise that this festival was observed every year. To get the water for these plants probably meant an extra journey to one of the relatively few fountains of Athens.

Apollo, the laurel bearer, a god of all vegetation to whom plane trees, tamarisks, apple trees, as well as laurel were sacred, had his principal shrine at Delphi. Dionysus, the tree-god, with ivy as his symbol, also had his shrine at Delphi. He also was regarded as the deity of all vegetation, not the vine alone. In addition to such principal gods and goddesses there were innumerable spirits in mountains, hills, caves, streams, fountains and lakes. Nymphs, beautiful young daughters of the supreme god Zeus, were not immortal as he was. They were everywhere; dryads, hamadryads, naiads, and countless more Every meadow, mountain, cave or stream had one or more attendant nymphs. They brought flowers to the fields and gardens; they restored the sick and gave aid and comfort to all in danger, fear or distress. Nature, for the ancient Greeks, had aspects vastly different from that of our sophisticated, modern, town outlook.

Flowers must have been grown for sale to supply the garlands and wreaths required for many solemn occasions. This pleasant custom was practised by Mediterranean peoples as it had been by Egyptians, although it was apparently unknown in Greece in Homeric times. Crowns made of leaves were then reserved for gods and goddesses but they were being called for by smart society in Sappho's day early in the sixth century BC, for she sang:

> ... offerings of flowers
> are pleasing to the gods, who hate all those
> who come before them with uncrowned heads

OPPOSITE Illustration from the 14th-century manuscript *The Romaunt of the Rose*, the allegorical French poem translated by Chaucer which celebrated the ever-popular rose

OVERLEAF LEFT The pool in the gardens of Madrasseh Madar-i-Shah, Isfahan, the glorious creation of Shah Sultan Husain completed in 1715

OVERLEAF RIGHT Emperor Babur supervising his gardeners who are measuring the flower-beds; 16th-century manuscript

Then also the rose was first introduced into Greece. Sappho's story that roses came from Macedonia was generally believed. A new spirit was then stirring in Greece to allow more regard to be given to pleasures such as the rose could offer. Throughout the 'archaic' period, however, the Greeks created no pleasure gardens for private enjoyment. Otherworldly, mystical, superstitious, religious or traditional rules required individual dedication to the service of the community, obedient respect for its leaders, and due reverence for gods, goddesses and all the unseen powers of nature.

Vase painting is among the few remaining indications of the cultural and artistic style of this 'archaic' or 'ideational' period. At first it was exclusively linear, purely geometric, and in one colour. When more than one colour began to be

درختهای انار بسیار هست کرد اکرد حوض تمام سه برگزار

باای من باغ همین است در وقت زرد شدن نارنجها بسیار

A gold wreath of oak leaves and fruit from the Dardanelles, 4th century BC

used, there was no blending or striving to create an illusion of reality. It was austere, because art then was not part of a conscious pursuit of pleasure of the kind sought later through more illusionistic, impressionistic, 'visual' art giving greater gratification to the senses. Throughout this early time, a private garden of delight is almost unthinkable.

During the sixth century BC and particularly in its latter half, the strongly ideational, otherworldly art of the archaic period weakened to allow somewhat greater concern with the things of this world. Social values remained strongly religious and ethical although the claims of sensate humanity were slowly getting some recognition. When these two conflicting tendencies became fairly well balanced, a marvellous, sublime, idealistic art resulted in the fifth century BC. It was calm and serene with an orderly beauty in sculpture making 'noble men appear still nobler'. Increasingly visual and realistic, it was still an art serving religion and civic and social morality. Artists, although recognized and honoured as leaders in a common national enterprise offering praise and gratitude to the gods, were not men apart, richly rewarded by material wealth and social adulation. It was not until this idealistic period that there could be any thought of gardens as a source of human refreshment, contentedness or pleasure.

A history of gardening, particularly if it stresses the aesthetic appeal of gardens as an art form, must explain why the Greeks, with their rich heritage of poetry and legend, with artists and craftsmen as creative of beauty with their hands, heads and hearts as any in the annals of humanity, with a keen appreciation of the glories of nature, yet failed to win renown as gardeners.

In the first place, there would have been little need for flower gardens, as distinct from herb and vegetable plots in the archaic and classic periods of the troubled history of Greece because, as Thucydides remarked: 'Most of the Athenians and most of their descendants down to the time of this [the Peloponnesian] war continued to live in the country where they had been born.' There they would have had a wealth of wild flowers in spring and autumn growing naturally

OPPOSITE An Indian princess in her garden. The peacocks were a common decorative feature of Indian and Persian gardens. 16th-century miniature

without watering or irrigation, and they picked them. To keep flowers alive in the summer heat would have required water and labour that could not be spared from the more serious business of growing food crops and vines. Greece has always been short of water, while much of the land, apart from fertile patches in river valleys, was singularly unrewarding to the cultivator.

In the early Homeric period of Greek history, moreover, defence and deference to the gods had the first call on human energies, allowing little margin for mundane, merely human satisfactions. Later, when concern for the favour of the gods was less evident among the more intelligent Greeks, fratricidal wars of Greeks against Greeks forced them to live shut up in cramped little huts and houses behind the stout city walls. Like Babylonians and Assyrians, the menfolk of Greece, who should have been cultivating fields and gardens, fought and died outside the walls. In relation to our own time, most Greeks were 'primitive' people in the sense that every family had to find their own food, to maintain if not to build their own shelter, and to make their own clothes. It is unlikely that they could have found time, beyond that spent on the daily round of exhausting toil, to embellish their homes by a flower garden. There were few, if any, cultivated varieties of flowers until late in the history of Greece.

After 500 BC wealth increased and with it slavery. Possibly a quarter of the population were slaves but most of them did not work on the land. There were not many very rich Greeks enjoying vast estates after the manner of the wealthy Egyptians. Greek city states were democracies, so the first step towards gardening in Greece was communal. It was taken by Athens, but not before the austerity and otherworldly preoccupations of 'ideational' archaic Greece had begun to yield and an 'idealistic' cultural development of human powers to meet sensate human needs was gaining more and more support.

Statesman and successful general, Cimon of Athens (*c* 512–449 BC), two generations before Plato (*c* 429–347 BC), is said to have been the first to look for natural beauty as an aid to civic amenity rather than as an honour to the gods. During the first half of the fifth century BC he was, said Plutarch, 'the first to beautify the city with the so-called "liberal" and elegant resorts which were so excessively popular a little later, by planting the Agora with plane trees and by converting the Academy from a waterless and arid spot into a well-watered grove'. The Agora was the great public place below the Acropolis where the men of Athens loved to gather and gossip. The Academy was an open space outside the walls of Athens which later became renowned as the place where Plato talked and reasoned about philosophy, ethics and life. It was, said a character in one of the plays of Aristophanes, planted with trees, olives, and others, to provide a gratifying scene

> All fragrant with woodbine and peaceful content and
> the leaf which the lime-blossoms fling
>
> When the plane whispers love to the elm in the grove
> in the beautiful season of Spring.

Old traditional beliefs in the complicated mythology of Greek gods and goddesses were slowly giving way, in the minds of more reflective Greeks, to a greater trust in the power of human reason.

The Greeks had the example of their great enemies, the Persians, before them, but Persian parks and gardens, often of great extent, were the creations of an autocratic king and a few of his staff and his court, often as game and hunting reserves. Democratic Greeks not only had no such great and powerful aristocrats but hated the thought of them. So stories about Persian 'paradises' remained travellers' tales for them. Such was that told by the Greek general Zenophon who described how, around 400 BC, a young Persian prince, Cyrus, took him through his 'paradise' or enclosed park at Sardis to admire 'the beauty of the trees all planted at equal intervals . . . in perfect regularity – the rectangular symmetry of the whole and the many sweet scents which hung about them'. Apart from this solitary reference, there is no description of a Persian garden at this early time and nothing to show whether these earlier inhabitants of Iran anticipated the often splendid gardens of their successors some 2000 years later. The ornamental reliefs on the magnificent stairway of the royal palace buildings in Persepolis built between 518 and 460 BC do however include reminders of the natural beauty of trees and flowers.

Outside Greece, in the Greek colony of Sicily, where the able Dionysius I (430–367 BC) overthrew democratic government to rule alone as 'tyrant', he is said to have created a royal park on the Persian model, but it was short-lived. It was not until Alexander the Great made his epic and victorious drive (334–323 BC) to the very borders of India that there was any mass contact between Greeks, Persians, Indians and other oriental peoples. It proved most fruitful to Egypt, where one of Alexander's Greek commanders, Ptolemy, founded a new dynasty and where Greeks settled to create the Hellenistic culture centred upon Alexandria.

Owing everything to the great Greek thinkers of the two previous centuries, Alexandrine cultural life was both more practical and inventive as well as being more extravagant and artificial in poetry and literature than that of the homeland. Gardens there became a striking feature of the landscape to impress later visitors such as Strabo, who referred briefly to them in his travel-book over 300 years later. This Hellenistic culture, fortified by the powerful contribution of the Ionian Greeks in Asia Minor, deeply influenced life in Mediterranean lands. It was able to stimulate a love of gardens as well. The great historian Rostovtzeff believed that 'even in the third century BC Greece was one of the best cultivated countries in the world. Her vineyards and olive groves, her fruit gardens and kitchen gardens were famous.'

He quotes no sources for this opinion and he does not mention flower gardens, pleasure gardens or landscape gardens. In time Greek love of flowers became more widespread. In addition to the rose, the Greeks greatly favoured the carnation, wallflower, narcissus, violet, crocus, gillyflower, sweet marjoram and lavender. They revelled in as many as they could afford and sought to perpetuate their pleasant odour through the arts of the perfume-maker. One sign of a greater effort to improve them is to be read in the story that Alexander the Great sent back to his tutor, Aristotle, seeds of flowers and plants he encountered on his victorious march to India.

Although mainland Greeks made no progress in domestic garden layout and design, in two ways they made some beginnings which the Romans were later to pick up and develop. They beautified public places and recreation grounds, such as the Academy, by deliberately planting trees and shrubs. That they adorned temples also was discovered by American archaeologists in 1936 when flower pots, regularly aligned with the columns, were discovered on three sides of the Temple of Hephaestus (formerly called the Theseum) on the west of the Agora. They have been restocked with myrtle and pomegranate. The Greeks

The Temple of Hephaestus, formerly the Theseum; pots of replanted myrtle and pomegranate stand in front of its columns

developed the domestic architecture of larger houses by adding a small interior square, colonnaded courtyard or 'peristyle' which could, like Minoan light-wells, contain flowers or shrubs in pots or be made into a small garden. Romans saw these houses when they captured Delos in the middle of the second century BC. Later they began to build in the same style.

The great achievement of the Greeks – and it revolutionized civilization – was more fundamental than their modest efforts at creating public gardens, recreation fields and fostering a love of trees and flowers with their ritual and social uses. The Greeks developed the life of the mind.

If gardening is to become an art, other considerations arise beyond the pleasurable sensations of a passing moment. It was therefore of the greatest consequence that one or two powerful Greek minds, not content alone with admiring and creating beautiful things, which they did in full measure, began also to puzzle over the inner nature or cause of their excellence and beauty. They taught mankind to think with general ideas, with concepts. By studying the due proportions which in music and architecture, for instance, go to make up a pleasant harmonious whole, they discovered that such harmony could be expressed by mathematical ratios. They were thus able to see more clearly into the manner in which pattern and symmetry of form give coherence and unity to complex wholes so as to make them appear fitting, intelligible and satisfying to all beholders. The converse of this positive achievement was a reduction and, in the best periods, an elimination of ugliness, deformity, sombre stiffness, ungainliness as well as the avoidance of the bizarre, the fantastic and the obscure. The result, in the 'idealistic' fifth century BC, was Plato's conception of perfect beauty and form as an idea or ideal of divine creation of which mere mundane objects could never be more than an imperfect copy.

Plato's austere idealism, modified by his pupil and immediate successor Aristotle, lived on to influence many other thinkers, notably Plotinus (AD *c* 205–270) during the Roman Empire. Soon after the death of Aristotle in 322 BC men's inclinations turned more eagerly towards the things of this world. Epicurus (*c* 342–270 BC) stimulated this trend by saying that 'we call pleasure the alpha and omega of a blessed life'. He had to hasten to point out that he 'did not mean the pleasures of the prodigal or the pleasures of sensuality, as we are understood to do by some through ignorance, prejudice or wilful misrepresentation'. Most people, sensuous by nature, did not wish to have their pleasures limited in such manner, so they accepted the teaching of Epicurus very readily but without his qualifications. Hedonism resulted, the pursuit of sensuous pleasure for its own sake.

Before it triumphed completely, there was a brief period in which the claims of pleasure, the call of duty, of obedience to principle and awe and wonder about the unknown seemed to have about an equal response, a period of perfect balance which produced the magic of the Greek artists of the fifth century BC. Standards were then set in art and science which had never before been attained. Garden art could not fail to benefit ultimately, with other arts, from this remarkable expansion of human powers of perception, appraisal and progress from which mankind has never ceased to benefit. It is true that Egyptian and Mesopotamian arts and crafts had much earlier, like Minoan, attained astonishing excellence, but they flourished and decayed in sequestered valleys and islands, leaving no heritage of speculative thought and, unlike the Greeks, these earlier artists had no successors and no continuity in the ancient world.

A clear link may be seen between this new outlook and garden arts in the practice of the famous philosophers of Greek idealism of holding their discussions under trees in what were essentially gardens, or the beginnings of gardens. They were not formally set out, assiduously cultivated, graced by flower-beds, statuary, fountains and the other embellishments of the gardens of much later times. Plato's garden at the Academy was in 'a gymnasium outside the walls of Athens', bought for him, so Diogenes Laertius recorded, by a friend. When Aristotle (384–322 BC) returned to Athens, he lived in the Academy area also and taught there 'in the shady walks of the divine Hecademus' named after some unknown hero. Theophrastus (c 370–285 BC) carried forward the scientific work of his master Aristotle as a successful teacher, particularly in the study of plants about which more of his writings remain than of any other Greek. He left his garden in his Will to his friends 'to study literature and philosophy there in common', with strict injunctions about its maintenance. Epicurus later made his 'garden and all that pertains to it' his first concern in his Will, urging his heirs and trustees 'to maintain the garden' and 'to preserve the common life in the garden'. Cicero, who saw it 200 years later, said it was outside the Dipylon Gate, showing that in later times when Romans began to study in Greece and when a tourist trade began, the gardens of the philosophers drew visitors in the same way as the former homes of famous writers do today.

Before the effects of their profound discoveries could be more generally realized and propagated, the Greeks had to influence other peoples whose abilities and resources made them willing to learn. Those strange, un-European folk, the Etruscans, seem at some stages of their history to have absorbed something from the Greek example, although their civilization was very much an independent development. It arose as early and was obliterated sooner than that of Greece, after attaining an impressionistic vigour and eccentricity foreign to Grecian ways. Some tantalizing traces of its nature, achievement and influence, mainly in jewellery, pottery, statues and wall paintings, have survived in tombs. From them alone, it is difficult to decide whether their evidence of a considerable Etruscan interest in flowers, trees and in landscape (which is not a feature of Greek vase paintings) was an original contribution, or whether it had been inspired by Greece or more probably, the Near East, whence the Etruscans are supposed to have come. Nothing otherwise is known about an Etruscan love of nature or of gardens.

When Etruscan civilization crumbled from internal weakness and massive attacks by Gauls and Romans, the Greek colonies in south Italy alone confronted the Romans with a cultural tradition comparable with and even superior to that of their enemies and former masters, the Etruscans. Soon the Greeks, too, were to fall before the tough combative Romans, who slowly qualified as the heirs, in parts at least, of the Greek humanistic tradition. But the Romans were tardy, recalcitrant and, for long, difficult and rather dense apprentices.

An unexpected, paradoxical contrast arises in the story of garden development in ancient Greece and Rome. The Greeks, one of the most artistic, most inventive people in the annals of humanity, failed to perfect gardens as an art form. The Romans, not endowed with much aesthetic sensibility, created splendid gardens in Italy and spread them throughout Western Europe. Why the Greeks failed, has already been explained. The Romans, by contrast, for all their love of hearth and home, their intense loyalty to their family and their country, their bravery and self-sacrifice, were all too often wooden-headed, clumsy-handed, cruel and heartless to their enemies. How was it that they were able to succeed?

Hard-working peasant farmers, the Romans were no strangers to the task of growing corn, vegetables, vines, herbs and fruits but, after the manner of peasants generally, they were long singularly obtuse about the world of art. Hard and dour, they had always led austere lives. Fighting was their trade. Etruscans to the north of them, Greeks to the south, were relishing worldly beauty to which the aggressive Romans long seem to have been indifferent and insensitive. During their conquest of Sicily in the Second Punic War (218–201 BC), Livy recorded that 'miracles of Greek art' were captured by the Romans when they sacked Syracuse in 212 BC and other Greek towns in south Italy a little later. It was during that desperately fought war that a few paintings were first recorded in Rome. They were battle scenes executed by Italians or Greeks and by the only republican Roman who gained fame as a painter, for which he got the nickname 'painter' – Fabius 'Pictor' – not a compliment.

The first signs of a change can be discerned in the second century BC among a few of Rome's aristocracy. During their wars in Asia Minor, Roman soldiers and their commanders had seen oriental parks, Hellenistic gardens and elegant houses. They had belonged to the wealthier folk, many of whom Roman army commanders took as captives, together with as much loot as they could carry to sell in Rome. Greek and west Asian men, women, boys and girls, many of whom were more cultured and intelligent than their coarse captors, were shipped like cattle to fill the slave markets of Rome. Their skill and good taste were something new in Roman life. Some of them became gardeners.

By the first century BC the leaders of Roman society were becoming more civilized and sophisticated, with a keen desire for more luxurious living. The first famous large private park or garden within the fast expanding city of Rome, although outside the old Servian walls, was that of Lucullus, who had campaigned successfully for Rome in the Near East from 74 to 63 BC, when he was superseded by Pompey. He then retired to Rome to live until his death in 56 BC in a style that has made his name a synonym for exquisite luxury. Situated roughly on the high ground above the present Spanish Steps in Rome, the palace and grounds of Lucullus long remained a splendid site, although nothing is known of its actual layout or contents.

Garden scene; stucco from the House of the Priestess of Isis

Pompey got back to Rome in 62 BC with spoils and booty greatly exceeding the vast haul of his predecessor. Some of this new wealth went into beautifying the city of Rome for, with Greek examples before his eyes, Pompey created Rome's first permanent theatre and adorned the large portico in front of it with scores of trees to form a leafy open space. He seems also to have enlarged his own grounds in the Campus Martius below the park of Lucullus, extending them over the northern end of the Pincian Hill. To the east of the gardens of Lucullus, the historian Sallust later created his own splendid gardens on the strength of the war booty he brought back from Numidia where Caesar had left him in command in 46–45 BC. Ever since those early times, the Pincian Hill has been a garden site.

A few millionaires grown rich by looting might start a tradition of luxurious garden retreats on this scale, but smaller men had to be content with much less. Cicero (102–43 BC), Rome's greatest orator, lived comfortably but his town house had no great garden, although he said that it satisfied him. On his country estates he had more space and he adorned his favourite Tusculan villa with a colonnaded and tree-sheltered walk, largely as a setting for some Greek statues which he commissioned his friend Atticus to buy for him in 68 BC. Cicero's brother, Quintus, had more lavish ideas. While he was campaigning with a Roman army under Caesar, slaughtering, enslaving and looting their way through Gaul in 54 BC, Cicero was supervising the embellishment of a new villa he had bought for Quintus near their family home at Arpinum. It was, Cicero told him, 'marvellously pleasant with a fishpond, spouting fountains, an open space and plantation. Your gardener has clothed everything with ivy ... so that your Greek statues seem to have been turned into gardeners selling ivy.' Flowers were not mentioned.

At last, at the end of half a millennium in the life of the Roman Republic, a new breath of art in garden design can be detected and its origin was Greek. In a single generation garden design had become a speciality, like landscape art.

47

Flora, the Roman goddess of flowers, depicted on a fresco from Stabia

Romans, who produced no original philosophers or theologians, shared the strong mystical feelings of the Greeks for the unseen powers of nature. From the Etruscans, the Romans had absorbed the cult of *Lares*, gods of cross-roads, whom they transformed into special protectors of the home and the garden. In that character they found later a rival in the strange god, Priapus. From other Italian and foreign sources the Romans, in their superstitious anxiety to protect their precious plots and homes, adopted other gods and goddesses: Flora, who cared for all the flowers, Pomona and Venus, among others. Like the Greeks, they had a deep reverence for the nymphs and the mysterious spirits, *numina*, who abounded in field and forest. It survived in the sacred groves of trees that were long maintained in the very heart of Rome, although by the time of Cicero they had dwindled to miserable remnants of their former size.

Cicero was not a religious man, but when he suffered a crushing blow by the death of his one daughter, Tullia, early in 45 BC, the only person for whom he seems to have had a passionate and tender affection, he could think of no other solace for his searing grief than to dedicate a garden in her memory. So many other Romans wanted gardens that Cicero, for all his urgent enquiries, seems to have been unable to find a plot and it seems unlikely that a memorial garden was found for Tullia. One garden he hoped to get was already reserved for Julius Caesar, then dictator of Rome.

Joy in the natural beauty of nature seems to have been growing, or, at least, first finding literary expression, among the Romans at about that time also. Catullus (*c* 84–54 BC), the first, the freshest, and the best of the Latin lyric poets whose works have survived, threw some shafts of light upon the Italian scene, for he rejoiced in the bright laughing wavelets on his beloved Sirmio (Lake Garda), the mountains, green woods, secret glens and resounding rivers, the bright streams leaping forth over moss-grown rocks to gush into the valley below. Similar touches are found a little later, in the *Georgics* and other works of Virgil, in the poems of Propertius, of Tibullus, and of Horace, but the sensual Ovid, for all his thousands of lines, and although the road to Rome from his home lay through the grand hills of the Abruzzi, had nothing to say in praise of scenic beauty.

So much of the literature of the Romans has been lost that it is dangerous to judge their character dogmatically from what remains. It seems true, however, that despite their superstitious awe and reverence for the unseen, most Romans lived severely practical, common-sense, positivistic lives. They were not much interested in the new Greek philosophical ideas about 'beauty', 'charm', 'artistry', 'urbanity' and so forth, about which Cicero wrote. It has never been easy to express abstract thought in Latin, as Lucretius and Cicero were the first to complain. Few Romans had as yet studied for a year or more in Athens as Cicero had done, to be exposed there to the glories of Greek sculpture, architecture, painting and music, or to the subtle refinements of Greek speculative and philosophical thought. Immensely impressive as that great artistic heritage should have been when it was still virtually intact in Cicero's youth, it was by then a mixture of very various styles.

During the course of its long development, Greek art had greatly changed from the austere, ethereal beauty of the archaic art of the ideational sixth century; to the perfection of the idealistic, humanistic art of the fifth century, and to the much more flamboyant, ornamental, often over-decorated art of the relatively decadent, sensate Hellenistic period.

Earlier than the Greeks, Rome's Etruscan neighbours had shown a broadly similar artistic evolution. Because the later Etruscan and Greek art was sensate in essence, it jibed badly with Roman ideas, still traditionally, austerely republican, simple, honest and unsophisticated. Cicero remembered his grandfather, who, in common with the rest of his generation, scorned and distrusted the Greeks – 'that race of babblers' as old Cato, his grandfather's friend, called them. Suddenly, through this mixture of the different styles of the immensely potent Greek production, Romans had to find their own way to a more cultural life.

Their perplexity can be better understood today when inhabitants of new countries and people newly awakened to an appreciation of beauty in old countries are confronted with an even greater jumbled mixture of the productions of artists and craftsmen from all countries at all the various periods of their cultural evolution. Like the Romans, they lacked direction because the clear distinction which might help them between the qualities and excellences of ideational, idealistic and sensate art is not generally made. It is not realized that each is the product of a different cultural period; that they are to be assessed by standards which are not merely different, but can be fundamentally incompatible. Lacking clear guidance, but dazzled by their sudden wealth and by the marvellous products of Greek and Middle Eastern artists which it enabled them to acquire, the Romans stumbled clumsily into their expanding imperial heritage.

During the Imperial Age, Romans, despite the artistic confusion of their time, had enormous advantages over other European people which enabled them to advance many of the arts of peace for the first time on a European scale. For over 400 years, Italy was never invaded by foreign enemies. There were, it is true, some frightful scenes of violence and horror during that long time but they were short-lived, and Italy as a whole was not overwhelmed by such upheavals. As soon as many Romans became rich – and relatively more Romans were able to boast of great wealth than any other European peoples until modern times – then soil, climate, water, everything favoured the development of gardens. Their nature and extent can be visualized thanks to references to them in some Roman writing and, still better, from actual garden sites uncovered in the two small country towns of Pompeii and Herculaneum south of Rome, which were suddenly buried by ashes, mud and lava from the fierce eruption of Vesuvius in AD 79.

Houses and gardens there show that many Romans and provincials were advancing in their quest for a pleasant life. The contrast between these two small towns and Olynthus, a Greek town in Chalcidice in southern Macedonia of the fourth century BC, gives some measure of Roman progress in the arts of living. No house there had a garden or a courtyard large enough for growing flowers, shrubs or a tree. Not more than one or two flower pots have been excavated among the ruins to which it was reduced by Philip II of Macedonia (348 BC). Both Pompeii and Herculaneum were insignificant places by imperial Roman standards, yet several of their wealthier citizens had enjoyed well-designed and reasonably large gardens for many years before they perished.

Such gardens were regarded as an essential part of the house itself, serving as a room in the open air for much of the year. They might be a square or oblong colonnaded plot with fountains, pools, pergolas adorned with vines, roses or other climbing plants and shrubs or other flowers growing in small flower-beds separated by narrow paths edged by close-trimmed box. Sometimes, as in the 'House of Menander', there would be a low wall between the columns on which country scenes would be painted, while ivy would be trained up the columns.

The peristyle in the garden of the House of Menander, Pompeii, before 79 AD

Larger houses would include fruit trees. A fine painting was found in one elegant house in Pompeii showing a grand garden scene and an orchard of plums, figs, pears, cherries and lemons. In their small houses, less well-to-do folk who had no space for a garden would often contrive to have a few rose bushes round the little atrium and would compensate for their lack of a real garden by having garden scenes painted on a wall.

The vast majority of the Roman citizens of ancient Italy were not rich, so, just as their successors today, they must have lived without gardens or at best with a plant or two in a pot. Window boxes became quite common after most city-dwellers were forced to live in large apartment houses that steadily began to replace detached private houses in Rome from the second century BC onwards. It was a housing development which by AD 350 reduced the number of private houses to 1782 against 44,173 great blocks of apartments. 'The common people of Rome offered the eye a reflection of the country with their miniature gardens in their windows,' wrote the elder Pliny (c 23/24–79), and the poet Martial (c 40–104) made fun of his own little window box which did not grow enough, he said, to nourish one caterpillar. To maintain even one or two plants, water had to be carried from a fountain. Martial lived near an aqueduct, but he had no tap in his rooms. The pleasure the Romans must have got from the sight of their growing plants was therefore more dearly bought than it would be in most cities today.

Their own little window boxes or gardens, where they had them, were by no means the only sight of growing plants and flowers which the Romans enjoyed. During the Empire more public gardens were added to the few, such as Julius Caesar's, inherited from the Republic. Soon others appeared in Rome, such as the grass and trees set out around the *thermae*, the great public recreation and social centres with their hot and cold baths, libraries, recreation grounds and other facilities.

Almost ringing the city as a 'green belt', moreover, were the large gardens, once private property but from the first century AD onwards mostly in the control of the Emperor. 'If such open spaces act as lungs to a city,' it has been said, 'no city ever breathed more freely than Rome.' Our own age of cement and glass buildings run up as cheaply as possible in morbid terror of decoration, as often as not lacking even a skimpy grass fringe at their base, an age in which civic beauty is often priced out of existence by cost-accountants and tax-gatherers, contrasts shabbily with Rome's sheer splendour in marble, gold and impressive public buildings, and with its gardens and open spaces. Romans, who were not themselves great artists, temporarily enriched the world of art to an extent that can now barely be imagined even from the vast and impressive surviving ruins that yet remain after more than 1500 years of decay and neglect.

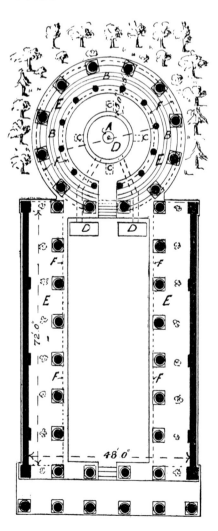

The plan of the Roman scholar Varro's famous aviary in the gardens of his villa at Casino

Away from the vast imperial city of Rome lay the villas, mansions and country estates of solid Roman citizens, many of them much larger and more impressive than the small gardens of a town such as Pompeii. Very little is known about them apart from remarks by the younger Pliny (c 61–114) and his uncle, Pliny the Elder.

The elder Pliny, who perished in his attempt to rescue victims of the fatal eruption of Vesuvius in AD 79, had spent his long life in eager study and writing. His *Natural History*, almost an encyclopaedia of Roman knowledge, does not deal with gardens as such but it contains a great deal of ancient lore, collected from other writings and his own experience about trees, plants, fruits, flowers and the use to which they were put in making garlands, perfumes and medicines. He was also keenly interested in the history of painting and sculpture. By his time many Romans had created a pattern of luxurious living which included the enjoyment of gardens, parks and large elegant villas. Already Cicero's great rival, the orator Hortensius, had a villa at Laurentum on the coast about sixteen miles from Rome set in a park stocked with many kinds of animals all of whom had been tamed and trained to come at the sound of a lute played for them during dinner parties by a slave dressed to personify Orpheus. Another of Cicero's friends, the scholar Varro, described his handsome aviary, 15 metres (48 feet) wide by 22 metres (72 feet) long, with a large circular dome at one end supported by two dozen marble columns. Fresh river water gushed through it, filling ponds and gutters for the birds, 'all kinds of which were to be found there'. Remains of Roman mural paintings survive to show how Romans liked to associate and enhance garden pleasures with the charm of birds.

There was therefore a considerable gardening tradition in Rome by the time of the elder Pliny, upon which he was able to draw and also supplemented by personal observation. He paid a great tribute to the eager curiosity of the men of old who, he said, had left nothing untried but had scoured the trackless mountains, the empty deserts and the very bowels of the earth in their search for plants either fascinating in themselves or valuable as food or medicine. 'We moderns', he pessimistically observed, 'have lost the habit of research for human good.' The Romans had never done much for botanical learning. Marcus Cato, the Censor, in the second century BC had been the first but, said Pliny, he did not do much and he had no successor.

There was at least one botanical garden in Rome, because Pliny used to visit it. He said that its owner, Antonius Castor, over one hundred years old, was still actively raising his specimens with no loss of memory and no physical defect. Nevertheless Pliny's own account of plants is literary as much as scientific. Among all herbs, moly was the most famous, he said, apparently for no better reason than that Homer had said so nearly 1000 years previously. It has been thought to have been *Allium nigrum* or *Withania somnifera* – sleepy nightshade. Next in reputation was the plant of the twelve major gods, *Dodecatheon*, possibly the primrose, *Primula vulgaris* (*P. acaulis*), not the *Primula veris* (*P. officinalis*), which is not known to grow in Greece, followed by the penteboron, *Paeonia officinalis*, and the universal healing plants, of which Pliny describes four varieties, including elecampane, sweet winter marjoram and giant fennel.

By his time the use of these old traditional herbal remedies was becoming as remote from the life of sophisticated Romans as Anglo-Saxon wort-cunning or medieval simples are to the average Londoner or New Yorker. Why should anybody bother with them, asked Pliny, when doctors abound on all sides? Roman kitchen gardens were also rather neglected. Pliny's contemporary, Columella, lamented that the poor diet of the average Roman lacked the improvement that fresh garden vegetables would bring. There was however a developed market-garden industry because there was money in it. Greengrocers' stalls probably looked then very much the same as they do in Italy today.

This Roman emphasis upon the commercial aspect of gardening is also very evident in the few Roman remarks about flower growing. Pliny's account is the fullest but he was mainly concerned with their commercial use in making up wreaths, chaplets or garlands and in making perfumes and unguents. At the same time he does not conceal the pleasure he got from the charm of their colours and scents. He began to run through the gardener's year beginning with the white violet, the first herald of spring, followed by the 'ion', *Viola odorata*, and the flame-coloured wild phlox which has been conjectured to have been the wallflower *Cheiranthus cheiri*, although Theophrastus described it as without scent. Cyclamen, Pliny said, bloom both in spring and autumn. Somewhat later came the narcissus and the lily. Of all Roman flowers, the rose was chief. There were few varieties. One was the wild rose 'sometimes growing on a bramble with a faint but pleasant smell'. More highly regarded were others distinguished by the number of their petals, from five to one hundred; by their smooth or rough stem, and by their colour or scent. Some lacked scent but others were renowned; none more so than the roses of Cyrene, for it was from them the best perfume was obtained.

From such tantalizingly meagre references and from one or two mural paintings some rough idea can be gleaned of the great appeal of the rose in the Roman Empire. In the middle of the rose season the lily, *Lilium candidum*, began to bloom in Roman gardens where it was second only to the rose in general favour. In the same breath, Pliny mentions the convolvulus, *Calystegia* (*convolvulus*), as 'a rough sketch which Nature made when learning to produce the lily'. After the lily came the anemone, usually the poppy anemone *Anemone coronaria* although the *Anemone apennina* was another variety. Then Pliny goes on to list a number of other plants less easy to identify. They seem to include wild vine or wine-flower, cassidony. 'gladiolus', probably corn-flag, rose campion, spike lavender, sweet marjoram, iris, crocus, spikenard, blue cornflower, periwinkle, yellow daisy (*Chrysanthemum coronarium*) and others. Difficulty arises over his 'hyacinthus', which has been taken to be a wild hyacinth or bluebell, a gladiolus, purple lily, or scilla, but not our garden hyacinth. Pliny broke off his catalogue before he had completed the gardener's year but it is evident that his list is not much more than a collection of wild flowers, although he did distinguish between wild and cultivated flowers, noting that those with most fragrance were usually wild. He said that 'cultivated saffron is better than other kinds, but it is not so effective'. Despite its cultivation, it was, he said, degenerating everywhere. Vergil had earlier pointed out that a constant effort had to be exerted by farmers and growers everywhere to beat back the universal tendency of everything to fall back into decay 'not otherwise than the rower who strives to force his craft against the stream, who, if he relaxes, is swept headlong down the tide'.

It is therefore difficult to reconstruct a Roman garden as a Roman would have seen it. Some plants have degenerated, perhaps become extinct, such as the 'petellium' which it now seems impossible to identify. Others have changed their character through long cultivation. The cypress, for instance, now so evocative of an Italian background, was an 'exotic' to Pliny, 'naturalized with the greatest difficulty'. Rome's first writer of renown, Ennius, had mentioned it, while Cato later in the second century BC gave what was, for him, a lengthy set of instructions about the way to raise it from seed. He said that the best seed came from Tarentum, which suggests that the Greeks popularized it in southern Italy, having derived it themselves from Anatolia. Theophrastus and Virgil after him regarded Mount Ida in Crete as the best known home of the cypress. Sacred to Dis, god of the last home of the dead, it was placed outside houses as a sign of mourning and it is still found in cemeteries.

Pliny saw little good in it. He said that its leaves and berries were bitter and useless, it yielded little wood and he objected to what he called its pungent smell. However, money could be made after thirteen years' growth by selling it as poles or props, so a cypress plantation gained the name 'a daughter's dowry', which it continues to bear in Crete in modern times. Little esteemed at first, it was beginning to find more favour in Pliny's day because of its decorative possibilities. 'It is clipped and trained to form hedgerows,' Pliny said, 'or else thinned and lengthened out in various designs in ornamental gardening, representing fleets, hunting scenes and various other objects' – a strange use for cypress.

In the next generation, around AD 100, his nephew, the younger Pliny, makes the first known clear distinction between the beauties of nature and the beauty of garden art. He left in his letters lengthy descriptions of two of his villas or country seats: one in Tuscany, the other on the coast five or six miles south of Ostia and only about sixteen miles from Rome. The countryside of Tuscany was, he said, so exceedingly beautiful that anyone would think it was a painted landscape depicted in the most gloriously beautiful manner. He also described with relish the natural beauty of the public park around the sacred source of the Clitumnus stream in Umbria which Augustus had protected. Yet he thought that

A fanciful 18th-century plan of the great Tuscan estate of Pliny the Younger, the first person to make a clear distinction between the beauties of nature and the beauty of garden art

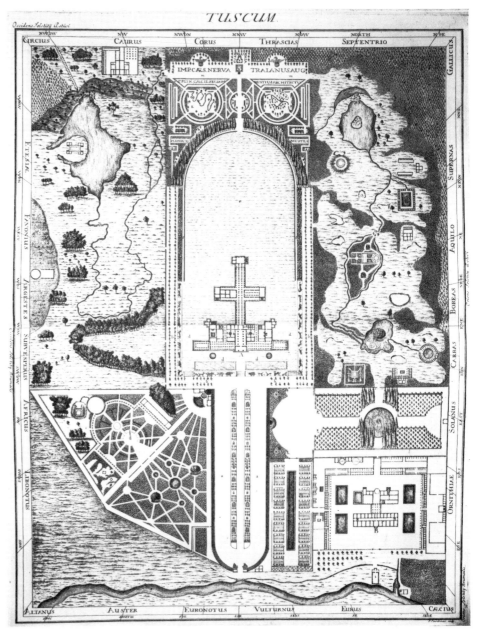

his own garden owed to art as many beauties as his fields and meadows owed to nature. Here is the germ of those theories of the picturesque and of the kinship of landscape art, gardening and painting which one or two Englishmen thought they were the first to proclaim in the latter half of the eighteenth century.

Although Pliny set out to describe his gardens fully, no two efforts to reconstruct them are the same. His favourite was a villa in Umbria, halfway between Rome and Lake Como, where he had two more villas. One, high above the lake, is thought to have been in the Serbelloni Park at the extremity of the Colunga peninsula, now owned by the Rockefeller Foundation. He preferred to be in his villa in Umbria:

Immediately upon entering visitors get a full view of the plane trees all round. They are so covered with ivy that their leaves and those of the ivy intermingle. The ivy covers not only the trunks and branches of each tree but runs from one tree to another, joining them together. Box trees are planted between each plane tree and behind them are bay trees adding to the shade.

54

A little beyond this ivy-clad entrance, the straight driveway ended in a semicircle over which cypresses cast a deep, dark shade while flower-beds were resplendent with roses. Paths are mentioned, lined with boxwood hedges 'and in between grass plots with box trees cut into all kinds of different shapes, some of them being letters spelling out the name of the owner or of the gardener who did the work'. Pliny also boasts of 'a level spread of acanthus so soft I might almost call it fluid'. The craze for cutting box hedges and other shrubs into odd shapes and sizes in which the younger Pliny indulged was, according to his uncle, something fairly new. 'C. Matius, a member of the equestrian order and a friend of Augustus invented the art of clipping rows of trees about eighty years ago', he said, which would have been around 5 BC. He also mentioned that the art of dwarfing trees was practised in Rome, indicating a distaste for the practice which his nephew did not share.

Pliny the Younger also described in some detail his elegant, solidly constructed open-air dining arbour with its four graceful vine-clad columns of Greek Carystian marble, and its curved white marble couches on which his guests and he reclined, around a stone basin faced with marble which was filled, though never overflowing, with water. Some of the lighter courses of the banquet were floated on the water in small ships and model birds. This was by no means the only fountain, for Pliny refers to others, some throwing a jet high into the air. Throughout the grounds there was the pleasant sound of rills and rivulets of water.

In Laurentum on the coast, where Hortensius had his country estate, Pliny

A modern reconstruction of the younger Pliny's estate at Laurentum. Box and rosemary lined the avenue and 'the garden is well planted with mulberries and figs'

had another smaller villa, to serve rather as a weekend cottage would today. There also box lined the avenue except where it was exposed to wind and salt spray. Then it was replaced by rosemary. 'The garden is well planted with mulberries and figs for the soil suits them very well but it isn't good for any other trees' except bay trees. They were considered to promote health. A hundred years later, Commodus, when emperor of Rome, was advised to retire there to escape the plague at Rome. 'A terrace fragrant with violets' is the only mention of flowers at Laurentum.

The century and a half which had elapsed between the days when Cicero was buying statues for a garden and having them decorated with ivy, and the lifetime of the younger Pliny saw therefore a great development in Roman country estates and gardens. They were larger, more richly endowed with trees and shrubs as well as with sweet-smelling flowers, roses and violets. In comparison, the garden Cicero described, like the pleasures of his country birthplace, was much simpler, almost austere. Pliny's gardens provided a new note of sensuous enjoyment. Yet it is clear from the description he gives of the way he passed his time in them that he was no sybarite. He walked, rode on horseback as well as being carried about in a carriage or a litter and he gave hours of toil to literature in the hope of becoming a great orator and writer.

What aristocrats such as Pliny achieved was modest in comparison with the splendour created for an emperor. Not all emperors were renowned for their great interest in parks and gardens, although by AD 100 many of the large gardens within Rome itself had been added to the imperial domain, through theft or more or less enforced legacies. The most spectacular new imperial parks and gardens were those of Nero (54–68) and Hadrian (117–138). Taking advantage of the havoc caused by a ruinous fire that destroyed the greater part of Rome in AD 64, Nero calmly annexed 200 acres in the very heart of the city covering the slopes of the Palatine and Esquiline hills and the eastern entrance to the Forum, to create a landscaped park of fields, vineyards, pasture and woodland with huge numbers of wild and domestic animals and a lake like a sea. It seems to have been a Roman version of a Persian royal 'paradise' or hunting park. Within it he built a new palace, his 'Golden House', on a scale of luxurious splendour to outdo anything hitherto attempted. But within five years, and before it was all completed, Nero met a violent end. Soon after, the estate was broken up and mostly returned to public use. Vespasian drained the lake and began to build a vast amphitheatre, the Colosseum, on its site.

The next huge new imperial park was that round the palace built at Tibur (Tivoli) for Hadrian, who became emperor in AD 117. Considerably larger than Nero's park in the middle of Rome, it attracted far less adverse comment because it was in the country and Hadrian was not a vicious megalomaniac. His enthusiasm for Greek culture comes out in some of the special features of the place, the Academy, the Lyceum and the Vale of Tempe. It was a chain of parks with pools, grottoes and a vast wealth of superb statuary, rather than a single unified whole. Neither it nor Nero's Golden House are typical specimens of Roman garden art, for nobody except an emperor in command of the riches of the world could have created them. They may however be taken as showing what the unstinted wish-fulfilment of a rich Roman with taste could involve. It is all the more unfortunate therefore that surviving evidence does not permit a plausible reconstruction in any detail of their probable appearance.

The art that went into creating the lesser parks and gardens of a wealthy Roman citizen in the Italian countryside around AD 100, in so far as Pliny's were typical,

Hadrian's villa at Tivoli; a partial reconstruction of the central ornamental pool, surrounded by statues and colonnades, for which his parks were famous

was compounded out of relatively few special features. The whole was planned to appear to good advantage from many points of view, including those from the house, from the walks, the lengthy drives, and the paths between the plots in which grew shrubs, bushes and trees cut into all manner of fancy designs, as well as tall cypresses and planes festooned with ivy. Fountains and running water were prized and inevitably pools or ponds were essential. Garden pavilions, shelters and marble seats were also elegant decorative features of large gardens. Flowers were not forgotten but they were secondary and simple – violets, roses and rosemary seem often to have sufficed.

By Pliny's day intensive cultivation was accompanied by efforts to improve plants and trees, especially fruit trees. Grafting had been tried for so long on so many trees that Pliny thought that all possibilities of improvement by that method had been exhausted.

While many flowers were well known in ancient Rome, they were evidently not much cultivated in private gardens, except, as Pliny said, violets and roses. Indeed they are not to this day. In Italy the emphasis has always been upon greenery, shade and water, diversified by stonework and marble. Many beautiful sculptures, antique Greek for preference, were set up as the owner could afford. Because the more famous originals were unobtainable, a great trade in copies developed. Over fifty have been discovered of the beautiful Cnidian Venus alone, which Praxiteles carved about 364 BC, and there were many others. Romans, as Cicero's example shows, were the first to set up that marble garden statuary which looks so well in an Italian summer but seems incongruous in a northern winter. It is sometimes said that the then new art of cutting evergreens into various shapes was a poor man's substitute for expensive marble statues. It is now known as topiary work from the Roman *topiarius*, meaning gardener, first used by Cicero, but was then called *Nemora tonsilia*, 'shorn' or 'trimmed glades'.

Roman gardens were larger, richer and more diversified by flowers, shrubs and trees than any previously seen in the Western world. Where the relatively confined space of a peristyle limited gardening design, the layout of the garden had to be formal, regular and symmetrical. Where ample space was available the formal element, although still there in the planned walks, drives, fountains, statuary and shrubberies, was less obtrusive. Pliny, on his Umbrian estate, seems to have been so smitten with the beauty of the surrounding countryside that he made his park merge to some extent with the fields and the sight of natural beauty. But the formal, planned, artistic aspect of his grounds was sufficiently pronounced to make it more akin to the mannered, architectural designs of Renaissance Italy and France than to the open, landscaped wild 'English garden' of the eighteenth century. In both its aspects the Roman garden served to inspire and instruct the aristocrat of Western Europe after the recovery of many of the Roman classics. They would have had far more, and probably far better practical guides had not Greek gardening literature perished with so much Roman writing.

In the course of two or three centuries the old Roman character had changed completely. It used to be the fashion, started by the Romans themselves, to try to explain such a revolution by the influx of slaves from the degenerate lands of Asia Minor and Greece. There were indeed vast numbers of them. In Italy they bred very many more. If they were not all brought up on stern old Roman lines it was because fewer and fewer Romans were either. Roman cultural life itself had become as sensate as, long before, had the cultural life of the countries from which the slaves had come.

Against such a very powerful tendency to go all out for pleasure, Romans with responsibility for the safety and welfare of their country and their Empire had to fight a dogged battle against the constantly mounting challenge to the Roman way of life from without. Barbarians with little concern for their own sensate ease and convenience of life but with a fierce determination to survive, even if they had to fight Romans in order to do so, were being forced westwards. For two or three centuries there was sufficient vigour in the Roman Empire to hold them at bay. It was fortified by the spread of Stoicism among more reflective Romans from the first century BC onwards. That vigour nerved many to resist the arbitrary rule of irresponsible emperors, and to die heroically as a result. It also inspired one emperor, Marcus Aurelius (AD 121–180), to become a Stoic saint.

A new challenge was also growing within Rome from people just as opposed to the feeble sensualists as any responsible Roman of the old school could wish. Yet they were an even greater menace to imperial Rome than were the feckless city mobs. Emperors as enlightened as Marcus Aurelius shared the distrust and resentment inspired by the new sect of Christians who would not honour the traditionally venerated gods of Rome. While the pleasure-loving Roman Empire weakened and decayed, Christianity was winning vastly more believers than had ever been attracted to Stoicism. They long expected, with eager anticipation, the imminent end of the world, a state of mind in which many of the activities and interests by which the Romans had formerly been animated lost their meaning and purpose and therefore their appeal. With the triumph of Christianity, the pleasures of the senses were condemned. A discriminating taste in designing and adorning an earthly home with gay gardens had no virtue in the Age of Faith that was destined to command the allegiance of mankind in Western Europe for the next thousand years or more.

Christianity effectively shattered much of the humanistic culture bequeathed by Greece and Rome. Barbarians might destroy the grand gardens of the wealthy citizens of the Roman Empire without exciting an urgent desire to see them restored. The history of garden arts, as of all other arts, cannot be understood without taking account of this revolution in cultural outlook and the values of civilization. Other periods of religious fervour had been characterized by a similar outlook, as a brief glance backwards in time will show, for the new way of life had antecedents in traditions formed centuries previously which were preserved in the writings of the Old Testament.

The barbarian folk who came as invaders in the fifth century AD and thereafter, or those who survived from the lower strata of Roman society lacked the skill and resources to maintain huge buildings, baths, water supplies, sewers and all the other technical equipment of a vast city, even if they felt any desire to do so, which is unlikely. As the splendid Roman palaces and houses decayed through long neglect, looting, burning and occasional earthquakes, squatters, bringing their chickens, pigs, goats and cattle, built their flimsy hutments amid the ruins. Slowly soil and rubbish mounted as drains were choked and as weeds, bushes and trees grew, withered, decayed, soon to be replaced by others.

As the centuries passed, a deep peace of ignorance slept over that great imperial city whose mere name had for centuries been able to electrify the minds of men. The notion aired in recent years, that the fall of Rome should be regarded as a 'myth', is not supported by the story of Roman gardening art. Neglected by political and social historians, gardening is so intimately a part of civilized life that it is a valuable index to the intensity and vitality of culture at any one time. When general poverty, civil discord, war and invasion bring human quality below civilized standards and nearer to an animal level of mere existence, then the arts of gardening no longer prosper. So it was in Rome.

So also was it in the provinces. Roman ways of life and with them Roman villas and gardens had spread throughout Western Europe. Flowers, roses and violets especially were widely cultivated as gardeners supplied the owners of large villas as well as the markets of towns with flowers, fruit and vegetables. Many a villa built in Gaul and Spain had ample gardens. Those in Britain were not thought to have been very notable until, in the 1960s, a very large courtyard garden, made for a vassal British king in Roman style, was discovered near Chichester. Its character was sufficiently evident to make it possible to restore it as it was once seen in Roman times. Where such provincial gardens are merely conjectural, literary sources confirm that they once existed.

As late as towards the end of the fifth century AD, Sidonius Apollinaris, near Bordeaux, and Fortunatus, a hundred years later, show that elegant Roman villas and country estates were still being maintained under barbarian rule in Gaul, but no detailed description of their gardens is known. Thereafter no secular writing has survived, and no more appeared for several hundred years. The Dark Ages intervened and when they lifted, all memory of the great pleasure gardens of Rome and its provinces had vanished.

A tenuous link between pagan Roman gardens and medieval gardens can however be discerned in the enclosed gardens of Christian monasteries and nunneries. Inheriting Roman-style houses with their porticoes and peristyle gardens, the monks and nuns used them to grow vegetables and medicinal herbs and perhaps flowers for the altar. The idea that gardening should yield aesthetic satisfaction, however, long fell under the stern disapproval with which all sensuous enjoyments were tabooed.

Fresco from Pompeii showing a villa with its characteristic court and formal, symmetrical garden layout

59

III

GARDENS AND THE GREAT RELIGIONS

Slight as are the traces of garden arts of ancient times, throughout many centuries men had worked hard to develop grand gardens, just as they had advanced civilization and created many other art forms of the very finest quality. Loyalties and the artistic efforts they inspired were at first given traditionally to religious and cult practices which seemed at the time to be essential for personal and communal survival. In more than one early civilization the hold which such habits and attitudes had exerted from immemorial antiquity began to weaken, probably with the growth of more confidence in human abilities and certainly with the increasing attractions of a more sensate, self-regarding, pleasure-seeking way of life.

Garden arts, like other arts, reflect such tendencies. They explain why garden art faded away in Roman lands as Christian principles of conduct were gradually given more honour at the expense of the pleasure-seeking daily round with all its diversions and material satisfactions. Tendencies they were; and no more, because cultural life is not a neat and tidy affair that can be divided up into a succession of packaged, independent and different styles. Millions of naughty pagans did not turn overnight, or in the fifth century AD, into worthy, spiritual, Bible-reading theologians. Cultural values, like the popular nymphs of Greek mythology, may not all be immortal, but many live a long, long while. So men continued to cultivate many gardens long after the ruin of the Roman Empire although the spirit in which many of them did so was new to the sophisticated Romans. It was a spirit with a long history in the Holy Land from which Christianity came.

Scanty as they are, the few references to gardens in one or two Books of the Bible have made a deeper impression on the minds of men in the English-speaking world than has any other garden literature of antiquity. The fact that the gardens to which they referred were nothing more than small plots of a few vines and

The garden of paradise; frontispiece from
Paradisi in Sole, 1629

olive trees, with a fig tree and possibly a pomegranate or two, did not lessen that impact, despite the fact that the vast majority of those who, in northern latitudes, gave earnest heed to every word in the holy Scriptures had never seen their like.

Wresting a living with difficulty from an often unrewarding soil, or struggling to create some small garden of their own, countless humble folk have been spurred on by the promise of Isaiah that the wilderness and the solitary place shall be glad and the desert shall rejoice and blossom as the rose. That 'rose', the rose of Sharon, with 'the lilies of the field', carried sacred overtones rarely evoked by the briar roses, the cowslips and the primroses of the British country-side, or by the new flowers of America, Australia or New Zealand. Modest ambitions for peace and prosperity cherished by such folk were fortified by reading that, once upon a time, Judah and Israel had dwelt safely, every man under his vine and under his fig tree from Dan, even unto Beersheba, all the days of Solomon; that once men had rejoiced in the rose of Sharon, the lily-of-the-valley and the flowers that appear on earth at the time of the singing of birds when the winter is past and the rain is over and gone.

But the garden message of the Bible was rarely of ease and luxury. The first Bible lesson told how the first woman and the first man fell from grace and were chased out of their home, a glorious garden graced by trees and their fruits pleasant to the sight and good for food, with the tree of life in the midst. In the sacred canon moreover, the hedonistic, sensate imagery of the Song of Solomon was followed by the stern words of Isaiah thundering against all those who, following the ways of the heathen, sought to create sacred trees or groves. 'Thou shalt not plant thee a grove of any trees near unto the altar of the Lord thy God,' he commanded, and the fate of Ahab, among whose crimes was to transgress this rule, re-enforced the lesson. 'They that forsake the Lord shall be consumed. They shall be ashamed of the oaks they have desired and they shall be confounded for the gardens they have chosen.' No wonder that Jews and Romans did not understand one another.

The folly of the pursuit of pleasure in gardens was moreover the message of that disillusioned preacher in the Book of Ecclesiastes who found no consolation from his gardens and orchards. 'I planted trees in them of all kinds of fruits. I made me pools of water . . . whatsoever mine eyes desired, I kept not from them. I withheld not my heart from any joy.' But, he said, 'when I looked on all the works that my hands had wrought, and on the labour I had laboured to do: behold all was vanity and vexation of spirit and there was no profit under the sun.'

So the garden stories of the Bible taught a moral lesson more often than they encouraged the human heart to rejoice in gardens or other delights of this world. Their message was not lost for many generations. Yet although the point of the story of Ahab King of Samaria and Jezebel his ruthless wife, who stole Naboth's vineyard to make a garden of herbs near the royal palace after he had refused to sell it to them, was to denounce the sin of covetousness, it also showed that gardens were very highly prized in ancient Palestine. A love of flowers and a deep feeling for natural beauty which lamented their short life was not absent from the grand solemnity of the prophet's admonitions: 'All flesh is grass and all the goodliness thereof is as the flower of the field. The grass withereth, the flower fadeth, but the word of our God shall stand for ever.'

Much effort, not always well informed, had gone into trying to identify some 150 plants, trees and shrubs mentioned in the Bible. When the early Hebrew

PREVIOUS PAGES The courtyard and garden of Chehel Sotun, Isfahan

62

writers and prophets were not more specific, it is impossible to do more than to hazard guesses about far less than a hundred of these flowers. Appreciation of natural beauty, which they could all take for granted, was subordinated to their deeper concern with the moral life and religious duty. Their 'gardens' were first and foremost orchards and vineyards into which there was little need and no pleasure-seeking impulse to drive them to transfer the splendid flowers which grew in profusion around them every spring. Many of these flowers were of a desert or semi-desert kind, spiny with small blossoms. During the Christian era when every word of the Scriptures was accepted literally as the word of God by countless millions who down the ages heard and read the Holy Bible, an accurate identification of species of flowers was of far less importance than the poetic emotions and the fervour their mere names inspired. When the Bible commanded them to 'consider the lilies how they grow, for Solomon in all his glory was not arrayed like one of these' (Luke 12:27), gardens and the beauty of nature became invested with a religious aura that remained a vital influence in their lives. The Bible story moreover began in a garden as Adam and Eve forfeited their earthly paradise, bringing temptations and sin and the curse of work and toil upon humanity, and it ended with the promise of the redemption of man, again in a garden.

For centuries the faithful of Christendom, deriving their values from the strong religious and ethical teachings of the Old and New Testaments, were commanded to renounce mundane pleasures. In the theocratic state of Byzantium the talents of its artists and craftsmen were directed into the service of religious themes. Where gardens might have had some show in the pious pictures with which alone Byzantine mosaic workers adorned the walls of some of the basilica churches and by which scribes and illuminators decorated their holy books, natural beauties are merely suggested by some often crude, conventionally stylized, symbolic trees and plants. Worldly concerns were strictly subordinated. Some gardens would have existed, because the Byzantines inherited a cultural outlook derived very largely from the Greeks and from the later Roman Empire.

When Constantinople was founded by the Emperor Constantine early in the fourth century AD, palaces and houses of the rich would have been Graeco-Roman in style. Many would have had peristyle gardens. Large as the original site was, Constantine's wall was later enclosed within a yet greater wall. Between these walls the land would have been cultivated for food, if not for flowers as well. Had there been a strong impulse to create gardens of delight, land, labour and wealth were not lacking. Yet no evidence remains to show that any Byzantine possessed pleasure gardens such as rich Romans had enjoyed. Books on garden art, if ever they existed, have not survived. Fragments remain such as the great herbal of Dioscorides, written and illustrated for Princess Anicia Juliana before AD 512. Like so much Roman and Byzantine scientific writing, it was a book made from other books instead of a study fresh from nature; nevertheless, for all its inaccuracies and shortcomings, it preserves pictorial evidence about the names, shapes and colour of many plants prized for medical reasons by Greeks, Romans and Byzantines. Flowers in its pages that might indicate some joy in gardening are very few. Some would have been needed for religious and other ceremonial occasions, if not for social embellishment, but no evidence now survives to say what they were or where they were grown.

The herbal of Dioscorides perpetuates the learning of an earlier age, although in an attenuated, unsatisfactory form. So does the one remaining agricultural treatise, the *Geoponica*, a poor thing in relation to the great heritage of farming and garden lore which the Byzantines might have been expected to have cherished and improved. Compiled around AD 600 and revised and recopied around AD 950, three short chapters are given up to garden matters. Some account of the nature and cultivation of fourteen evergreens to provide wreaths and a few notes on about a dozen common garden flowers – rose, lily, iris, viola, narcissus, crocus, etc. – are about all it offers. If there ever had been a more developed, more subtle, Byzantine appreciation of garden art, no evidence of it has survived. As in ancient Palestine, Archaic Greece and early republican Rome, the predominantly austere, otherworldly attitude characterizing the religious and social leaders of the theocratic Byzantine state seems to have discouraged gardens of delight.

One or two later Byzantine secular works have been preserved which strike a more lyrical and romantic note. The most famous in the popular eleventh-century epic story of Digenes Akrites, who accomplished incredible deeds of valour against his and Byzantium's enemies in a manner anticipating some strong-man, 'wish-fulfilment' fantasies of later ages. He was not fighting all the time and there are some tender scenes in a garden of the park or 'paradise' type which he created in a glorious meadow full of marvellously coloured and scented flowers, many trees, bushes and vines abundant with fruits, through which a stream meandered with many beautiful pools set off by ornamental birds, peacocks, swans, parakeets and others. On the sole authority of this fanciful tale written when possibly Byzantine austerity was beginning somewhat to relax, it has been asserted that all Byzantines 'loved beautiful scenery. Gardens and parks and flowers were a delight to them.' But like the story itself, the scenery is little more than a literary stereotype of the sort that began with Homer's garden of Alcinous and recurred, for example, in the Greek pastoral romance *Daphnis and Chloe* written during the height of the Roman Empire in the second or third century AD.

On the cross-roads between East and West, Iran, Iraq and the Mesopotamian lands shared a tragic history. From the fifth millennium BC, pottery and other remains in Iran attest a succession of primitive and early art styles of Sialk, Susa, Hissar and others. In the first millennium BC Medes fought with Assyrians and Persians, who emerged victorious under able Achaemenian kings in 550 BC. Then, already, Zoroastrianism had become the chief religion of the land. It differed from the strict Jewish faith by allowing more recognition to human sensate inclinations. Its followers were enjoined to a life of toil on the land, ploughing, sowing, planting trees and irrigating. They were also expected to raise a family. In striking contrast, the doctrine preached by Mani in the middle of the third century AD, in an attempt to adapt and combine Zoroastrianism with Christianity, advocated a strict asceticism which denied its more dedicated followers all such human sensate joys as meat, wine, eggs, milk, baths and matrimony. Many human activities including work on the land were also forbidden to its leaders or priests.

Zoroastrianism prevailed and with it a more tolerant attitude to mundane pleasures. The faithful were encouraged to believe that they would, unlike those who followed Ahriman, the Evil One, find themselves on the third night after their demise among flowers, inhaling fragrant odours and greeted by a beauteous maiden who, among other comforting attentions, would praise them for not having cut down trees. Not all religious or 'ideational' beliefs are therefore as

Friends meeting in a garden; Moghul painting *c* 1610–15. The private nature of this garden and its use as an extended living area are characteristic of Persian gardens

opposed to sensate garden joys as was the doctrine of Isaiah.

Those who dwelt on the Iranian plateau certainly had greater temptations to make gardens than had the children of Israel, for splendid as was the native flora of the Holy Land, that of Persia was yet more grand. It is a land of strange contrasts, of fertile valleys among the mountains issuing upon waterless salt deserts and wide steppes, long the home of nomads. In favoured areas, such as in the Bakhitari and Elburg mountains, in Fars to the south, and also near the Caspian Sea in the north, flowers of exquisite perfume abounded in profusion.

About the middle of the fourteenth century AD a Persian, referring to the meadows of Fars, where the plain was covered with wild narcissi, said, 'It is most famous, and such is the sweet smell of the narcissus in these meadows, that while it goes to the head, the heart is rejoiced thereby.' Among this wealth of wild flowers were also delphiniums, iris, daffodils, jonquils, tulips, hyacinth, lilies-of-the-valley, marigolds, gillyflowers and red ranunculi. Here was the treasure house from which European gardens were to be enriched until they were able to draw upon the floral wealth of China in the nineteenth century. The Persians took these flowers and many others and planted them in their gardens. But there is no evidence that they devoted much effort to improve any varieties.

From around 700 BC the renowned Achaemenian kings were supreme until Alexander the Great overthrew Darius III in 333 BC to instal Greek domination under the Seleucid line. That in turn was replaced by Parthian domination for 400 years, from 200 BC to AD 226 when the national Iranian Sassanids took command. They finally established the religion of Zoroaster as the religion of the state. In the seventh century AD their empire began to crumble. It was overthrown by the onrush of the Mohammedan Arabs in AD 651, but already the land had been a battle ground between Turks and Arabs. Zoroastrianism survived under Moslem rule and also by migration to India, where it is still sustained by Parsees, 'men from Fars' or Persia.

Between the eighth and thirteenth centuries the amalgam of Iranian and Turkish rule produced a brilliant Islamic culture throughout west Turkestan, using the Turkish language. Still the invaders came, notably the Mongols, who under their dreaded chief or 'Very Mighty King', 'Genghis Khan' (Temujin, 1162–1227), established the Empire of the Great Khan from the China Sea to the Oxus, so bringing the first great periods of culture in Iran to an end. Various dynasties succeeded until they were again overthrown by Timur (Tamerlane), who re-established Mongol rule until 1469. Persia and its gardens were thus exposed over the centuries to many and various strands of cultural influence.

The common pressure of climatic conditions; the common experience of nomadic life on the arid, treeless steppes of the Iranian plateau shared alike by Persians, Arabs, Turks and Mongols; the compelling need for water and shade as much as for food and shelter; the contrast between desert drought and glorious spring flowers in the mountain valleys; all these help to explain the great significance of gardens in the lives of the people of Iran and to account for the leading features of Persian gardens as well.

Even less than Zoroastrians were the Arabs inhibited from garden joys by the rigours of an ascetic religion. There was indeed a strong ideational side to the pure Moslem faith because true believers were sternly forbidden alcohol, gambling, swine flesh and much else as well. On the other hand the sacred book, *Quarān* or Koran, records again and again in minute detail the enjoyments which await the faithful in paradise and they are sensual to a degree to astonish and revolt puritanical minds. In the context of gardens as an aspect of the world of art, the full force of this clash of values has an importance which the fate of gardens in medieval Europe will make clearer.

Persian gardens deserve greater thought and remembrance than they usually evoke. Many nations, many cultures contributed to their formation; many were to be influenced by them directly and many more indirectly as gardens they inspired were copied in various national idioms from the plains of India to the rivers and hills of Spain. Persian flowers created a sensation as, centuries later, they endowed many a European garden with lavish colour, scent and glory. They then gave new subjects to artists and new delight to all who adorned their living rooms with floral displays. They made more fortunes for traders than losses in the veritable economic upheaval they caused when the Dutch succumbed· to 'tulipomania' in the seventeenth century.

Persians also collected rare plants. They had long been linked with the yet greater storehouse of floral beauty to the east. Excavations at the old port of Siraf on the Persian Gulf in 1969 revealed Chinese porcelain container jars brought there in Sassanian times. Great as was the ruin, misery and destruction caused by the Mongol invaders, they came from lands whose natural wealth in immense varieties of wild flowers still astonishes the rare visitor able to travel to Ulan Bator between April and October. Flowers and shrubs were not the only novelties that the Persians owed to such invaders. Paling fences of a Chinese type began to be depicted on Persian miniatures in the fifteenth century.

What most invaders brought was of small account in comparison with what they found and were able to achieve in Persia. When the desert Arabs arrived in the seventh century AD their ignorance of garden art was but one aspect of their lack of culture but they made astonishing progress, sustaining, and here and there advancing, the intellectual achievements of the Greeks at a time when the Latin West was sunk in ignorance. They took over Persian gardens, captivated by what they found. In particular, they perpetuated the traditional Iranian garden design of a wide, right-angled cross believed to symbolize the four quarters of the universe separated by four great rivers. Of immemorial antiquity, this ancient symbolism has endured down the centuries, despite invasions and the overthrow of one ruling class by another.

Among the artistic achievements and splendours of Iran, the Persian flower-carpets connect garden art and another aesthetic form more closely than any other art or craft elsewhere links gardens to the world of art. No carpets earlier than those of the seventeenth century have survived, but there are Persian miniature paintings of an earlier date in which carpets are depicted in the traditional design. Flowers and floral motifs are also very generally found on carpets, in paintings and in architectural decoration from an early period. Before the Arab conquest, the most illustrious of the Sassanian kings, Chosroes I (Anushirwan the Just, 531–579) had a magnificent carpet, said to have been 55 metres (180 feet) square and lavishly adorned with precious stones, in which every beautiful, sweet-scented flower was depicted, to solace him in winter when no flowers bloomed. The tradition of the floral carpet long endured. It was evident more generally in the seventeenth century, when Persian gardens provided the design of many Persian carpets. Then again the old motif of the four quarters of the universe and the four rivers reappeared. The need to fill in the pattern was met by depicting flower-beds, but whether such beds were already prominent elements in a Persian garden, or whether they were introduced into gardens to copy the carpets, seems to be uncertain. What is clear however is that garden art and the art of designing textiles were closely linked and that they influenced each other.

Cultural tradition was so strong in Persia that new styles, new forms familiar to successive occupants of the country, made little headway in any of the arts although increased resources made it possible to expand and enlarge traditional types, particularly of gardens and buildings. Many of the more fortunate Persians probably had pleasant gardens round their homes in the troubled centuries of remoter history, but it is not until late in Mohammedan times, in about the fourteenth century, that actual evidence of their nature can be gleaned from literary sources, from miniature paintings, and from archaeological remains.

Certain characteristics by then were well marked. The central feature of every Persian garden was the pool of water often raised above the level of the ground. It might take any shape, except that a round basin was rarely found. There might be more than one such pool in a large garden. At the cost of immense labour in tapping a subterranean water supply and establishing a channel (or 'Qanat line') from this source, usually at the foot of a snow-clad mountain, garden pools were successfully kept brimful. To ensure this effect the rims and edges of the pool had to be level. With subtle skill they were made part of the garden in the sense that by mirroring the plants and trees they contributed to heighten the charm of the scene with their deep, clear reflections. 'In the twilight, by the edge,' Mr Pope and Miss Ackerman point out in their monumental *Survey of Persian Art*, 'the dimensions dissolve, there is no height, depth or far extent, only the all-encompassing darkly shimmering foliage'. Such gardens were still designed in the form of a wide right-angled cross, that old design with its religious, cosmological significance.

In larger gardens, pavilions or kiosks were built by the pool. Some of these kiosks, which may have been inspired by memories of the tents of their nomadic ancestors, became more elaborate, with a second storey to gain a better view and fresher air. Generally, the Persians merged indoor space or shelter so subtly with the open air outdoors that a clear division between them was not apparent.

Elegant, frequently elaborate garden pavilions were built by the rich for entertaining and also as a retreat. Often large octagonal buildings, sometimes decorated with lavish magnificence, with mirrors, silver and gold fittings and other embellishments, they might be built out over the water or on small islands. This natural development in any country where water is precious and the sun is very hot has been attributed to the Mongols, familiar with Chinese ways of life. Their occupation of Persia after the mid-thirteenth century led to the introduction of Chinese styles and practices, among which lacework wooden garden screens, papier-mâché and Chinese porcelain were included. Poetical names for gardens in which the Chinese excelled began to be applied to Persian gardens such as Garden of Heart's Ease, Garden of the Glory of the World, Garden of the Nightingale, Paradise Garden and many others. It is noteworthy that the Persian word *Bagh* was used for 'garden' later in India where the Mongol invaders took it when Babar (1483–1530) of the fifth generation of the descendants of Timur conquered the Kingdom of Delhi.

Pools and their fountains, kiosks and pavilions were two essential features of a Persian garden. Trees were a third. They were needed for their shade, and for the pleasant reflections they threw on the surface of the garden pools. Plane trees and cypresses were the favourites, with poplars often also as a surround, as well as elms, willows, pine, ash, oak and maple. Fruit trees also, alike for their shade and glory of their blossoms in spring quite as much as for their fruit, were also very much in evidence; almonds, cherries, apricots, peaches, plums, figs, oranges and limes were among the commoner kinds, but hazelnuts, pistachios, filberts,

OPPOSITE Persian flower-carpet of the 18th century, with the ancient motif of the four quarters of the universe separated by four great rivers; flower-beds are depicted in the rest of the pattern

A Persian painting *c* 1550 depicting the story of the 'Duel of the Roses' – the rose, the 'Queen of Flowers', was given pride of place among the many flowers beloved by the Persians. Note the gardener at work in the background

pomegranates, lemons and quinces were also frequently to be found. Flowering bushes and shrubs, lilac and myrtle were also plentiful. Grass lawns, being difficult to maintain, were unusual. Flowers which are concentrated and massed in innumerable English gardens were a feature of Persian gardens also. Miniature paintings of the fifteenth century onwards show flowers glowing brightly in the shade under trees and along water courses rather than planted out in formal beds in Western style. In Persian civilization as in that of later Egypt, Greece and Rome in their sensate age, flowers were the accompaniment of feasting and rejoicing.

Another especially striking feature of Persian gardens since the twelfth century AD, before the first Mongol invasion therefore, is the lavish use of coloured glazed

70

tiles and the skilful manner in which they are placed to adorn the outside walls of houses and in gardens to blend with the blossoms and the trees so as to heighten the colour and attraction of the scene, particularly under the hot Persian sun in the clear light of summer. Similar embellishments are found in many a courtyard and patio, wherever 'Arab' influence penetrated.

From the sixteenth century onwards, travellers' tales become more numerous in the West. Persian gardens then became as proverbial in Europe as the gardens of Egypt had been in ancient Greece and Rome. Tulips, pinks, carnations, jasmine were among the flowers especially noted, but pride of place was given both by the travellers as by the Persians to the rose, the queen of flowers. A Portuguese traveller in the sixteenth century reported that in one garden alone in Shiraz over 12,000 pounds of roses were gathered during the season, in one day.

In addition to the water, the trees and flowers, Persians often enlivened their gardens with decorative animals, reminiscent of the old royal paradises. Swans, pelicans, pheasants, pigeons, ducks, aviaries of singing birds as well as deer were kept. The larger parks were sometimes hunting grounds as in the days of Cyrus.

Whether it was due to Moslem influence after the seventh century AD or to a native tradition which Moslem practice fortified, Persian gardens were very private, as they yet remain. Sometimes the tops of the enclosing walls were crowned with little beds full of the loveliest flowers. Within these small 'paradises' the Persian soul rejoiced. 'The colour and succulence of fruits, flower-perfumes, birds' songs, the rustle of leaves and water, the coolness; the light in its varying qualities and angles; the changing sensation of air, still or in motion; the sheen of birds' feathers ...' such are the evocative words with which Mr Pope and Miss Ackerman summed up some of the delight experienced in their great study of Persian art.

Reflective Persians sought more from their garden retreats than mere sensuous delight. Mysticism, a blend of religious and aesthetic emotions, inspired generations of Persian poets to celebrate flowers and gardens in much the same spirit as that evident in the poetry of other lands, such as that of Herrick and Wordsworth in England.

> O God! I, from a desert of troubles and afflictions
> Am freed. I am seated in the Garden of Iram.

So runs a verse referring to the fabulous garden, Gulistan-i Iram, supposed to have been made by a king 'Iram bin Omad' in Arabia Felix as a perfect model of that paradise promised to the faithful in the Koran.

'So essential is the garden to the Persian conception of life,' Mr Pope and Miss Ackerman observed, 'that both the first reality and ultimate bliss have been interpreted in garden terms.' The 'moving beauty of flowers', as they describe it, was felt by the Persians to be 'a signal to the soul of a dimly remembered community'. Time is lost in an illusion of eternity. When, as among the Persian mystics, 'ultimate reality can be intensively realized in the still but penetrating contemplation of a red rose ... the mystic sees God in the garden and himself in the grass'.

In the seventh century AD, when the Arabs set out on a career of conquest which was, in two generations, to put them in command over an area larger than that once ruled by Rome, they knew nothing of garden arts. All that their prophetic tradition had to say about garden joys was that Adam, the first man, had been hurtled down from heaven with but three possessions, 'a myrtle tree, the chief of sweet-scented plants; an ear of wheat, the chief food of the world; and a date, the chief of the fruits of the world'. They had, however, improved upon this tradition by growing a few highly prized flowers, notably jasmine, gillyflowers, narcissus, lily, iris and rose.

The desert Arabs were nomads, perpetually on the move in search of pasturage for their animals. They had no other wealth than their slaves, their tents woven out of the hair of their camels and sheep and what they could steal by raids upon the caravans of traders to the East. For most Arabs, the word 'garden', although not unknown, stood for 'any spot wherefrom we bring forth grain in full ear; the date palm from whose pith come clusters within reach, and grapes, olives and pomegranates'.

One of the first conquests had been of Alexandria in AD 641. More ancient and more richly endowed than Constantinople, it had been, next to Rome, the wonder and the pride of the ancient world. It glistened with marble buildings, columns, pavements and colonnaded streets and was said to be adorned with beautiful gardens of which, however, no description has survived. When the desert Arabs saw the prize they had captured, they valued it so lightly that some five years later, after an unsuccessful revolt, the imperial city was put to fire and the sword. Thereupon, as already in Rome, a slow decay began as the uncared-for buildings and monuments collapsed through age or earthquake. Gardens, no longer maintained and irrigated, wilted under the fierce Egyptian sun, sharing a decay as swift as that which, many centuries earlier, had overtaken the Hanging Gardens of Babylon.

If the civilizing influence to which the Arabs had been exposed in Alexandria had made no immediate impression upon them, in time they proved willing to learn from the Persians to the East. Two hundred years after their first amazing leap forward to master the Middle East and Egypt, the successors of the caliphs were building palaces in other capitals than their stony, arid, holy city of Mecca and were adorning them with gardens in true imperial Persian style. The gardens of the 'Palace of Eternity', Qsar al-Khuld (AD 762), outside the walls of al-Mansur's new capital, Baghdad, on the Tigris, built as the 'Abode of Peace' (Dar-al-Salam), were said to rival the paradise gardens of the Koran (25.16.17). The caliphs' rule there lasted for 500 years, until 1258. The land around Bukhara in Central Asia, under Arab rule, was 'turned into a veritable garden' growing not merely a rich variety of fruits and vegetables, but many flowers. In private gardens, around splashing fountains, roses, water-lilies, violets, myrtle, iris, sweet marjoram, lemon and orange trees were grown, some in great quantities as saleable crops, particularly for the manufacture of perfumes. Thirty thousand bottles of the essence of red roses were sent each year to the caliph of Baghdad. They came from Fars, one of the four 'earthly paradises', the other three being the gardens south-east of al-Basrah (Basra), the orchards of Damascus and the gap of Bavvan in Faris. From Fars also came narcissi, as highly prized by the Arabs as by the Persians before them. Like the religion of Zoroaster, that of Mahomet was 'founded upon the enjoyment of material pleasure and it appealed to the sensual'.

When the more skilled and intelligent of the learned Arabs fell under the spell of Greek civilization, Greek science as well as the art of Iran were spread as part of the legacy of Islam. Arabs made good use of the artistic talents of the skilled artisans whom they gained as subjects, many of whom learned Arabic, became Moslems, and called themselves Arabs to gain security. To refer to such a motley amalgam of peoples as 'Arabs' would give the misleading impression that Arab civilization was the invention of desert Arabs or their descendants. The dominant

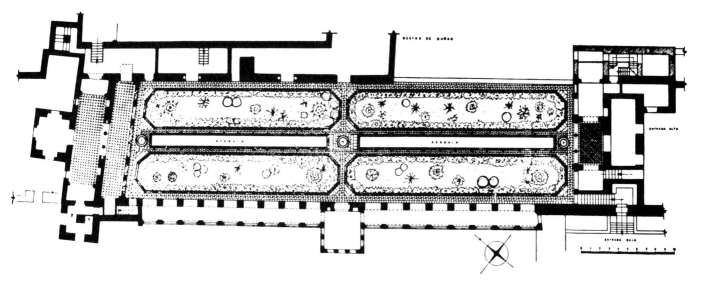

Plan of the Generalife above the
Alhambra showing the recently
uncovered medieval garden – one of the
few existing traces of Arabic gardens in
Spain

Arab aristocracy had the merit of encouraging the cultural interests and skills
of their mixed subject peoples, not the vast Moslem majority alone, but also the
Jews, Christians and Berbers as well as Byzantine minorities.

So successfully did the caliphs foster the arts of civilization that throughout
the early Middle Ages the lands they ruled were materially and culturally in a
'modern' sense well in advance of those of every European people. Where they
succeeded in gaining and maintaining a foothold in Europe, as they were able
to do in Spain for nearly 800 years after AD 711 and in Sicily between 827 and
965, far from diminishing what little then remained of the cultural inheritance
of Rome, they surpassed it on many fronts.

Within two or three generations after its foundation around AD 750, Cordoba
(or Cordova) began to rival Baghdad in splendour and magnificence. By the
middle of the tenth century it had attained great heights of prosperity. Of all
the boasted glories of Cordoba which, probably with characteristic Arabic
exaggeration, were said to have included 200,000 houses, 600 mosques, 900 baths,
besides a university and many public and private libraries, nothing now remains
save the vast mosque. No trace can be found of the 50,000 gardens which were
said to exist in and around the city. The Moslems brought with them, to grace
their Spanish homes, Persian ideas on planning and ornamenting a garden with
fountains, glazed, coloured tiles and garden houses, as well as decorative birds
and animals characteristic of the old Persian paradises. They had, moreover, a
skill in irrigation and in terracing, which, on the hills around Cordoba, is said
to have resulted in an agricultural productivity far beyond the wit of the relatively
barbarous, less cultivated native Spaniards.

For over 300 years, Berbers (or Moors), Jews and Christians lived in Spain,
said Salvador de Madariaga, 'in cordial intimacy in peace and war'. Eventually
the power and energy of the caliphs of Cordoba weakened. Christian knights
from the north captured that Moslem city in 1034, after which Moslem Spain
was gravely weakened. Such reverses brought fanatical Moslems from the wastes
of the Sahara and beyond, Berber tribesmen and Negroes who succeeded for
a time in throwing back the invading Christians.

A small domain at Kamatta or Granada, hidden in its rich valley and protected
by surrounding mountains, alone survived for a time the collapse of the Moslem
Empire of the West. Granada then succeeded Cordoba as the wealthiest city of
Spain as many skilled refugees flocked there after the Moors were driven from
Cordoba, Seville, Valencia, Murcia, and other Moslem domains. Among the few
relics of Arab civilization still to be seen in Granada are the Palace of the Alhambra

73

The Palace of the Alhambra, Granada, with its shaded pool and secluded walks

and the Generalife higher on the hill above the Alhambra. Despite popular notions, none of the gardens there continued the Arab tradition in gardening. After reviewing all the available evidence, Mr James Dickie reported in 1968 that the gardens of the Partal in the Alhambra are no more than forty years old and that their design in the style of Le Nôtre 'is diametrically opposed to the Muslim sensibility with its emphasis on the intimate and the within'. Similarly the gardens of the Alcazar at Seville, reputedly those created by Moorish gardeners for Pedro the Cruel in 1350, are neither Arab nor Spanish, 'but represent the typical Italian garden introduced into Spain during the Renaissance'.

Despite the constant invocation of flowers and gardens in Arabic poetry Mr Dickie could find no more than two passages, of the eleventh and fourteenth centuries respectively, which gave any description of the nature of the old, vanished Arab gardens. Archaeological investigation during reconstruction after a fire in 1958 revealed the nature of the original Arab garden in the Patio de la Acequia of the Generalife before it was again obliterated by a modern garden. What was then discovered, when interpreted with the aid of literary texts, indicates the essential features of true Arab gardens. Their close affinity with the gardens of Iran, already stressed above, is evident both in their fundamental cruciform design with its fourfold division of the garden space and the ample provision of water, shade and scents. They were private and utilitarian, being cultivated for flowers, vegetables and fruits. The modern idea of a garden as a pleasurable show place was a product of the Renaissance, much later, which a primitive Moslem would not have understood.

Shade and water as an antidote to the aridity, heat and death of the desert were the first requirements. When gardens were made into a paradise on earth, they became a foretaste of the paradise to come after death, which was a way of regarding gardens which the Arabs took over from the Persians, one of whose words for garden, *firdaus*, stands also for paradise. Just as in Egypt, centuries earlier, those who had revelled in their gardens during their lifetime wished to be buried in them when dead. 'May rain clouds water his grave and revive it and may the moist garden carry to him its fresh perfume,' is, says Mr Dickie, an Arab funerary inscription. It perpetuates the sensate outlook of the Arabs who, already in the eleventh century, sought in their gardens a voluptuous gratification of the senses from their shade, water and scents, in which, despite the orthodox ban on alcohol, they alternated 'the pleasures of sobriety and inebriation'. When a whole people can anticipate the paradise of after-life as a garden as the ancient Egyptians and the early Moslems did, there can be little doubt about their enthusiasm for gardens on aesthetic grounds and still less doubt about their high significance in the everyday life of those times.

A special feature of Islamic gardens, little remarked upon and never generally adopted elsewhere, was their sunken flower-beds. In the medieval Moorish garden of the Patio de la Acequia the flower-beds were half a metre (18 inches) below the surrounding paths. Mr Dickie points out the advantages of such an arrangement. When the flower blossoms were at feet level, they gave anyone walking on the paths the illusion of treading a floral carpet. At the same time such a design accentuated the geometrical form of the gardens, leaving the architectural features of the adjacent buildings clear and unobscured by vegetation. In heavy rain, the soil would not be washed on to the path, as happens with raised flower-beds. An obvious disadvantage of such raised paths would be the hazard, especially to 'the inebriated', of stumbling off the edge and falling into the flower-bed below.

A water staircase alone remains of the informal Moorish garden on the hill

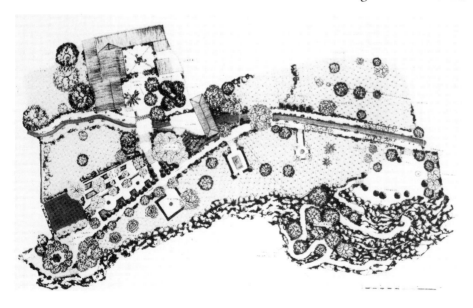

Plan of the garden at Velez Benaudella, the only surviving informal Islamic garden in Spain

75

The richly decorated Moorish arches leading to the Courtyard of the Lions, Alhambra, which would have been filled with trees and flowers at the time of Moslem rule in Spain

above the formal garden of the Patio de la Acequia. One informal Islamic garden has survived elsewhere in Spain, that in Velez Benaudella between Granada and Motril.

From early Arabic manuscripts, Mr Dickie compiled a list of the fifty-two common flowers mentioned by Arabs up to the eleventh century. Pleasurable scents as well as colour were sought with jasmine, narcissus (pheasant's eye), violet, mauve stock, yellow wallflower, red rose, white lily, blue iris, water-lily, almond blossom, marguerite, camomile, trumpet narcissus, poppy, pomegranate blossom, myrtle, basil, lavender, carnation, orange blossom, marjoram, oleander, thyme, mint, saffron, lupin, as well as other flowering trees and shrubs – laurel, pear, plum, mulberry, medlar, quince, apple, fig, cherry, vine, cypress and willow. In Andalusia some of these plants had a fragrance far more pronounced than they would be likely to yield further north in a harsher climate.

The Moslems have been credited with having introduced some of these plants into Europe that were already well known long before the end of the Roman Empire. They may have reintroduced some plants known in Roman days which had disappeared during the Dark Ages. They probably brought apricots, bananas, spinach, artichokes, rice, sugar-cane and the silkworm. Further to the East, Arabs are more frequently execrated for their destruction of trees and for the depredations caused by their herds of goats.

Casual visitors to Spain find it difficult to believe that the magnificent villas and gardens of Moorish Spain ever existed or that they were not taken over and enjoyed by some at least of the Christians who came to occupy and rule the land. Such notions are misplaced because they rest upon the tacit assumption that it would have been 'natural' for Christian victors in the holy war against the followers of Islam to have enjoyed gardens as much as the Moors did or as most people do today. Spanish Christians were sternly forbidden some of the garden joys of the Moslems. To be able to show that anyone had washed in a pool near a mosque, as Moslem ceremonious practice required the faithful to do, might set inquisitors to work. Such was the danger that the very name of the Court of the Pool at Granada had to be changed to the Court of the Myrtle Hedges. Railings and barriers were erected to shut away the charm of such Moorish garden pools that were allowed to remain, while the rigidly orthodox displayed that aversion to water that remained for too long among their less pleasant characteristics. Bigotry threw a dark shadow over the land. Granada fell to the Christians in 1492. The Jews and Mohammedans were given the choice of conversion to Christianity or expulsion, thereby involving Spain in the loss of many, if not most, of its skilled workers, gardeners included. By the first decade of the seventeenth century even the Christian Moriscoes were driven out of Spain with a vicious cruelty that indelibly disgraced their bigoted oppressors.

It was another example of that clash of sensate and ideational cultural values that explains why the gardens of the Roman Empire perished as the early Christians gave all their loyalty and devotion to things not of this world. The Moorish gardens of delight with their bright tiles, their fountains and their deep calm pools that had brought a breath of the far-distant Orient to the western limits of Europe faded away. In their place came the glum austerity of monasticism, progressively degenerating by spiritual inbreeding and ritualistic monotony. Its nadir is to be seen in the funereal gloom of the Escorial, while in Cordoba the great Mosque along with the remnants of courtyards and patios still contrive under the southern sun, amid the scented glory of orange blossoms and golden fruits, to recall some of the pleasant features of Islamic paradises and to stir thoughts of distant lands and ways of long ago, of muezzins and camel bells, when the caliph's word was law from the Indian to the Atlantic Ocean.

Garden art flourished in Egyptian, Hellenistic, Roman, Persian and Arab civilizations during their later pleasure-seeking, 'sensate', cultural history but was slight or absent in their earlier, traditional, religious, 'ideational' cultural life. So also the Israelites who listened to their prophet were given no encouragement to create pleasure gardens, or to seek other satisfactions of the senses. After the destruction of countless fine European homes and gardens that had been occupied and enjoyed for several hundred years under imperial Roman rule, many more centuries elapsed before garden pleasures again became a precious element of civilized existence. Where invading Visigoths had already gained a familiarity with Roman ways, as in southern Gaul and Spain, they seem to have shown little or no interest in maintaining the civilized ways of living of the Romans among whom they came to live and to rule.

Sidonius Apollinaris (*c* 430–*c* 480), the Christian bishop whose letters are the sole source of first-hand information about that part of Gaul at the time, shrewdly observed that the Romans, having lost military and political power, would have to rely upon Roman culture if peace, unity and settled civilization were to continue. Evidently the gap to be closed was too wide, even in the south, for cultural values to achieve such an integration. In northern Europe and in the British Isles no hope at all existed of any communication, least of all of cultural values, between the Romanized Britons and the primitive, barbarian invading hordes. They and their descendants came to kill, to loot, to burn and to destroy. Nothing more conclusively demonstrates the low cultural level of these invaders than the slow pace with which they were redeemed from near savagery. In England gardening to ornament a villa or to provide a pleasant retreat, as distinct from mere crop-raising, died out soon after the departure of the Romans. When the few hardy garden plants which survived were given names in Anglo-Saxon they were almost all adaptations of Roman plant names, probably because the clergy alone could write. A garden however was called 'herb yard' or 'plant yard', *wyrtzerd*, and an orchard, *ortzerd* or 'orceard'.

The only civilizing influence remaining in the West was that of the Christian Church. It had a plan of action in the Rules drawn up, traditionally in AD 529, by St Benedict in the monastery he had founded on the crest of Monte Cassino in Italy. Shortly afterwards a great missionary campaign was begun by Pope Gregory the Great. In AD 596 St Augustine brought the Christian message to England, some 200 years after its Roman defenders had withdrawn. He, and generations of priests who followed him, had to struggle with vast numbers of illiterate folk little susceptible to the higher values of the human spirit. To influence or to control them was exceedingly difficult.

While the barbarian newcomers were living in mean wooden huts little better than a good nineteenth-century hen-house, or in caves and rude tents, with many natives as their slaves, the Church began to build very much more impressive structures. Monasteries were being founded and wherever there was a monastery or a nunnery there was likely to be some sort of garden. The Rules of St Benedict which set the tone for much monastic endeavour allotted six hours of every working day to manual toil, against four hours of reading. Hitherto work in the fields and gardens had been undertaken mainly by slaves. Now counts and nobles were to be found in slaves' dress carting manure and driving pigs. It was an immense revolution in social and cultural values.

Illustration from the 14th-century manuscript, *The Romaunt of the Rose*, the earliest of all poems to celebrate the beauty of the rose

In those far-off days when the example of the Church was all important, monastery gardens were strictly for use and not for pleasure. A few herbs and vegetables with one or two fruit trees were tended as a source of food and medicine to supplement the crops grown on the lands which the Church was often steadily acquiring. Flowers were also grown to adorn altars and shrines and to provide crowns and garlands which the priests often wore when performing services or during processions. By the beginning of the eighth century it has been said that one third of the land of Gaul was owned by the Church and leased to independent cultivators who had found it less and less possible to survive on their own.

The economic resources of the Church were becoming relatively enormous. At the same time many cultivators had bartered their freedom and their land for the protection of a larger landowner so that numbers of petty lords and barons became more powerful. They usually sought to add to their power and to their estates by attacking their neighbours. In time the Church inherited some of the augmented properties.

In Italy, it has been said (by H. O. Taylor in *The Medieval Mind*) that 'no complete break with the Roman past ever occurred, that antique reminiscence and tradition never passed away and that the literary matter of the pagan past never faded from the consciousness of the more educated among the laity and clergy'. Of very few this may be true. An essentially agricultural community continued to grow food crops and a few flowers, but without the monasteries and nunneries, learning could hardly have survived. They housed celibate men and women, at first probably in large private houses where the colonnaded covered walk of their peristyle enclosed a plot of land within which a few trees, shrubs and flowers could be kept alive. Food crops were mainly grown outside, at first by the monks themselves.

One or two documents of the ninth century indicate the nature of monastic gardens when some cultural interests began to become evident in Europe's Dark Ages. One is the plan of the Benedictine monastery and its garden of St Gall in south-west Germany. Another is a much more human document by the energetic young Abbot Walahfrid Strabo, a German (*c* 809–849), of the neighbouring Benedictine monastery of Reichenau, about twenty-five miles distant from St Gall on the lake of Constance. In some respectable Latin hexameters about 'the little garden', *Hortulus*, that he made there, he shows that his predecessors had not 'chosen to labour' or to have his 'experience of hard work and sacrifice of many days when I might have rested'. St Benedict's commands were already being forgotten, because the new young Abbot found a bed of nettles long undisturbed, with matted roots 'like a hurdle grooms make from osiers'. Moles had been active also and their 'tunnels' had to be destroyed. At last the plot was cleared, then, 'so that it should not be washed away', he 'faced it with planks and raised it in oblong beds a little above the level ground'. He then prepared the soil for planting and sowing by raking down the clods of earth and digging in a rich top dressing of manure. From some other garden in the following year, perhaps that of St Gall, he got seeds and some half-dead stock. After the spring showers had come again, he had the satisfaction of seeing 'the garden carpeted over with tiny young shoots'. He described twenty-three of his plants, adding that 'I could describe many more flowers for you if my hasting Muse (Thalia) did not make me shorten sail and run for harbour'. Medicinal plants and flavouring herbs made up his list, with the lily and the rose.

Brief and practical as the poem was intended to be, it glows still because of the intense satisfaction which Walahfrid derived from his labours. Here was a man in the so-called 'Dark Ages' of early medieval Europe recounting traditional herbal lore and old wives' tales yet adding his personal appreciation of the aesthetic appeal of a garden and of the plants he had lovingly raised in it. Because his resources were so limited, and by modern garden standards so pedestrian, he observed them the more attentively, relishing the colour, taste and scent of wormwood, catmint, sage, the natural beauty of southernwood, the entangled tendrils of gourd which reminded him of the task of girls spinning wool. And the melon, too, 'the growth it makes is beautiful' as it creeps over the dusty ground. He notes the beauty of his purple-flowered iris, but the climax of his poem was reserved for praise of the lily and the rose: 'two flowers so loved and widely honoured that have throughout the ages stood as symbols of the Church's greatest treasures, for it plucks the rose in token of the blood shed by the Blessed Martyrs and it wears the lily as a shining sign of the faith ... pluck thou roses for war, for peace the smiling lily' because 'Christ left peace and war for his church on earth'.

Such were the simple qualities of a garden in an ideational cultural time when sensate enjoyments were not indeed unknown but were unquestioningly made to serve overriding religious aims. Those who in a sensate age think of the 'romantic' sybaritic allure of gardens, may find it difficult to recognize a 'garden' in Abbot Walahfrid's neat rows of herbs and 'weeds' as some of his cherished plants would now be regarded, but no such difficulty arises when a broad socio-cultural, aesthetic view is taken of garden history. We can take leave of the young Abbot in the words of his dedication to Father Grimald, his tutor and mentor: 'I can picture you, sitting there in the green enclosure of your garden, under apples which hang in the shade of lofty foliage where the peach tree turns its leaves this way and that out of the sun, while your happy band of pupils gather for you fruits with tender down and stretch their hands to grasp the huge apples.' No such intimate, personal a description survives of other monastery gardens known to have existed in the ninth century.

By the tenth century the food the monks needed was usually grown for them in their fields by customary tenants bound to the soil, or by slaves, of whom in England there was about one for every ten householders before the Norman Conquest of 1066. There were also many free labourers. By 1090 the abbey of Evesham, for instance, employed three hired gardeners.

Monastery gardens were utilitarian without the mystic overtones that in pagan times had brought goddesses and nymphs into gardens. Not from the monasteries and nunneries were pleasure gardens ultimately developed but from the manors, although without the work of the monks and nuns it would have taken the owners of the manors much longer to acquire the rudiments of civilized living. Early in the ninth century also what seems to be the first evidence about secular gardens survives in the famous series of rules for the management of the royal estates of Charlemagne, the *Capitulare de Villis* of 812. Some seventy plants and trees are mentioned, but all belong to the herb garden, the vegetable garden and the orchard. Sage, rue, rosemary, caraway, pepper, cress, parsley, lovage, dittany, chives, garlic, mustard, capers, are among the plants cultivated for their power to relieve the tedium of a diet of bread, meat and fish, which, in winter, especially when fresh meat was replaced by salt meat, became very monotonous. Cucumbers, melons, gourds, celery, endive, beetroot, carrots, parsnips, beans, cabbages, onions, radishes, peas and leeks were among the vegetables to be grown. Fruit trees included apples, pears, plums, medlars, quinces, mulberries, cherries and figs. Chestnuts, walnuts, almonds and hazelnuts are also listed. Flowers however were limited to little more than the lily, the rose and the poppy. When imperial majesty was no better provided, it is unlikely that the gardens enjoyed by the Emperor's subjects would be richer. That the *Capitulare de Villis* should be ascribed to Charlemagne's son Louis, in Aquitaine, around 794–795 was argued by Dopsch. Doubt arises on this point because a number of the garden plants and trees enumerated are southern and cannot easily be raised in northern France or in Germany.

Progress beyond these early efforts to recreate something worthy of the name of a garden was very slow. In the terrible situation of Europe during the Dark Ages the record was often one of decline rather than of progress, for the great work of Charlemagne did not long survive his death in 814. Monastic gardens no more than monasteries and nunneries were pleasure gardens or romantic retreats. Towards the end of the tenth century a great impetus to build monasteries and churches endowed Europe with very many grand Romanesque ecclesiastical buildings. The rivalry of emperor and pope provoked a competition in which the secular power in turn produced some splendid palaces. After nearly a thousand years, little of all this remains and it is impossible to reconstruct even in imagination just what the full picture may have been, particularly how far it may have developed gardens and gardening.

Some historians of gardening have supposed that medieval knights who went crusading to recover Holy Places from 'the Saracens' between the eleventh and thirteenth centuries saw and admired Persian-style gardens and resolved to copy them. At that early period any such cultural transfer is most unlikely. Christian soldiers who went onwards into war in Palestine or Spain by command of the Pope and the Holy Church did not embark upon their dangerous voyages as sightseers, curious to learn about new refinements in the art of living. They had no more sympathy for the way of life of the Saracens and Moors than the Fathers of the Roman Republic felt towards Etruscans or Greeks or the American Indians for the habits and amusements of the English colonists of Virginia.

Little better than in the Dark Ages, the conditions of life for the average man and woman all through the early Middle Ages were pitifully meagre, hard and uncomfortable. Stone houses were uncommon, possessed by none but a very few wealthy citizens and the houses of the great majority of Englishmen showed little progress beyond the one-room mud hut of the primitive Anglo-Saxons, until in the later Middle Ages wooden frame houses in small towns became rather more general. Each might then have a long narrow strip of garden behind it in which vegetables and pot-herbs with perhaps a fruit tree or a flower or two would be grown. But such towns were a later development.

In England, the Domesday Book (1086), William the Conqueror's famous inventory of the resources of his newly-won kingdom, gives little account of other than arable and pasture farm land but it does mention gardens and little garden plots (*horti* and *hortuli*), so small patches of vegetables and pot-herbs were not uncommon around larger houses before the Norman Conquest. It also records some thirty-eight vineyards, the largest of which, in Berkshire, covered about twelve acres.

The minor country gentry in the early Middle Ages were also very meanly housed by modern standards and when well-established families lived in sparse conditions, a harder life would be that of all the free labourers and above all the slowly diminishing semi-free villeins tied by customary duties to their manorial lord, and the actual serfs or slaves. Opinions about the quality of life in those primitive days vary. It seems clear however that the great majority of the people of Europe from the fall of Rome almost until the dawn of the Renaissance had a very thin time and that it would be idle to look for gardens of the sort that the Romans knew or those with which we have become familiar. Life for the great majority was, in the words of Thomas Hobbes, nasty, brutish and short, so that no cultural values of any significance, no love of well-ordered gardens, graced the life of the masses in Europe in the early Middle Ages.

The long stretch of some five or six hundred years or more in which the men, women and children of Europe lived without the gay gardens to which their predecessors in the land had long been accustomed is an interlude; a negative period which however demands notice if the story of gardens and gardening is to be related to the wider story of the development of civilization and culture.

During the early Middle Ages relatively few people could read, still fewer had access to books. For advice about gardening and agriculture, they would most probably have relied upon tips from the older generation, friends and neighbours. One or two of the greater monastery libraries might have had a work by one of the old Latin writers about agriculture: Cato, Varro, Virgil, Pliny, Columella, or some later compilation based upon them.

For centuries these old texts were occasionally copied without improvement. Such was the herbal of Apuleius Barbarus of the fifth century AD, based upon Pliny and Dioscorides and the old wives' tales to which they had given heed. Another herbal often copied was that in Latin verse known as 'Macer', composed by Odo of Meune-sur-Loire around 1161. After six or seven hundred years Apuleius began to be superseded by the herbal of Rufinus in the thirteenth and fourteenth centuries, four-fifths of whose text dealt with herbs and vegetables. But Apuleius was reprinted several times after the invention of printing. In so vital a matter as the curative value of herbs no progress whatever had been made in scientific endeavour for over a thousand years. On the contrary, there had been a decline from the best wisdom of the ancient world. Some of the old classical mythology survived. Walahfrid Strabo, for example, Christian abbot though he was, wrote of Vulcan's forge on Mount Etna, Apollo's high altar and the sad fate of Hyacinthus, obscene Priapus, Ceres' poppy and Thalia, the muse of poetry.

In that pre-scientific age, curiosity was by no means absent but the means of satisfying it did not exist. Men were prisoners of fixed ideas such as that earth, water, air and fire were ultimate elements of all things so that the explanation of a question such as what makes plants grow had to be resolved by some reference to these elements. Thus according to Adelard of Bath, who wrote early in the twelfth century, in his *Questiones Naturales*, 'Plants are nourished from the earth but from a compound not a simple earth, but from the earthy. The hot plants taking that which is hot; the cold that which is cold; the dry what is dry; and the moist what is moist.'

For any great improvement upon this word-locked 'science' it was necessary to wait until the seventeenth century.

In the twelfth century, secular gardens began to be improved in a cultural advance. Some revival of humanistic interests and endeavour then began a development which was to outstrip anything achieved by the monasteries. The Benedictines, the Cluniac monks, the Cistercians were no longer taking the lead in intellectual endeavour, neither were their monasteries the sole centres of culture. When a remarkable religious revival began in the following century under the

A typical walled town garden with its neat beds of flowers and herbs; from a 15th-century manuscript

impetus of the new orders of itinerant friars, the Franciscans and Dominicans, it lay outside the world of monks and nuns and further accentuated their growing isolation. Nevertheless they continued in control of a large part of the economic life of the country. In England, as in Europe, they had grown rich. They had some 600 houses scattered all over the country; they owned much of its wealth and some of them resembled an idle aristocracy but one largely withdrawn from active participation in secular national affairs.

In England during the thirteenth century, agricultural production began to rise. The Benedictines were thickly settled in the best corn-growing areas and some of their more enterprising abbots developed a marked economic interest and skill. Long before the great enclosure movement during the sixteenth century that was to cause so much distress in England, large tracts of land were being bought up by the abbots from the fourteenth century onwards. They turned some of this land into parks and some hunted and rode to hounds like any sporting squire. They aimed at a more productive agriculture, even if they did not themselves plough and sow, or forgo all worldly pleasures.

At the end of the twelfth century some of the citizens of London living outside the walls were gardeners. FitzStephen, who wrote the life of Thomas à Becket not long after his murder (1170), said of London: 'On all sides the houses of the citizens who live in the suburbs there are adjoining gardens planted with trees and pleasant to the sight.' New standards of comfort and convenience were slowly coming into evidence. Alexander Neckham (1180–1217), in his well-known *de Naturibus Rerum*, advised that 'the garden should be adorned with roses and lilies, turnsole [heliotrope], violets and mandrake; there you should have parsley and fennel and southernwood and coriander, sage, savory, hyssop, mint, rue, dittany, lettuce, garden cress'. He also mentions poppies and daffodils as well as other plants, some of which cannot be grown in an English climate.

By the time that written records and accounts begin to be made about monasteries and their finances, their gardens, to judge by one or two samples, seem of small importance. In the *Observances in Use at the Augustinian Priory at Barnwell Cambridgeshire in the Middle of the Thirteenth Century* (edited by J. W. Clark in 1897) there is no record of gardens or priory gardeners, although the duties of cellarers, graingers, and of several other servants are mentioned. The painstaking analysis by R. A. L. Smith of medieval monastic administration, *Canterbury Cathedral Priory* (1943), throws no light upon monastery gardens or their management. When their accounts and records begin at the end of the thirteenth century it seems evident that the Canterbury monks were already far from the ancient rule of St Benedict. There is no mention of the cathedral gardeners any more than of the sweepers and cleaners or other menial servants, of whom no record remains except of their large numbers.

A similar negative finding relating to gardens and gardeners can be reported from Leicestershire during the fourteenth and fifteenth centuries in the light of R. H. Hilton's *Survey of the Economic Development of some Leicestershire Estates in the 14th and 15th Centuries* (1947), although it contains a reference to 'the garden round the castle' of Donington in 1421, then leased to two farmers.

Here and there however an energetic man endowed with that natural love of making things grow and grow well, would not be above taking a hand himself in the monastery garden. Far north in Scotland in the pleasant plain of Kinloss, near Forres, there is an account in *Records of the Monastery of Kinloss* (edited by J. Stuart in 1872) of just such an abbot, as late as the year 1500, who, like Walahfrid Strabo 700 years earlier, 'was wont to do much with his hands ...

View from the cloisters of the Abbey
garden of San Domingo de Silos, Spain

sometimes he worked even to perspiration in the garden, uprooting and planting
trees or in work of that kind'.

By that time the early contribution of the monasteries towards the acquisition
of the rudiments of gardening practice and knowledge had long since been made
and absorbed. By the fourteenth century, the friars were no longer poor itinerants
living on the charity of the faithful but had settled in their friaries. As these were
usually built inside the towns and cities their gardens, if any, were small. When
Mr G. Baskerville in his well-known book, *English Monks and the Suppression
of the Monasteries* (1937), sought to draw up a list of all the values which disappeared on the dissolution of the monasteries and friaries in England, he deplored the immense destruction of buildings, of art treasures and libraries of
manuscripts; he noted that some contemporaries lamented the religious losses
resulting from the cessation of the prayers and ritual of the monks and nuns,
and he added the loss of pilgrimages. He made light of the relatively insignificant
hospitality, almsgiving and doles; he noted the change in religious services; the
pensioning-off of abbots, priors, monks of whom there were only about 3000,
and he has nothing to say about their alleged medical and healing skills. Their
gardens with the gardeners who cultivated them were usually taken over by those
who acquired the abbey and monastery lands. The Dissolution as a whole was
a relatively painless operation, apart from the grievous destruction of ancient
relics.

All traces have long since disappeared of the gardens of the great abbeys of
Glastonbury, Rievaulx, Fountains and others. Here and there the form of the
monks' fish ponds may still be seen and there are some large walled gardens such
as that at Milton Brodie in Morayshire which was once a monastery garden,
according to local Scottish tradition. The monks' parsley, still to be found there,

is said to be a relic of its medieval occupants. Elsewhere the peaceful, brooding quiet of the grounds of many an ancient monastic site, such as Port Royal in France or around the ruins of the Abbey of Elgin, seems still to breathe a numinous air recalling the long vanished days when a Christian brotherhood worked in harmony to maintain them and to serve the religion by which they were inspired. Their gardens are no more but the spirit in which they were created to be long and lovingly maintained cannot be said to have completely vanished from the earth.

England was about a century behind the continent of Europe in its cultural development and it was probably not until the thirteenth and fourteenth centuries that its gardens began to equal those of France of the twelfth century. Progress on the Continent is evident from the one respectable treatise on gardening produced during the Middle Ages, that by Petrus de Crescentiis or Pietro Crescenzi of Bologna in Italy, *Opus Ruralium Commodorum*. Written around 1300 and often copied and later printed, it devoted considerable space to gardens, describing in turn the main features of a small herb garden with its mint, sage, marjoram and rue and the usual few flowers, the violet, lily and the rose; of medium gardens for people of moderate means of about an acre in extent, and finally of the gardens of kings and other illustrious and rich lords which might be parks of twelve acres or more.

Both the advice it gave on the design of gardens, and the type of crops recommended are evidence of its southern European or Italian origin. But it is not easy to say how much of the book was based upon the author's practical experience and how much was taken over in the normal medieval manner from Cato, Virgil, Columella, Varro and Palladius. Some of it was medieval, such as the recommendation to build seats of turf and to make hedges of roses, pomegranates, plums or quinces. A much more ancient feature was advice on the stocking of the royal or lordly park with hares, stags, roebucks, rabbits, pheasants, partridges, nightingales, blackbirds, goldfinches, linnets and all other kinds of singing birds. Such a park had to be well planted with trees to afford cover and shelter for the livestock. A fish pond was also included, so that fish were available for the meatless days observed by all good Catholics. The fruit trees recommended were much the same as those prescribed for the royal domains of Charlemagne five hundred years earlier.

This somewhat elaborate treatment of garden design and layout was something very new. Medieval gardens were almost all small and restricted, especially in Europe where many people lived in walled towns. Many began as small herb gardens, and were but slowly extended for vegetables and fruit trees. Ornamental flower gardens were not developed until the Renaissance and often much later. Few nowadays are likely to award the name of garden where there are not lots of flowers. In comparison with the gardens of the sixteenth century, these earlier medieval gardens were pitifully bare. Efforts were concentrated upon raising nosegay flowers, particularly roses, lilies, violets, clove-pinks, cornflowers and periwinkles. All were little better than wild flowers but they were widely used in the decoration of altars and shrines as well as for chaplets or wreaths for the head after the antique Roman manner. They were valued also as an antidote to the stench of unwashed bodies and uncleaned clothing that was so general until almost modern times.

The utility value of flowers was not exhausted by their perfume and decorative charm. Some were also eaten. Violets were in demand as salad herbs, as a garnish, as colouring material and as a relish. Primroses, hawthorn, violets and rose petals were cooked with milk, honey or sugar. Rose hips, whose nutritional virtues were rediscovered in the British Isles under the stress of wartime shortages of other fruits, were also collected.

As wealth and humanistic interests grew with the slow decline of the spare, strict ideational spirit of the early Middle Ages, a greater interest began to be taken in the things of this world, notably flowers and gardens. Festive occasions in the Middle Ages as in Greek and Roman times began to call for flowers, and so above all did romantic affairs.

Froissart set his delightful description of his encounter in the springtime of his youth with a fair dainty maid reading a romance 'in a fair garden in the month of May among the young trees that rose so thick around while in the early morning the small fowls vied with each other in melody'. Later in another garden where there were 'many delights of roses, of lilies and other flowers' he plucked a crimson rose for her. Froissart's English contemporary, Chaucer, who had a true poet's eye for natural beauty, often feasted upon flowers and trees. If his *Canterbury Tales* speak the idiom of the people as they are generally supposed to do, then English men and women also coloured their speech with references to garden lore. The Miller, for example, told a tale about an elderly carpenter's gay young wife of whom he said:

> She was ful more blisful on to see
> Than is the newe pere-jonette tree.

Evidently English gardeners were experimenting with new pear trees from France, even then the source of splendid pears.

What remains of Chaucer's translation of *The Romaunt of the Rose*, that long French allegorical poem written around the rose, is relatively short but it includes the description of the rose bush, the 'roser':

> A Roser charged full of roses
> That with a Hegge about enclos is

It proved to be an irresistible attraction for, said Chaucer:

> Toward the roser gan I go
> And when I was not fer therfro
> The savour of the roses swote
> Me smoot right to the herte root
> As I hadde al enbawmed be.

It was from no lack of joy in flowers that some people in the later Middle Ages at least did not fill their gardens with them and continually search for new varieties. They concentrated their enthusiasm on what they had already and what they could see growing wild in the fields. Here is a new note in European literature, a sign that thoughts were turning more and more towards earthly joys.

When gardens begin to be illustrated in medieval European manuscripts from the thirteenth century onwards, they are mostly unimpressive. This may to some extent be due to the artist's lack of skill and perspective, so that their indications of a garden were largely symbolic. Yet when greater technical skill had been developed in the early Renaissance, gardens made little better showing. The only real difference between early medieval and pre-Renaissance gardens is one of size.

In the castles of the nobility, where the romantic secular garden ultimately attained a free development it could not have in monastic cloisters, gardens grew with the changing character of the castle itself. Until the end of the twelfth century

A garden in the Middle Ages, an
illustration to Chaucer's translation of
The Romaunt of the Rose, c 1340–1400

the European castle was often a hard-pressed stronghold, upon the stoutness of
whose walls and provisions of meal and water many human beings depended
for their lives. In Europe they were first built upon hill tops, and on other sites
by no means easy of access. Gradually as life assumed a somewhat more settled
form, they became more agreeable residences and it was then that gardens began
to be added to them.

At the end of the fourteenth century, orchards and gardens, often on a considerable scale, were found to be close outside the castle walls. A hundred years later
still, the nobles no longer fortified their homes which they now placed, as the
monks had always put their monasteries, on low ground near a river or stream.
Thereafter the gardens slowly became somewhat larger and much more elaborate. That they were also coming to be very much more highly regarded as
a part of the good life may be seen in the fact that religious scenes in medieval
miniatures were often depicted in a garden setting.

Medieval pleasure gardens, as distinct from the plots of land given over to
herbs and vegetables, were an expansion of the small orchards where a few trees
were grown amid wild flowers. The 'flowery mead' was gradually cultivated
by bringing in more wild flowers: roses, violets, lilies, columbine, poppies and
others. In England wallflowers were a popular addition in the fourteenth century
and carnations in the fifteenth century, although the Normans have been held
responsible for both.

86

Whether pleasure gardens in England ever attained any development comparable with that of some European gardens during the Middle Ages seems unlikely. Occasional pictures in illuminated manuscripts come from France, Italy, Germany or the Low Countries. There also contemporary illustrations are few before the Renaissance when men began to develop gardens on a scale hitherto unknown. Many houses of some pretension probably lacked a garden, and the general impression of the gardens of the Middle Ages is that they were few and small, devoted almost entirely to plants as foods, savouries and medicines and to fruits, with a few nosegay flowers rather as an afterthought.

How far back it would be safe to project into the earlier Middle Ages the features depicted in French and Flemish early Renaissance miniatures is conjectural. In England the sole trustworthy bit of evidence about them is a manuscript account attributed to a certain Master John Gardener written during the first half of the fifteenth century. It is a short practical manual based upon personal experience probably in Kent, in which he mentions just under one hundred plants, about a quarter of which are not native to England. Few flowers are in the list, and all except one or two, such as roses and madonna lilies, were wild flowers.

In the mid-fourteenth century the Black Death reduced the population of Western Europe by at least one third. Labour was in great demand, so wages tended to rise. The level of living from which they rose was, by modern standards, very low indeed. Gradually, however, wealth began to increase, despite the long unrest during the struggle between York and Lancaster in the Wars of the Roses. In England some of the rich were becoming more expansive. Between 1432 and 1437 Humphrey Duke of Gloucester transformed his new estates at Greenwich near London into a magnificent park of about 200 acres enclosed by a wall and planted with trees. He was a king's son, it is true, but he set a standard. It was the dawn of a new age, an age in which men were to take vastly more thought for the amenities of their daily life, including the construction and adornment of their houses and the land around them.

In the history of the aesthetic, philosophical aspect of garden arts as distinct from the record of garden craft in many lands, relatively little can be said about the thousand years of medieval times. Earlier models from the gardens of Rome or of Islam had little relevance to Europe. Brief, then, as the story of medieval gardens is, over a huge stretch of time, it confirms the view, already suggested, that in an age of predominantly ideational culture such as the greater part of the European Middle Ages, in which otherworldly values claimed the principal, spiritual allegiance of the community, pleasure gardens, pure and simple, were absent. For centuries the best of the leaders of society, religious and secular, professed, and, subject to much weakness of the flesh and to turbulent human passions often out of control, acknowledged the claims that religion made upon them. Crude and primitive as much of the culture of those early times has appeared to be in modern eyes, there can be no doubt about the consummate success of anonymous Byzantine and medieval craftsmen in forms of art deemed at the time to be of supreme importance. The supreme beauty of many a cathedral, abbey and monastery with the sculptures and windows, reliquaries, shrines and other treasure was all work, at vast cost, for the glory of God, not for personal renown and certainly not for private sensuous pleasure.

Had the same effort gone into pleasure gardens, Versailles in the eighteenth century would have been no source of astonishment. But no way was open to dedicate gardens or garden arts to the service of the Lord as they had joyously been devoted to the local, pagan gods in the cult practices of early Egypt. Isaiah had not denounced groves and gardens in vain.

Despite the first stirrings of more worldly interests in the 'Renaissance of the twelfth century', it was not until the thirteenth and fourteenth centuries that a fresh note of lyrical joy in the beauty of flowers began to be heard in Chaucer's *Romaunt of the Rose* (c 1340–1400), in the pages of Boccaccio (1313–1375), and of Froissart (c 1337–1410). Change was in the air, audible in mutterings of doubt, discontent and revolt. Symptomatic of the new spirit stirring in Western Europe was the Jacquerie uprising in France (1358) and the rebellion of Wat Tyler and John Ball 'the mad priest' in England (1381) at about the same time that John Wiclif (d. 1384) and the Lollards alarmed the Church. It was a revolutionary change; one to be accounted for as part of a general secular development as the ideational cultural pattern seems to have begun to lose momentum.

Such having been the broad development of gardens in the social and cultural life of Western Asia and in Europe down to the waning of the Middle Ages, the question naturally arises whether any similarity or parallels can be detected in garden arts in the Far East?

Dravidians, the earliest known inhabitants of India, lived in remarkably well-constructed towns along rivers in the Indus Valley, as excavations of the sites of Mohenjo-Daro and Harappa revealed after 1920. They appear to have been an agricultural community revering goddesses and Mother Earth after the fashion of such early folk. Remains of their writing have not yet been deciphered.

Invading Aryans after about 1500 BC were nomadic herdsmen worshipping male gods. They brought the Vedic religion and culture and the Sanskrit language. Knowledge for them, *Veda*, was purely religious, concerned with sacrifices to the many Vedic gods, with hymns of praise such as the *Rg-Veda*, and with prayers and incantations. Their elaborate theology and ritual was developed over a thousand years by the priestly class of Brahmans whose monopoly of sacred power elevated them to social superiority. Their ideas are to be found in the *Upanisads*.

Then began that grading of the population into castes, denounced in modern egalitarian times as one of the curses inflicted upon India. Mankind had been divided from the earliest times, according to the *Rg-Veda*: the Brahman was the mouth; the arms were the prince and his warriors; the thighs, the common people; the feet, the serfs.

Life was not a boon to many in Vedic India. Some left social life for an ascetic existence of meditation in caves and forests. They did not go, as some Chinese and Western solitaries have done, to rejoice in the glories of nature, but to escape by a kind of self-hypnosis, a blank state of mind, spurning, not pleasures of the senses alone, but sensations in general. They had 'looked close at objects of desire, at pleasant things and beautiful' but, following the teaching of the *Katha Upanisad*, they 'had cast them away and had not entered the net of riches in which so many men sink to perdition'.

None but a minority in overpopulated India could have resigned the struggle for existence in such a way. The great majority looked to religion for practical benefits, for protection against demons, enemies and disease, for good crops and for a more agreeable life generally.

In the sixth century BC, after about a thousand years of Vedic supremacy, a new belief arose which was to exert a profound and far-reaching influence throughout east Asia. Gautama received the name Buddha, the 'Enlightened', for his teaching about the nature and purpose of life. It was a development of Brahmanism, otherwise it would not have found a hearing. Buddhism also sought to escape from the evil and suffering of life, its pleasures and pains, by meditation, by leading a moral life and by achieving wisdom. Nirvana or nibbana was the word for the Buddhist ideal. It stood both for the type of person Buddhism sought to produce and for the ultimate state in which he found himself in this life and in the next. In this life a devout Buddhist had to become 'unprovokable, of unclouded mind, free from all lustfulness, of all indolence, a guide to passionate natures, a master of life and death'. He would then arrive 'where no thing is, where no grasping is, that is the isle of no-beyond, *nirvana*, where decay and death are no more'. That desire should fail was their hope; desire was the enemy, for it provoked lust, greed and anger, 'the three gates of hell'.

Buddhists worshipping the Bodhi tree, beneath which the Buddha received enlightenment

Instead of fleeing to the forests to live as hermits in a traditional Vedic way, Buddha's converts formed communities, ultimately monasteries, a thousand years before such retreats became the refuge of Christians in Egypt and Western Europe. Buddha was not at first regarded as a god. Adepts in the wisdom of Buddhism were called Bodhisattvas. Any of them able to surmount all obstacles, those who 'could scale the heavens and pluck immortal wisdom from its resplendent source', became a buddha, an omniscient being. None is more renowned among Buddha's converts than the great King Asoka (*c* 264–227 BC), two centuries after Buddha's time.

Like the mendicant friars of Catholic Europe a minority of wholly dedicated Brahmans and Buddhists depended for their food, clothing and survival upon the hard work and generosity of the rest of society whose ways they scorned to follow and even reviled. Gifts of food, clothing and medicine were provided for them, sometimes on an elaborate scale. Just as the Christian Church benefited by legacies of houses and land, so also did the followers of the Vedic and Buddhist faiths. One inscription records that a 'house and house garden of 12.5 metres (41 feet)' together with land, were made over to support a school or college where grammar was taught. Many similar gifts endowed charities for religious purposes, including the support of Brahmans and Buddhists.

Under the Gupta monarchs (*c* 320–535) Hinduism, the cult of Vishnu, Krishna and Siva among the principal deities, entered its golden age in northern India. Buddhism and Buddhist monasteries declined with any gardens they may have possessed. By about AD 1200 Buddhism was no longer an institutional religion there. Buddhism in India shared the fate it encountered later in China. Losing its hold on a reflective elite which sought instead satisfaction from the traditional faiths, which were Vedism in India, and Confucianism in China, Buddhism degenerated into a superstition of the uneducated classes.

Western thought was centred upon man. Even the idea of God seemed to be an idea of human powers infinitely magnified. In the thought of the ancient Greeks, worldly, human problems were far more actively pursued than were questions about nature. A very different standpoint was taken in the Far East. There, religions did not exalt man. Whereas reflective minds in the West accepted and glorified the effort to master and possess the world, those of the Far East had no such ambition, cultivating instead a passive, receptive state of mind, content merely to listen and to meditate. Where the Christian tradition encouraged activity, but not sensuous enjoyment, the religions of India, although they did not crusade against sex, passion and pleasure as did the ascetic puritan element in Christian thought, made it clear that the highest honour was due to those who mortified the flesh to the virtual suspension or extinction of the life of the senses. No encouragement to create gardens of delight is therefore to be expected from deeply religious, 'ideational', cultural leaders of either East or West. They alone are in question because the ordinary run of people did not concern themselves with religious or philosophical thought. As long as the tough executive warriors and politically powerful men also honoured such leaders of thought, the general trend of cultural life would be guided along 'ideational' lines, as it predominantly was in the Middle Ages of Europe. In India the caste system allowed a sharper division of society so that a strongly marked sensual, sensuous, 'sensate', way of life characterized many of the governing and military leaders, as it normally would the great mass of their subjects. How far their worldly interests were reflected in gardens of delight can only be conjectured from very scrappy references in the few secular 'sensate' writings that have survived from that early period, such as the *Kama Sutra* written at some time between the fourth and seventh century AD.

In all the remains of early Indian writing, whether Sanskrit or Pali, there is no detailed description of gardens or of garden art. Incidentally amid the mass of Brahmanic and Buddhist literature, some few faint references indicate the existence of gardens. Such are the collection of 'Stories of the Buddha's Former Births', *Jataka*. Some of these parables and fables tell about real or mythical kings who possessed a park cared for by many gardeners. All such tales bore about the same relation to reality as did many of the 'Lives of the Saints' of medieval Christendom, but even fables and parables depend for their effect upon some links with the realities of the everyday world. Royal parks in Aryan India seem to have served the same purpose as Persian 'paradises', except that they were not always for the exclusive use of the king as the Persian hunting preserves must have been. They seem, on the contrary, to have been the home of any homeless wanderer. Mystics coming from their mountain retreats 'to buy salt and seasoning in Benares', for example, were said to have dwelt 'in the king's grounds' during their stay. One 'false ascetic' set up a vegetable garden in a corner of one such park, taking his produce to market. A glowing account of these parks, taken from earlier writers, was written in Greek by Aelian (c 170–235):

... there are reared in the royal parks tame peacocks and tame pheasants. Within that park are shady groves, grassy meads planted with trees and bowers woven by the craft of simple woodmen. So genial is the climate that the trees are ever green and never show signs of age or shed their leaves. Some are native to the soil, while others which are brought with great care from foreign parts, contribute to enhance the beauty of the landscape.

Nowhere in the ancient world were flowers more in demand than in India. In Buddhist times, especially, they were revered. One of the most repeated formulas in the excessively repetitive Buddha stories tells of the 'showers of divine flowers' which were supposed to have fallen from the upper sky whenever Buddha, the Lord, spoke to the faithful. Garlands of flowers adorned temples, shrines and monuments. They were hung round the necks of revered and distinguished persons, as indeed they are in India today. They adorned homes and their inhabitants on festive occasions. Indian women loved to put flowers in their hair, a practice which fortunately also survives.

No single flower was held in greater reverence than the lotus. It seemed specially symbolic to devout Buddhists. Born amid mud and slime, it rises through the dirtiest water to the clear light of day, there to open its beauty to the sun, as though seeking heaven. So also, moralized the Buddhists, can mankind, despite its sordid earthly condition, rise with Buddha's aid to a higher plane. *Lotus of the True Law*, *Saddharma-Pundarika*, is a specially revered treatise on the Buddhist faith.

India's torrential rains made the cultivation of small herbaceous flowers such as those which grace Western gardens so difficult that the supply of flowers came largely from flowering shrubs and trees. What these most probably were and what an Indian garden of the period 200 BC to AD 700 was likely to grow, have been graphically described by Mlle Jeannine Auboyer in her excellent short account of *Daily Life in Ancient India*. Where a family could afford a garden, it would have been, she believes, at the back of the house for greater privacy. A stream or access to an irrigation channel would have been essential, not only for the garden but also for the daily ceremonial, religious wash. Then there would be lotus pools together with brilliantly coloured tropical flowering shrubs, trees and plants. Mlle Auboyer lists a few among many possibly commonly grown varieties, such as the scarlet or orange blossoms of the asoka or coral tree (*Saraca indica*), the sweet-scented kadamba (*Anthocephalus indicus*), the scarlet kimsuka (*Butea frondasa*), honey-scented jasmine, white atimukta (*Hiptage madablota*), sweet-smelling yellow champaka (*Michelia champaca*) and hibiscus, not forgetting roses, of course, among which the 'China rose' was prominent.

Ladies of the household, who traditionally had to spend most of their time at home, were in charge of the flower and vegetable garden, the layout of which they might have been able to plan, with its pool, arbours and seats. For many a young Indian mother the garden she tended must have come to be valued for more than its utility as a source of seasonings, mustard, parsley, fennel, green vegetables, sugar-cane, figs, mangoes, dates, limes and other fruit trees. In none but larger gardens or royal parks would it have been possible by means of leafy, shady groves to stir memories of forest scenes beloved by Indians.

Little is known about the daily life of millions of people in India during more than three thousand years. From the snow-clad Himalayan peaks in the north to the lush tropical and jungle vegetation of the south with its great variety of flowers, trees, shrubs and types of landscape, it will for ever be unknown whether and in what way gardens were formed out of it all. In an exotic Eastern setting, idyllic garden scenes can only be imagined, such as the moonlit gardens in which high-caste Indian ladies were said to appear after a cool evening breeze made life tolerable in the open air. A poetic imagination conjured up pictures of such gardens of delight:

> Through the shady palace garden where the peacock wandered free
> Lute and lyre poured forth their music, parrot flew from tree to tree
>
> Through lines of scented blossoms which by limpid water shone
> And the rooms with seats of silver, ivory bench and golden throne.

A fortunate few of India's teeming millions may have been able to luxuriate amid such operatic scenery, but, for the vast majority, life offered no such relaxation. They lived, and still live, in countless small villages, scattered all over India, exposed in former times to the attacks of rival villagers, roving robbers and invading armies. Twice only, between 250 BC and AD 700, did one ruler succeed in controlling the greater part of India: Asoka was the first, Candragupta the second. Oppressed by chronic overpopulation, taxes and the exactions of the money-lenders, the villagers lived on the margin of a pitifully meagre subsistence. Poor soil, polluted water, intense heat, terrific monsoon rains contributed to the spread

The lotus, most revered of all Indian flowers, and particularly symbolic to Buddhists who saw in its growth towards the sun from mud and slime a lesson for mankind

The Emperor Babur receiving envoys in his garden at Agra, renowned for its magnificence and unrivalled beauty; Moghul painting, early 16th century

of virulent infectious diseases, and all sapped vitality. Pleasure gardens do not arise in such circumstances, any more than they did in the walled towns, to any considerable extent, in times of peace. Here and there, as below the great rock palace of Sigirya in Ceylon, where a royal garden was made in the fifth century AD, a garden still remains, but such evidence is rare.

A new era in the history of Indian gardens opened with the conquest of north and eastern India by the Moslem Turks from Afghanistan. In 1524 Zehir-ed-Din Muhammed Babur invaded Hindustan. He was not a Moghul, a people whom he detested, although he claimed descent from the great Mongol conquerors, Genghis Khan and Timur Beg, or Tamerlane. Foreigners from the north, Tartars and Persians, were generally called Moghuls by the Indians, hence came the 'Moghul Empire' to describe Babur's dynasty. Babur was by no means the first Moslem to invade, occupy and loot northern India, attracted by its enormous wealth in gold, silver and gems. A man of great energy and daring, towards the end of his life he founded an empire which endured until the English became paramount in India in 1761.

In the limited sphere of garden history, Babur won distinction by his eager quest for flowers and trees and his equal enthusiasm for creating fine gardens. It was a taste he bequeathed to his immediate descendants with such success that the very origin of gardens of delight in India has often been credited to him. His long and fascinating *Memoirs* tell the story of his life, with five unfortunate gaps, from his accession at the early age of twelve to the small kingdom of Ferghana east of Samarkand until within fifteen months of his death in 1530. As welcome interludes in the dismal story of conspiracies, revolts, battles and murder, he makes many references to flowers, shrubs, trees and fruits, comparing their various attractions in one place or another. Journeying eastwards from Samarkand he celebrated the violets, tulips and roses of Ush which grew, he said, in gardens on both banks of the river there. Of Samarkand he said that in the whole habitable world there are few cities so pleasantly situated. With its gardens and suburbs it was a wonderfully elegant city. He commended the 'Heart-Delighting Garden', the 'Perfect Garden', the 'Northern Garden', the 'Paradise Garden' and others. After the loss of his kingdom and many desperately perilous adventures, he captured Kabul in 1504. He records that the hills to the south of the city were entirely covered with gardens, but they seem to have been mainly orchards. Consolidating his position there, he built in 1508, beyond Kabul to the east in a much better climate, his great garden, the Garden of Fidelity, overlooking the river. Following the old Persian gardening tradition which the Mongols assimilated, it was designed as a fourfold field plot, with a large pool or water reservoir in the centre, planted round with orange trees and clover. This spot is the very eye of beauty of the garden, said Babur.

As he campaigned he had a keen eye for flowers and gardens. He records two occasions when he had a collection made of tulips growing wild. West of Kabul he came across a foundation near which were some beautiful plane trees and, what was more remarkable, some oak trees which were nowhere else to be seen in the area. A flowering shrub with red or yellow blossoms, probably the Judas tree, *Cercis siliquastrum*, greatly enhanced the charm of the scene, which Babur improved by having a cistern or pool made there with a stone surround and stone seats. When the Judas tree bloomed, Babur said, 'I do not know that any place in the world is to be compared to it.'

When he eventually arrived in Hindustan, bent upon war, conquest and loot, he carefully described the country, its climate, animal and plant life. New flowering plants, trees and shrubs caught his eye as he commended hibiscus, oleander, white jasmine and others. Otherwise he found very little to please him.

Arriving at Agra, where he planned to reside, he looked for a garden site where he could 'construct water-wheels to produce an artificial stream' because 'one of the chief defects of Hindustan is the want of water-courses'. It was with great difficulty that he found a site. The whole of the Jumna river area, he said, 'was so ugly and detestable that I repassed the river quite repulsed and disgusted. Because of the want of beauty and of the disagreeable aspect of the country I gave up my intention of making a charbagh [a garden with a fourfold plot], but as no better situation presented itself near Agra, I was finally compelled to make the best of this same spot.'

He recounts the sinking of a well, the construction of the essential pool, and the laying out of the garden. 'In this way, without neatness, without order, in the Hindu fashion, I produced edifices and gardens which possessed considerable regularity. In every corner I planted suitable gardens; in every garden I sowed roses and narcissus regularly.' His son later said he named it the 'Flower-scatterer' and few places were equal to it in beauty. This was in 1526, after which he is said to have made other gardens near Agra, the Archanak Bagh a mile south of the city, and two more, on one of which, on the Agra side of the river in the Citadel, is his great well, sixty-seven metres (220 feet) in circumference, from which fifty-two people can draw water at the same time. Gardens on such a magnificent scale were evidently unknown in Hindustan, although Babur testifies to the existence of some garden plots when he complained that 'the country and towns of Hindustan are extremely ugly. All its towns have a uniform look; its gardens have not walls; the greater part of it is on a level plain.' Such gardens may have been commercial flower gardens or groups of shrubs or fruit trees. Despite insurrections, rebellions, treachery and war, he continued to find time to create and beautify gardens. In 1530 he died at his great garden, at Agra. His body was taken to the garden he had built east of Kabul and there buried on the slope of the hill.

Babur's civilized gardening tradition endured. He recorded that at Agra his followers whom he enriched from the vast spoils of war also created gardens. Khalif, Sheik Zein, Yunis Ali and several others made regular and elegant gardens and pools, constructing water-wheels as at Lahore and Debalpur. 'The men of Hind, who had never before seen places formed on such a plan or laid out with such elegance, gave the name of Kabul to the side of the Jumna on which these palaces were built.'

That such gardens of delight were indeed a novelty in Hindustan seems to be confirmed by linguistic evidence. Today the Persian word *bagh* for garden is still used there; moreover in Sanskrit the word *bhaga* was not used for gardens until after the Moslem conquest. Sanskrit words denoting coppices, sacred groves, flowery glades, a flower enclosure, a place for play and a plot for cultivation are also mostly later than the first Mohammedan invasion of the country in around AD 1000. Before then 'garland-maker', 'royal and monastic park-keeper' occur in Sanskrit as well as words denoting the work of girls in culling wild flowers.

Moghul gardens were Persian in style because there was no Mongol tradition of gardening for pleasure. Converted to Mohammedanism, the Moghuls amplified the fourfold division of the ancient Persians symbolizing the four rivers of life by adopting the Moslem Garden of Paradise of the Koran with its eight

'The Garden of the Fairies', a Moghul
painting of the period of Emperor Akbar

divisions ascending to the 'Garden of Eden' at the highest point. They followed
the Persian style also in being completely enclosed and secluded, graced by a
large pool which was also a reservoir and was called a 'tank' in India. If it were
sufficiently large, a grand pavilion would be built out into the pool. Moghul
gardens often had the characteristic sunken flower-beds resplendent with gaily
coloured, massed flowers, each usually filled with a special flower, tulips in one,
narcissus in another, roses in others, and so on.

Gardens of delight on the Moghul Persian plan had their greatest development
during the growth and consolidation of Moghul rule under the reigns of the
Emperors Akbar (1556–1605), Jahangir (1605–1627) and Shah Jahan (1627–1658).
It was then also that Moghul art, architecture and literature attained their highest
levels despite wars, rebellions, conspiracies and violence which continually
brought untold misery to India at that time. Nothing but the might and resolution

of men such as Babur and Akbar allowed any flowering of the arts of peace. Akbar inherited a love of flowers from his grandfather Babur. He was assiduous in bringing new plants to India as well as skilled gardeners from Kabul to grow them. This remarkable ruler consolidated Moghul power in India leaving some splendid monuments to his good taste and grandeur of conception.

Akbar himself did not create as many gardens as Babur or as his own son Jahangir was to devise. Nevertheless, several were his work, as at Fatehpur-Sikri and Sikandara. In the glorious valley of Kashmir, which he annexed in 1586 and was able to visit three times, he built a fort and palace in which a small garden had been made. There Akbar loved to sit to enjoy the view over the lake. During Akbar's long absences it was neglected, so that his son, Jahangir, who had learnt to love the country also on visits with his father, had to restore it. Meanwhile gardens were being created by those who had prospered in the emperor's service. Babur recorded some and Akbar's son mentioned others, notably a garden in Gujarat: '. . . In the whole of Gujarat there is not a garden like this,' wrote the Emperor Jahangir.

Despite his reverence for the Koran and his frequent pious invocations of 'Allah, the merciful and the clement', Jahangir became an opium addict and a drunkard. He left much decision-making to trusted officials, especially to the father and brother of his favourite wife, who merited the title he gave her, Nur Jahan, 'Light of the World'. With greater energy and taste than Jahangir and a love of political power greater than her love of flowers, Nur Jahan was able to achieve more for Indian gardens and for India than Jahangir would have accomplished alone. It was to please her, it is said, that he brought the great Asiatic

Emperor Muhammed Shah riding through his splendid garden; Moghul painting, 16th-century

95

plane tree, *Chinar*, from Persia. Not she but her mother invented the powerful essence or attar of roses, which greatly pleased Jahangir. His interest and enthusiasm made her work possible.

All the splendid Moghul gardens were made for the personal delight of their royal or aristocratic owners. But Akbar and his son Jahangir spared some thoughts for their subjects by ordering that trees should be planted along some of the most frequented roads, such as those from Agra to the Indus and to Bengal. These works of peace were undertaken despite desperate threats of war, revolt and struggles for power. Jahangir's sons at length rebelled against their father and fought each other. Prince Khurram emerged victorious on the death of his father to rule from 1628 to 1658 as Shah Jahan, sending his stepmother, Nur Jahan, to live as a pensioner in Lahore.

Jahangir's father, Akbar, by his renunciation of the faith of his fathers, by his tolerance and willingness to listen to missionaries of other faiths, and by his love of nature for its own sake, gave the first signs of the development of an increasingly self-regarding way of life. Jahangir, who revered his father, was more inclined to invoke Allah. He was resolute in maintaining and in enforcing obedience to principles, but in doing so, he followed his father in being tolerant and in being eager to hear about the beliefs of others. Moslem ideational cultural traditions were rapidly passing from an impersonally directed life to one more and more guided by personal sensations and ambitions. Perhaps Babur's love of gardens was the first sign; certainly it had not characterized previous Moslem conquerors of India, for there seems to have been no sign of any garden development, not even in Kashmir, before Babur. Sensuous garden art came to a splendid flowering under Jahangir and Nur Jahan. The prominence of such a gifted woman is also strong evidence that cultural and social ideas were changing. Yet finer art came with Jahangir's son, Shah Jahan.

Not in gardens alone did Moghul art then reach its grandest development. In painting, in literature, with histories, memoirs and especially with poetry, high standards were established by a people barely two centuries away from the life of barbaric nomadism. Between the building of the tomb of Humayun, the second 'Moghul' Emperor of Northern India, and the completion of the Taj Mahal nearly a hundred years later, a succession of splendid buildings gave proof of a grandeur of conception and a freshness of style and execution that contemporary Europe was hardly able to match. Especially notable is Akbar's 'ghost city' of Fatehpur Sikri about twenty-six miles from Agra. There, almost as though they had been finished a few years ago, still stand a variety of splendidly ornate and spacious buildings including the glorious Jami' Masjid Mosque of 1571. So the Moghuls continued; the fort and citadel at Agra, the entrance gateway to Akbar's tomb at Sikandra of 1612–1613 and the great Jani' Masjid Mosque at Agra (1644–1658), the largest in India, were all proof of a power that had its most convincing expression in the Taj Mahal, the tomb of Shah Jahan's beloved wife, Mumtaz Mahal, one of the architectural wonders of the world. Shah Jahan left many other notable buildings, any one of which would have conferred great distinction upon him.

Shah Jahan's splendid Shalimar Gardens at Lahore were inspired by his father's great garden at Kashmir which he also crowned with a grand black marble pavilion. He was the wealthiest of all the great Moghuls. Within the fortress of New Delhi his magnificent royal residence had large, enchanting gardens amply supplied by a canal seventy miles long bringing water from the Jumna river for its pools and fountains. This was but the largest of several gardens strung along

the river bank. The Pearl Mosque in the citadel at Agra and the celebrated Peacock Throne with other monuments to his taste and genius tend to suffer eclipse by the shining glory of the Taj Mahal (1630–1653). Its idealistic style is self-evident, for although it was traditional in form, it was no slavish repetition of previous achievements. Instead of merely following precedent, Shah Jahan broke away from it by placing it, not as a centre piece to a great garden, but on a marble platform high on the bank of the river Jumna, making the garden the approach to it with a long central canal instead of a pool, admirably proportioned and flanked by cypresses. His plan was to have been completed by his own tomb, a similar Taj in black marble on the opposite side of the river, a splendid idea which his son Aurungzeb refused to honour. Shah Jahan was buried with his wife later.

The glorious Taj Mahal, with its long central canal leading through the gardens towards it; built by the Shah Jahan

Idealist Moghul culture, like the culture of idealist periods in other lands and at other times, was relatively short-lived. Its decline may be symbolized by the pathetic vision of Shah Jahan in the last eight years of his life, imprisoned by his usurping son Aurungzeb in the citadel at Agra. Visitors to the fort and citadel buildings there are still shown the window from which he could gaze every day at the brilliance of the distant Taj Mahal as it glowed, with changing colours clear and glorious, between the rising and the setting sun.

Shah Jahan's pathetic end symbolizes the decline of Moghul might. Aurungzeb made a tremendous effort to consolidate his rule and sternly to repress rising sensate tendencies always latent in Moghul society. As though conscious of impending weaknesses, his vigorous, ruthless spirit reacted strongly in support of traditional values. He spent most of his reign under arms with his troops in camp. A devout, ascetic Moslem, his zeal was too great. In 1669 he prohibited Hindu religious exercises, attacking temples with an iconoclastic fury as grim as that with which, a few years earlier, Cromwell's puritans had assailed the artistic heritage of Catholic England. Aurungzeb added two rich kingdoms to his Empire by conquest, enlarging it to its widest extent, but internal weakness left his Empire in no condition to repel all the enemies he had aroused. Of these the wild Mahrattas were the most formidable. After his death in 1707, the ruin was fearfully rapid. Not political chaos only, but a cultural breakdown was also evident. It was not apparent in gardening arts alone, but also in architecture and painting.

As the Moghul leaders yielded to the lures of lust, liquor and drugs, Persians, Jauts, Sikhs and Mahrattas soon demonstrated that without firm government, chaos ensues on all sides. Hindu traditions, solidified by the caste system, were more tenacious. Brahmanism continued to command reverence, but even if the Hindus had been able to shake off their hated Moghul overlords, grand gardens would not have greatly multiplied because there was no deep Hindu gardening tradition. Gardens had become associated with foreign domination.

Moslem decline did not ensure Hindu ascendancy, but the Moghul garden tradition and the expulsion of Hindu craftsmen from the Moslem court stimulated some wealthy Hindus to create gardens in their own style. Whereas the Moghuls created sun gardens, the Hindus preferred moonlight gardens because, as Mrs Villiers Stuart relates in *Gardens of the Great Moghuls*, 'Hindu ladies ... rarely entered their gardens except at night', and except during 'one month in the year, July, Sawan [the middle rains] when the palace ladies went down to see how their gardens fared by day'. That was the one time of the year when the few herbaceous flowers of Hindustan, zinnias, cannas, balsam, marigolds, cosmos, amaranth, orchids, lotus, caladiums grow riotously, providing blazing masses of colour on a scale not to be seen in more temperate climates.

One grand Hindu garden inspired by Moslem examples was made at Dig, or Deeg, built by a Raja of Bharatpur, on flat land outside the Rajput palace-fortress. Begun in 1725, it was enriched after 1765 by marble thrones and seats looted by the Raja's people from the great Moghul Imperial Palace at Agra. Although constructed by a Hindu, it bore evidence of Moghul antecedents as was inevitable, because a strong tradition of Hindu gardens did not exist. All had not been forgotten, however, as Mrs Villiers Stuart recorded:

According to an old Indian treatise on gardening [which she does not name], five trees should be first planted, as they are luck bringing: – phalsa (*Grewia asiatica*), bhila or marking-nut tree, punag (*Rottlera tinctoria*, now *Mallotus philippinensis*), sirisha (*Mimosa sirissa*, now *Albizia lebbeck*), and nim (*Melia azardirachta*, now *Azardirachta indica*), after them, plantations of any kind can be made. The auspicious sides for planting

ABOVE AND OPPOSITE Floral borders depicted on Moghul paintings of the School of the Emperor Jahangir, *c* 1610

are: on the east the bur (*Ficus indica*, now *F. benghalensis* or *F. sundaica*) and Karanda (*Carissa carandas*); on the south gular (*Ficus glomerata*, now *F. racemosa*) and bambu; on the west amalka (*Emblica officinalis*) and bila (*Aegle marmelos*); on the north pakar (*Ficus infectoria*, now *F. virens*), bhor (*Ziziphus jujuba*), and Kaitha (*Feronia elephantum*, now *Limonia acidissima*). The bur tree should not be planted at the gate of the house or in such a place that the shadow of it may fall on the building. All large trees are inauspicious within the house, i.e. in the central courtyard, particularly those of a thorny nature.

When the breakdown occurred after Aurungzeb which ended the grand days of glorious Moghul gardens and vigorous cultural life generally, Sir Thomas Roe's prophecy nearly a century and a half earlier was verified. 'The time will come', he said, 'when all in these Kingdoms will be in combustion, and a few years war will not decide the inveterate malice, laid up on all parts against a day of vengeance.' In the middle of the eighteenth century, the great struggle between England and France that long raged in Europe, overflowed into North America and India, where, for two centuries, that 'fearful day of vengeance' inflicted upon the Moslems was postponed.

British military supremacy in India was achieved by Robert Clive and Warren Hastings in the latter half of the eighteenth century. Political control was essential if a military ascendancy was to be maintained. British administrative rule was enforced from about 1805. From then onwards Indians were exposed to the authority of another alien, very different culture. Garden history indicates how alien it was.

Ostensibly, and often in reality, devout Christians, the British were then on a rising sensate tide of utilitarianism in economics, ethics and law, whereas the guides revered by Indians were in theory, and often in practice, strongly opposed to all forms of sensate indulgence. They were also passive and contemplative at a time when the British were intensely energetic and determined, not for trade, economic and political advantages alone, but in other spheres, including a zeal for missionary Christianity and education. The new impulse which the British brought grew stronger and more positivistic throughout the nineteenth century, influencing India towards a predominantly Western way of life. Among its by-products were the determined and often successful efforts made by a relatively very small number of administrators, missionaries, the military, and traders from Great Britain, and notably by their often redoubtable wives, to establish European-style gardens wherever they lived in the Indian peninsula, uninfluenced by any gardens they may have found there. Indian princes, aristocrats and wealthy folk retained any they may have had, but those of former Moghul emperors were neglected.

Despite political decay and near anarchy many old Indian gardens were daily enjoyed. A British observer in the 1840s records how Indian 'ladies pay and receive visits in the evening, passing from garden to garden, in covered litters'. They were not to be seen, hence the high garden walls and the covered litters. Many large gardens perished. Apart from Pinjor and Dig, there is no note of any new garden in the eighteenth century able to stand comparison with those created during the great period of the Moghul Empire. The great days of Moghul gardening were long since over. Even to maintain many that had been created was too big a task.

The buildings in the Shalimar Garden with Shah Jahan's black marble pavilion remained in 1830. On holidays 147 of its fountains could still be made to play, but all that makes a garden of delight was in a lamentable state of decay: a few turfed walks, some shrubberies of wild plums, kept for their white blossoms,

View of the garden from the Rang Mahal in the Red Fort, Old Delhi

ivy-covered walls, a ruined bath, alone remained to give melancholy hints of its former magnificence. Akbar's Garden of Delicious Breezes was in a worse state and the noble groves of plane trees had been largely destroyed by the Sikhs. Despite such neglect, nothing could dim the beauties of Kashmir to the least observant eye.

Too few of the British sent to India had the eager curiosity and keen sympathy which that remarkable pioneer, Sir William Jones (1746–1794), exhibited towards the cultural life to be found there. Law was his profession but philology, literature and botany were among his many enthusiasms. No man did more to attract attention to the study of Sanskrit than he. Vivid pictorial notes of his such as that about the gold-coloured champac flower (the strongly scented *Michelia champaca, swarma champa*) which contributed to the elegant appearance of Hindu women as they rolled the flowers in their long black hair after bathing in the holy Ganges, added a glow to his writings which English romantic poets were very ready to borrow.

Despite such incentives, British interest in Indian gardens developed very slowly. In 1913 Mrs Villiers Stuart was a pioneer in calling attention to their merits and in lamenting the sad neglect of the great Moghul gardens. As she realized, their vast size made them a formidable problem. Lord Curzon whom she, as all others who write upon Indian antiquities, justly praised, had very much more in that respect to rescue than gardens. 'The grand old terrace gardens of India and Kashmir', she said, 'lie for the most part forlorn and neglected, or so changed that nearly all their charm and character are lost.' Yet she thought 'the average Englishman in India takes a far more practical interest in his garden there than he would do at home in England'. There was however a 'divorce of horticulture and design'. Gardens were regarded by most of the English, as were other aspects of life, from a practical, economic, horticultural point of view, a desire to see results rather than to relish a well-designed garden. With candour and truth she recorded that 'wherever English influence has been strong, as in British India and in the so-called "progressive" Native States, the typical Indian gardens have been the first to go, and the old symbolic garden craft the first of all the traditional arts to disappear', a good illustration of the mistake of attributing the decline of Moghul painting to 'a failure constructively to assimilate European art'. There was no 'assimilation, only decay'. The British were not alone to blame. There were rich Indians who could better have afforded a lavish expenditure on a garden of traditional design.

A decline in Indian gardens evident in the eighteenth century was therefore not remedied in Indian style in the nineteenth century, although gardens then again began to be made under the British Raj but in a British manner. Inevitably it was a development which changed the character of existing garden forms. Many Indians then began to be themselves influenced by Western ways. Large, elegant Indian homes in New Delhi and elsewhere now have gardens that resemble, with their lawns, shrubberies and flower-beds, an equivalent English garden; the only difference is the possibility of picking grapefruit and other exotic fruits and of relishing the flowers and scents of many trees, shrubs and sub-tropical plants and birds unknown in an English landscape. Long-neglected gardens as in Kashmir and Lahore are being rescued and restored. A visitor gets the impression that gardening is now being undertaken with zest as an art adapted to local conditions, as in the new Buddha Jayanti Park, and Gandhi's memorial gardens in Delhi, without any narrow nationalistic motives of reviving Gupta or Moghul forms and without scorn of European styles or plants. Many Indians share the gardening enthusiasm of their late President Husaain, who like his eminent predecessor Sir Sarvepalli Radhakrishnan found in the palace of the former viceroy splendid gardens of an Anglo-Indian form designed by a British architect. Indian gardens, as most modern gardens everywhere, are often of a mixed character resulting from the impact of various gardening traditions, an account of more of which may begin by considering some other gardens in the Far East – those of China and Japan.

IV

GARDEN ARTS OF THE FAR EAST

In their mad onrush, the Mongols, whom nothing seemed able to halt, swept across Asia to strike a deadly blow at the empire of the Arabs in Persia as at all other peoples in their path and to threaten the very existence of the warring, jarring peoples of medieval Europe at the beginning of the thirteenth century. They came bringing memories of a very distant land, resplendent with the blossoms and the scent of myriads of flowers of a glory, variety and splendour completely eclipsing the wild flowers that were about all the West then had in its few and tiny gardens.

The natural floral wealth of China even in modern times has been found to be so vast that it may well be believed that in those ancient days, before the acute pressure of population growth had driven the Chinese to intensive hand-cultivation of every available spot of ground, the tremendous spread of the most gorgeous wild flowers must have made the country a floral paradise. It was estimated by Ernest H. Wilson (in *China, Mother of Gardens,* 1929), who spent altogether eleven years on plant-collecting expeditions in China's remote areas between 1899 and 1911, that some 15,000 species of plants were to be found there, which is about three times the estimated plant wealth of Greece. About half of them are native to China alone. The whole of the north temperate zone of the world cannot rival China's trees either in number of different kinds or in their ornamental beauty.

To no other single country are gardeners of the rest of the world more deeply indebted for beautiful flowers than they are to China. Outstanding among them are roses, camellias, magnolias, wistaria, azaleas, primulas, gardenias, chrysanthemums, asters and peonies.

Long before the Mongol invasion of China the Chinese were making their country a cradle-land of human civilization. Early as these Chinese beginnings had been, they were later by two or three thousand years than the civilizations

Intensive cultivation of the land outside the walled city; an illustration from the *Shu Ching* ('Book of History'), one of the books in the Confucian canon

PREVIOUS PAGES Rikugien garden, Tokyo; a typical garden of the Japanese Feudal Period originally laid out by Yanagisawa Yoshiyashu in the early 18th century

of Egypt and Mesopotamia. Apart from a very few oracular inscriptions cut on bones during the Shang Dynasty (around 1500–1000 BC), historical information has not survived from ancient China to rival the hieroglyphics or tablets of baked clay which have thrown light upon the quality of life in other dawn-lands of culture in the middle of the second millennium BC. At that period the Chinese began gradually to build up and establish the rites, ceremonies, customs and ordered social etiquette which long persisted, despite periods of desperate violence, confusion and chaos. A traditional way of life emerged which did not appear to give emphasis to otherworldly religious beliefs, however much the mass of people were terrorized by fears of evil spirits and other superstitions. Yet even at that early period lyrical poems show a depth of sensitivity and feeling that had no equivalent in Europe outside Greece until centuries later.

The ideas and values by which the Chinese were guided for many centuries arose in troubled times. After the fabled Five Rulers came the seminal Feudal Period of the Yellow River basin (*c* 1030–221 BC) during which civilized order collapsed, resulting in the horrors of the Warring Kingdoms from about 480 to 221 BC. Occasional references to gardens occur in the lyrical poetry of that period.

At about the same time that Zoroastrism was winning converts in western Asia and Gautama was founding Buddhism in India, new ideas about the meaning and value of life also became manifest in China. It was against a background of human helplessness and despair in the sixth century BC, that two great rival schools of thought about the world and human life were formed whose influence continued to guide reflective Chinese until modern times. Confucianism was the first.

Confucius, the latinized form of Khung Fu Tzu or Master Khung, was born around the middle of the sixth century BC. His prudential and moral teachings, preserved in a record of his conversations and discourses, the *Analects*, tell of his efforts to bring peace and harmony among discordant, discontented people. Chinese society was traditionally made up of lesser nobility, knights and scholars, peasant farmers, artisans and merchants. Presumably as the only way of maintaining order, Confucius counselled 'loyalty' to the emperor, 'forgiveness' or toleration and mutual esteem among everyone. Such were the main principles of the Confucian *Tao* or way of life. Otherworldly influences were rejected. He confined his own teachings, said one of his followers, to culture, by which he meant literacy with a knowledge of the Odes, of history and the maintenance of traditional rites; to the administration or conduct of affairs; to the duties of loyalty to superiors and the keeping of promises. He never spoke about unusual natural phenomena or spiritual beings.

Education should, he said, be generally accessible to all, the first man known to have said so. Then the best and most able boys would be available to serve the emperor. Confucius became the patron saint of scholars and public officials, honoured during the centuries to come in Confucian or literary temples in every town and city in China until they were denounced during the crude Marxist repression of 1973. Usually each had gardens with many fine old trees and a semicircular pool spanned by a ritual bridge.

It has been suggested that the teachings of Confucius hindered rather than promoted the development of gardens because once when asked for advice about agriculture he replied, 'I am not so good for that as an old farmer,' and when the enquirer went on to ask him to teach him gardening, he gave the same answer, 'I am not so good for that as an old gardener.' As there was no science either of agriculture or of horticulture he was undoubtedly right in sending his enquirer to a practical man. A certain snobbishness may perhaps be detected in these replies for they might have been given by a republican Roman notable, who, with Cicero, despised manual work as the task of slaves. Perhaps Confucius intended no slight upon gardening, for he seems to have shared the general Chinese joy in flowers, judging by his praise of the orchid or *Ran*, which, he said, 'produces the King's fragrance'.

Indirectly his teaching promoted gardening in later times more than the words of any other philosopher in the history of thought because he stimulated the creation of a class of practical administrators, officials or civil servants, who down the centuries were to have leisure, good houses, the means to embellish them with gardens and the worldly wisdom which directed them to seek treasures on earth rather than in heaven. Confucius had a positive, progressive philosophy of success through effort in practical mundane affairs. He gave no encouragement to idle dreamers or to curiosity about natural phenomena so he is thought to have hindered rather than helped the progress of scientific thought.

As in periods of idealistic culture everywhere, Confucius strove for a balanced harmony or integration of the chief values of the human spirit. With the advice to seek the mean in all things went that aversion to manual labour which has characterized most leaders of early agricultural and patrician aristocracies. There seems to be no evidence of any luxurious expansion of gardening at least until the downfall of the old feudalism and the rise of a new nobility of wealth. In idealistic times in China, as later in ancient Greece, gatherings of wise men often took place in gardens where a few officials and other serious-minded folk also joined in the discussions.

With the continuance of civil war, bloodshed and murder it must have seemed to many that Confucianism had failed. From ancient times, the Chinese, in common with other races of men, faced with the mysterious forces of nature, developed in spite of Confucius superstitious beliefs in magic and other worldly forces. About a hundred years after the death of Confucius in 479 BC, these millennial yearnings were recognized by Lao Tzu, who presented a new way, or *Tao*, which sharply challenged the practical, worldly counsels of Confucius.

Difficult as it is to make out any very coherent doctrine from his pronouncements which are often as cryptic as those of the Delphic Oracle, the spirit of Taoism fundamentally rejected and opposed the life of the times. Taoism favoured retirement, contemplation and peaceful withdrawal from the world. It extolled the virtues of that mystic reunion with nature which was to become part of the soul of the educated Chinese, to inspire some of their greatest poets and painters. The state of mind induced by Taoism, although disastrous in government and administration, was therefore particularly favourable, Joseph Needham argued, to the birth of the spirit of scientific enquiry which Confucianism stifled. Certainly Taoism much later seems to have stimulated the development of gardens – but gardens of a rather special kind; gardens to mirror the natural beauty of landscape rather than merely to minister directly to the satisfaction of the senses by the colour and scents of flowers, shrubs and formal patterns. Nature itself at first sufficed. A mountain retreat with a small hut from which to view the majestic spectacle of natural beauty became the ideal for many whom Taoism inspired with aversion to the horrors made by man. Millions of Chinese in succeeding centuries strove to keep such sentiments alive by planning miniature gardens simulating distance and mountains, streams and trees.

Needham pointed to the way that these two major, profound, incompatible influences illustrated the dualism which the Chinese found in nature. There was the positive male principle, Yang, and it was inseparable from the yielding, negative feminine principle, Yin. For the Taoists, peace of mind was the most desirable human attainment, but it was not to be won by strife, competition and worldly success towards which Confucianism pointed; it was to be found by yielding, by withdrawal. The rival Confucian or Taoist influences on Chinese styles of gardening can often be identified.

When peace was at last brought back to the long-suffering Chinese under the Han Dynasty (202 BC–AD 220), the arts of civilization were able to expand more generally, and among them the art of the gardener. The traditional force of mystical, otherworldly sentiment stimulated by Taoism, ensured that many town gardens would not be mere pleasure resorts for idle hours alone, but that they would be intense with allegoric, symbolic and religious overtones. Many early Chinese believed that there were principles in nature which garden design ought to reflect. As in Persia, the universe was divided into four quarters, each of which was under the sway of its own special god. Taoist inspiration may have produced the Chinese striving to reflect nature and natural wildness in their gardens and to avoid regularity and formality in arrangement. As the teachings of Lao Tzu gained increasing admiration, he began to be venerated as the founder of a new religion. Temples were founded and sacrifices were made in his honour. A new monasticism began, as though inspired by the contemplative hermits in their mountain retreats, away from the wear and tear of a Confucian society.

Confucian influence on the other hand, by extolling the supremacy of the emperor and by providing him with willing, obedient and educated officials, was a permanent influence tending to counteract the religious mysticism of Taoism.

Well, therefore, did the Chinese look upon life and human affairs as subject to the equal and opposite pull of Yin and Yang. Gardens could be made to flourish continuously to cater both for the more ideational, otherworldly reveries of the Taoists as well as for the more sensate, mundane ambitions of successful officials, merchants and others whose more robust natures did not crave for the consolation of a mystical, religious kind. Confucians and Taoists, true to type, naturally did not exhaust the great variety of character to be found among the Chinese people, millions of whom were able to relish the beauty of flowers and trees without looking for divine inspiration from every leaf.

Gardens were already being made in China during the first millennium BC. Some of the largest resembled the great parks of western Asia in which rulers kept animals for show and for hunting and where they grew flowers for the ladies of the harem. Some of them did so at the expense of the poor. 'They destroyed homes and habitations and dug up the cultivated fields,' said Meng Tzu (Mencius), a Confucian philosopher in the fourth century BC, 'turning them into gardens and pleasure-parks', so much so that many people lacked clothing and nourishment. The great mass of the people, then as at all ages, had little thought except for the necessities of life. They cultivated their millet, rice, vegetables and fruit. Flax was grown for linen and the mulberry was already widely cultivated to nourish silkworms as well as for its fruit. Peaches, apricots, cherries, pears, plums and chestnuts were among the other trees commonly to be found. Everywhere the bamboo was in evidence, reverenced for its beauty and used for every conceivable type of construction. Vines were unknown or little prized, alcohol being made from rice. Tools and implements were of a primitive kind: forks, hoes, hatchets and light wooden ploughs. Such was the general poverty of the country that although the wheeled cart had been invented, the great bulk of the fetching and carrying was always the task of human labour. The land was not private property; it belonged to the emperor.

During the Han Dynasty the first contact was made with India. Chang Ch'ien was sent in 138 BC on a mission in the course of which he reached Bactria, returning after ten years or more with the grape vine and alfalfa. His master, the Emperor Wu Ti (*c* 140–86 BC), was a great plant collector. The magnificence of his palace at the Han capital of Ch'ang-an, the City of Eternal Peace, was legendary. The Imperial park and gardens tended by 30,000 slaves were said to have been bounded by a wall 150 miles in circumference. However exaggerated such a story may be, Wu Ti is credited with the establishment, in 111 BC, of a botanic garden. To it specimens of strange plants began to arrive from every direction as other envoys joined in the hunt. The improvement of plant species by cultivation began. Chrysanthemums, for instance, were developed from two species of small wild flowers to become perhaps the most popular, most revered plant of the Far East, renowned in ancient Chinese classics.

It was about this time that the peach was taken to Persia and from there to Rome and Western Europe. It was not the only export, for beyond the traffic in plants and trees went the export of ideas about garden arrangement and decoration. As remarked already, memories of the pavilions and pagodas of China may have directly inspired the kiosks and pavilions of Persia quite as much as would a nomadic experience of tent life. Among the novelties subsequently taken to China were peas, broad beans, flax, walnuts, cucumbers, figs and pomegranates, some of which acquired a Chinese significance of their own. The pomegranate was regarded as a symbol of fertility; grape-vines were appreciated for their decorative charm and as shade-giving creepers rather than for their grapes, while the hard shells of walnuts were polished by being rolled in the hands of countless bookish folk to help them to keep their fingers supple and thereby to enable them to wield their writing brushes to better effect.

From India and Nepal during the 250 years after the second half of the first century AD, a stream of missionaries of the new Buddhist faith made their way into China to set about translating the Buddhist writings and to win converts. China seems to have been a fertile field for such a faith, for the Chinese had no coherent, transcendental religious beliefs. They were plagued by all manner of crude superstitions arising from astrology, divination, signs and omens, and gave immense ingenuity to attempts to rationalize their primitive folklore.

In the celebrated Book of Changes, *I Ching*, probably of the third century BC, the whole body of traditional beliefs had been reduced to sixty-four symbols, composed by various combinations of six long and short rods to make hexagrams. They purported to furnish a general scheme of classification for everything of ultimate significance in the world of nature. Needham stressed the misfortune for China that such a manipulation of essentially empty symbols should have become a substitute for the study of the phenomena of nature. The whole exercise, he observed, was evidence of a search for peace of mind and the belief that it could be promoted if all human knowledge could be classified. When the best educated minds of China were thus blinkered, progress in technology, including horticultural science, was left to rule-of-thumb methods of practising gardeners.

Buddhism from the second to the fifth centuries AD fortified to some extent

Flowers were particularly valued by the Chinese both for their beauty and their traditional meaning. This porcelain ewer and bowl of the Two Sungs period, 12th century, is in the form of a lotus, symbol of purity and truth

Confucian efforts to improve morality, but in its aversion to worldly affairs, which it dismissed as illusory, it outdid Taoism, although it did enrich the family-ridden Chinese society by a more universal compassion. In its impact upon cultural life Buddhism exerted a restraint upon sensate indulgence as powerful as if not more powerful than the sternest puritan in the Christian West. As such it did nothing to encourage gardens of delight which Confucian ways of thought tended to encourage.

Meanwhile Taoism was transformed into a religion by the exaltation of the Way into a kind of absolute, the One, the source of all life and illumination. Buddhism had some mildly positive influence on gardening by exaggerating the earlier Taoist aim of cultivating the inner powers of men through mystical contemplation and withdrawal from the world and by encouraging a monastic way of life.

As in Western Europe, monasteries fostered gardens both for the food and herbal medicines they provided for the inmates and for the flowers needed for the shrines of altars in the temples. Many countries in the Far East still maintain the characteristic Buddhist liturgical offering of flowers that perish and incense that burns. In *China, Mother of Gardens*, Mr E. H. Wilson, in drawing attention to the contribution of monastic gardeners to our present wealth of resources, said that Europe owes to them the best varieties of pears, which were not introduced into England until after the Battle of Waterloo. In more ancient days, the temple gardens of China and Japan preserved the maidenhair tree. Flourishing generally throughout the north temperate zone in Mesozoic times, as shown by geological fossil remains found in Europe, Greenland and America, the maidenhair tree is the sole relic of an ancient species whose origin can be traced back to the primeval age of the earth. China and east Asia generally escaped the last Ice Age, so a vastly greater floral wealth is to be found there than that inherited by the Western hemisphere.

More than once strong Confucian opposition to Buddhism succeeded in closing the religious houses and in driving the monks and nuns back into the world to contribute to the economic activity and to the wealth of the nation. After the eleventh century however such opposition dwindled and Buddhism, with its love of flowers, spread very generally throughout the vast empire. Among the novelties and inventions of the Han Dynasty were the introduction of tea, first mentioned in AD 273; the study of botany and mineralogy; the use of water mills and of the wheelbarrow, a familiar garden aid which was unknown in the West until the Middle Ages, a thousand years after its invention in China.

The Han Dynasty collapsed in violence in AD 220 and the country was split into the Three Kingdoms and later rent by many warring dynasties until AD 618, when the first emperor of the T'ang Dynasty began what was to become a century of marvellous human achievement in which Chinese art and literature rose to new heights of power and sublimity. In that great idealistic period, Chinese artists first began to paint pictures of flowers, although painting upon silk, which began probably at some time between 500 and 300 BC, had already reached a high pitch of excellence. The Buddhist paradise was commonly represented with flowers, but the Chinese did not need Buddhist missionaries to teach them that flowers were beautiful. Many T'ang paintings of flowers and of landscapes have survived, but few of gardens as such, although they sometimes figure as a setting for a picture of court ladies amusing themselves with some traditional game or merely enjoying themselves socially.

The all-too-short idealistic art of the T'ang Empire was succeeded in the eighth

The San Tan-yin garden, Hangchow – 'Three Pools that Mirror the Moon' – with surrounding pavilions and bridges; Ming Dynasty

and ninth centuries by another 'time of troubles' of the sort that China had too often known. Yet the indomitable will to survive, to restore and to create kept alive the spirit of Chinese culture and maintained the Chinese gardening tradition. Order was not very successfully restored by the Sung emperors who ruled as the Northern Sung from 960 to 1127. The love of flowers and of gardens again had fresh scope, and the oldest Chinese book on orchids, and indeed on any single flower, dates from the tenth century.

Savagely assailed by the Tartars (or Tatars), the Sung emperors were driven south to rule as the Southern Sung Dynasty between 1127 and 1279 from Hangchow, a paradise with a lake set in a circle of blue hills, rich with bamboo, lotus, magnolia, chrysanthemums, plums, peaches, almonds, apricots and other gorgeous flowering plants and trees. At almost the same time, other Mongol hordes surged westward into Europe, raping, slaughtering, looting and burning as they went.

In China as in western Asia they slashed and hacked at a millennial civilization they neither valued nor understood. There also they ended by settling down to absorb many of the cultural values they had so wantonly and savagely assailed. In south China particularly, the love of flowers, of trees and of ordered gardens was among the charms of the new and civilized ways of life which they were to learn from the defeated Chinese. An inborn feeling for flowers may have characterized their racial traditions, for their homelands were wonderfully rich with an immense wealth of flowers. In modern times the Magyars, who were of Mongol stock, although that did not save them from near-annihilation by

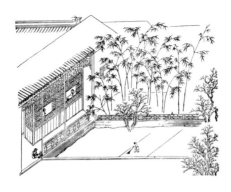

The neat and charming little garden of Lin Ch'ing in Ch'ing-chiang-p'u, to which this civil servant retired

the Mongol hordes in the thirteenth century, have preserved in country districts a tradition of highly decorative and rich flower-patterned embroidery on women's clothes.

Eventually the great Mongol emperor, Kublai Khan, a convinced Buddhist, overcame the last of the Southern Sung Dynasty and became emperor of all China in 1280, when the country reached new heights of power and domination. During this alien Mongol rule, Marco Polo with his father and his uncle arrived at Shangtu in 1275, where they encountered Kublai Khan, at the end of their great trek from Italy.

Marco Polo astonished Europe after his return (1298) by recounting the advanced arts and civilization of China. Hangchow was, he said, 'the greatest city in the whole world'. 'All along the main street running from end to end of the city, both sides are lined with houses and great palaces and the gardens pertaining unto them.' From the lake it was possible in barges to 'take in the whole prospect in its full beauty and grandeur with its numberless palaces, temples, monasteries and gardens full of lofty trees sloping to the shore'.

Marco Polo also mentions certain pleasure gardens in which the elegant social set would 'divert themselves the live-long day, with their ladies, returning home in the evening in their carriages'. In his description of the emperor's palace he said that there were 'groves and lakes and charming gardens planted with fruit trees and preserves of all sorts of animals, such as roe, red-deer, fallow deer, hares and rabbits'. He found the same kind of royal park at Kublai Khan's palace at Xanadu, where the wild life was kept largely for the sport of the Khan's falcons. When he got to Peking, Kaan-baligh, the City of the Khan, which he called Cambaluc, he encountered the same kind of royal game reserves. 'There are fine parks and beautiful trees bearing a variety of fruits. The parks are covered with abundant grass.' The whole place, he said, was full of animals.

Kublai Khan was a great collector of trees. He planted many on the famous Green Mountain

which has been made by art from the earth dug out of the lake. This hill is entirely covered with trees that never lose their leaves but remain ever green. And I assure you that wherever a beautiful tree may exist and the Emperor gets news of it, he sends for it and has it transported bodily with all its roots and the earth attached to it and planted on that hill of his. No matter how big the tree may be, he gets it carried by his elephants and in this way he has got together the most beautiful collection of trees in all the world.

Kublai's passion for trees led him to give orders 'that all the highways... should be planted with rows of great trees... even the roads through uninhabited tracts are thus planted and it is the greatest possible solace to travellers.'

It is clear from Marco Polo's accounts both of Hangchow and of the north of China that private citizens had gardens also, but he is silent about their character and gives no description of any plant.

Despite their success in assimilating and fostering Chinese culture, the Mongols, who ended by trying to share the government of the Empire with the Chinese, were always looked down upon as barbarians. After their tough fighting spirit had been softened by their new settled civilized way of life, the Chinese rose against them in the middle of the fourteenth century and they were overthrown.

Emperors of the Ming Dynasty then ruled China from 1368 until the middle of the seventeenth century. Romantic gardens were then widely developed, per-

The famous Pan Mou garden, Peking. Originally designed by the Ming poet Li Li-weng, it was restored in the 1840s by the Chinese official, Lin Ch'ing, one of the large class of wealthy, cultured civil servants of this period, seen here with a friend admiring his garden

haps somewhat exaggeratedly, in the effort to provide settings of a magnificence comparable with that of the gorgeous palaces created by the emperors in the 'Forbidden City' of Peking.

By this time an immense garden lore and ritual had been created in China. The largest group among the class of wealthy, well-to-do, cultured Chinese spread throughout China was that of the professional civil servants. As a class they were alive to the charm of gardens, and the gardens and the elegant homes of these households of high officials continued to form a splendid feature of Chinese life. As late as the year 1915, the garden of the viceroy or local governor of Lanchow, according to Mr Reginald Farrer in *The Rainbow Bridge* (1921), was almost a park in size, stocked with pheasants, rabbits and storks, with noble old trees, mounds, rockworks, pools, gazebos, terraces, towers, summer houses and pots of gay flowers along the parapets.

From comparatively early times, beginning in the eleventh century during the Sung Dynasty, books were written in China upon individual flowers and trees as well as more general works such as the *Records of Flowers and Trees of the Prince of Wei* which dates from the second and third century. Over one hundred older books written before 1850, most of them before 1750, are listed in the bibliography of Mr H. L. Li's *The Garden Flowers of China* (1959). In the seventh century, during the Ming Dynasty, more comprehensive Chinese manuals on gardening began to appear such as the *Hua-Ching* or *Mirror of Flowers* and *Yuan Yeh*. The latter, one of the most complete treatises, advised a very private, out-of-the-way site, 'if possible among trees in the mountains'; such was the traditional, Taoist-inspired site for a garden which 'should be made to last a thousand years'. Surrounded by a creeper-clad wall, it should have a stream running through it with irises and orchids on its banks. A bamboo grove should also be planted there 'to provide a stillness to captivate the heart' and there should be willows also for 'when the morning breeze blows through the willow trees, they sway like the slender waist of a dancing girl'. There, too, a straw-thatched hut should be erected so that in the heat of summer 'one may drink ice-cooled wine while the breeze plays among the bamboo canes. In winter one may sit in a heated room there, by the brazier and melt snow for tea-water. One quenches one's thirst and all worries vanish.' At night, 'The moonlight lies like glittering water over the countryside. The wind sighs in the trees and gently touches the lute and the book that lie on the bed.'

When escape to enjoy the peace that is to be found amid natural beauty was impossible, a garden could still be planned in the city, but if so, 'it should be situated in a sheltered corner; even if the neighbourhood is vulgar, all noise is shut out when the gate is closed. One opens a path that is uneven and undulating. Over the tops of trees and bamboo canes, the crenellation of the city walls appear as if floating on air.' A city garden required ample space for the large trees, a stream, flowers and a mound to give the illusion of a mountain that the Chinese regarded as indispensable. If they had little space the garden had to be proportionately reduced to a miniature garden, for then 'a little mountain may give rise to many effects; a small stone may evoke many feelings'.

To achieve such an illusion, with winding paths offering new perspectives at every turn, with miniature hillocks and mounds concealing new aspects, was the aim of many Chinese gardens; 'the winding path leads into dim distances', carrying the mind on beyond the cares and worries of the moment. To produce these effects, a garden required daily patient toil so that the result was a more studied, complex and intricate art than was that of the 'English garden' of the eighteenth century, although that was supposed to have been inspired by the Chinese example. Chinese garden design, like Chinese painting, was the product of a matured aesthetic philosophy which sought to reveal the general in the particular and to discover the particular in the general. Long before any such notions were current or practical in Europe, they had been assiduously cultivated in China. It was not until after the middle of the eighteenth century that some notions about the nature of Chinese gardens, as of Chinese art and decoration in general, apart altogether from the deeper theories upon which they were formed, began to reach Europe, where they were eagerly, if not very intelligently, imitated.

A few such generalities give a very inadequate impression of the immense variety of China's gardens, if only because the vast size of China and its various climatic zones make it most unlikely that there was anywhere 'the' Chinese garden. Whatever the location and quality, there can be no doubt about the assiduous care that went into their making. From M. Halphen's translation of parts of the *Hua Ching* of 1688 as *Miroir des Fleurs* (Paris, 1900), it is possible to follow in some detail the constant hard work in China willingly devoted to gardening. Detailed instructions were given about grafting, propagating, transplanting, pruning, sowing, manuring, erecting trellises, watering, weeding, harvesting, potting, digging, and so forth which its main practical purpose was to expound. The details with which flowers were studied is indicated by the description of some 150 different kinds of chrysanthemums. The author, Ch'en Hao-tzu, also described garden kiosks and verandas, and his aim seems to have been to provide a complete manual for the gardener and for country house life, which had then clearly reached a highly developed stage.

The strongly marked poetic feeling for flowers which is so characteristic of the Chinese does not seem to have led them to make flowers a central attraction of their gardens in the way that they are of the very essence of the average English garden. Grass lawns also were never a prominent feature of most Chinese gardens. Far greater interest was taken instead in flowering trees and shrubs. The Chinese had, however, strong favourites among flowers, some of which were admired and cultivated for more than the immediate enjoyment of their beauty because they were endowed by tradition with symbolic meaning and importance in all Chinese life. A flower symbolized each month.

Orchids often symbolized feminine charm because of their delicate beauty and fragrance. The lotus, as a symbol of spiritual purity, truth and noble endeavour, was an emblem of the righteous man; the chrysanthemum, of long life; while the peony, the king of flowers, and a badge of high rank and of wealth, signified material prosperity and happiness. Chinese girls were nearly all named after a flower.

Poets and painters never tired of extolling the glory of their favourite flowers. Each had faithful admirers including whole schools of painters devoted to their celebration. There was the artist Tao Yuan Ming (365–427), whose passion for chrysanthemums and their cultivation became a legendary theme in Chinese painting and poetry for more than a thousand years. So strong a poetic feeling for flowers, which could be satisfied by growing a few, or, as often, a single bloom in a pot, was rarely felt with similar intensity in Europe.

Throughout two-and-a-half millennia or more, a very varied plant lore accumulated. Many other flowers were equally beloved and renowned and carefully cultivated. Such were the rose, peach blossom, the Japanese apricot, viburnum, magnolia, azalea, wistaria, narcissus, or sacred lily, and jasmine. All these last-mentioned plants were natives of China except the narcissus and jasmine which are believed to have been imported by Arab traders from western Asia at an early date.

Trees were equally renowned. The bamboo which grows wild all over southern and western China stood for pliability through strength. The peach, regarded in much the same way as the Greeks thought of the apple of the Hesperides, as able to confer health and long life, was also a talisman against demons. Peach wood was therefore used as a lucky charm on doors and on panelling. Many betrothals were made when the peach trees were blossoming, so it became a symbol of congratulation.

The beauty of plum blossom aroused tremendous enthusiasm. Wang Ming at the beginning of the Ming period would stay outdoors in the cold night air to revel in its beauty, singing proudly, 'I live in poverty and paint plum trees'. A great lore developed about the most artistic form of the trunks and branches of plum trees. Pines were similarly revered. They stood for silence, solitude and revered old age and they conjured up visions of venerable old hermits in those mountain retreats that were most favoured as garden sites.

While it is probably fairly generally known that oranges, lemons, limes and wild citrons grow wild in South-East Asia, notably in southern China and the southern slopes of the Himalayas, there has been much uncertainty and vagueness about the manner in which they reached Mediterranean lands. According to Tolkowsky in his *Hesperides*, in the second half of the third century BC the botanist Hsi-Han praised oranges in his treatise on the plants of the south. The citron was not imported until the fourth century A D when it was called 'Buddha's hand'. At that time also tea-drinking became popular and the dried petals of chrysanthemums, roses, or jasmine as well as orange peel were used, as some are still, to flavour some kinds of tea. Lemons, although native to South-East Asia, were not generally known in China until much later.

The fame of orange blossoms and their glorious fragrance spread from the south of China to the north, where the winters were too cold for orange trees to survive. By the twelfth century the trade in oranges was well organized and boat-loads of oranges were sent to the North. A great lore about the medical virtues of oranges and orange peel was developed and the fruit, the tree and its blossoms were justly celebrated in countless verses and depicted in paintings.

Clearly the Chinese made much of their riches in flowers and trees and shrubs. They also adored rocks, sand and water. Hundreds of years before Western eyes were invited by daring sculptors of yesterday and today to seek aesthetic satisfaction from the contemplation of strange shapes of stones and wood, the Chinese had developed a great cult of weather-worn and water-chased rocks and stones. By the seventeenth century it was already difficult to find good specimens. Limestone blocks formed into curious shapes by the action of water were especially prized. The rocks stood for 'mountains', for everlasting permanence in a garden 'made to last for a thousand years', and were commonly set up in the middle of garden ponds. Where water was not available, however, sand and small stones were used instead to create the illusion of water. No other people employed rocks and sand for purely aesthetic reasons in this way and they form a distinctive characteristic of the gardens of China and of others modelled upon them.

The best rocks were cherished with an almost religious veneration. To erect them at precisely the best point in a garden called for great taste and discernment. 'Only scholars and real amateurs of gardens', it was said, were able to accomplish so exacting a task satisfactorily. Landscape painters were regarded as the best designers, as they were again to be in eighteenth-century England. They, too, were a product of the long blending in Chinese culture of schemes of values created over a thousand years and more previously by Confucius, Lao Tzu, and by the Buddhists. Taoism was still a vital force in Chinese ways of thought.

The Chinese idea of a perfect garden was not fully realized, even when the best possible use had been made of the whole range of available trees, shrubs, flowers, rocks and stones. Just as important were the buildings, walls and galleried walks, for they also were regarded as essentially a part of the garden as a whole. When Western Europe began to copy Chinese garden pavilions in the eighteenth century, they were already the product of a long evolution in China. Of all kinds of sizes and shapes, round, square, polygonal, with and without supporting pillars, they were to be found in vast numbers all over China. Many were skilfully and most artistically provided with graceful roofs projecting far beyond their sustaining walls or pillars. They were often roofed with coloured glazed tiles – yellow, green or dark blue to add to the charm of the landscape. Chinese pagodas, which became popular as adornments to the parks and large gardens of Europe during the late eighteenth century, served no such purpose in China, where they were local versions of Indian *stupas*, holy towers built over the relics of Buddha or of some saint. They were to be seen in the grounds of the temples or on isolated hills outside the cities.

Galleries were not merely sheltered walks uniting different parts of the garden but they formed an indispensable part of the whole garden scheme. Great skill and artistry went into their lattice-patterned walls, doors, balustrades and win-

The Jade Girdle Bridge at the Summer Palace, Peking, built by the last empress of China, Tz'u Hsi

dows, for the open stonework of a wall could become a window by being pasted over with rice-paper.

Walls were rarely straight or strictly rectangular, but subtly curved and shaped. Doors and windows in them were similarly treated. The round moon-gate was especially popular, and it was often varied, sometimes rather extravagantly, to provide strange and exotic apertures.

Characteristic also of the Chinese scene are the arched bridges thrown over streams and pools. Their exaggerated rounded form resulted not merely from the utilitarian desire to ease the passage of small boats and craft below, but often to enhance the effect when they were mirrored in the water they spanned.

So much beauty, so skilfully provided, demanded considerable insight and powers of perception if it was all to be properly appreciated. An old Chinese poet wisely said that one should enter a garden in a peaceful and receptive mood, study its general plan and when all its varied features have been thoroughly assimilated 'one should endeavour to attain to an inner communion with the soul of the garden and try to understand the mysterious forces governing the landscape and making it cohere'. The garden world of China was a world for reflection, meditation, withdrawal; a world in which the individual found his greatest solace in the privacy of his garden in devotion to the five pure things: water, rock,

The pavilion and lotus ponds of Cho Cheng garden, Soochow, over half of which is made up of pools; late Ming Dynasty

bamboo, pine, and plum blossom. It was a world seen with a painter's eye and described with a poet's pen, evocative alike of delight and philosophical insight. For some followers of Lao Tzu such a garden could be the boundary of their world, at least for a time.

Even summary accounts of some of the main features of Chinese gardens can hardly fail to convey something of their compelling charm, some feelings of admiration and respect for the men and women whose taste and discernment created such exquisite retreats centuries ago to minister to that love of beauty, that reverence for nature which all mankind seems able to acknowledge, however distinct and different may be their race, cultural background and historical development. Through the mists of time such kinship through a common human interest in the natural beauty of gardens links garden-lovers today with court officials of the pharaohs of Egypt, with the monarchs of ancient Persia and their Greek enemies, with Epicurus, with Cicero, Pliny and Hadrian. It also provides a bond with the ancient Chinese. 'To ramble in my garden is my daily joy,' wrote a Chinese poet of the fifth century at a time when, far to the West, the Roman Empire was going down to ruin.

Garden delights were naturally the special privilege of the wealthier folk. Certainly most Chinese emperors did not lack for gardens, perhaps more exquisitely beautiful than those enjoyed by any other monarchs of history or of fable. The Imperial Parks of the Sea Palaces, dating from the twelfth century, on the shores of three lakes or 'seas'; the seventeenth-century 'Perfect and Brilliant Garden' of the Old Summer Palace at the foot of the Western Hills near Peking; the New Summer Palace and the Park of the Jade Mountain, restored at the end of the nineteenth century, were all among the vanished glories of imperial China. The poetry of their titles is only exceeded by the descriptions of many of their beautiful aspects: 'The Pavilion Riding upon the Rainbow', 'The Tower of Profound Peace', 'Pavilion of Purple Glory', 'Hall of Sweet Dew', 'Grotto of the Secret Clouds', 'Terrace for the Invitation of the Moon', 'Hall of Greatest Brightness and Goodness' and many more.

Tragic ruin overtook the glories of these imperial Chinese gardens. The fanatical T'ai-ping rebels of the 1860s caused a greater devastation than did the Mongols 600 years previously, for the havoc they made of the wonders of Hangchow and of Peking has never been repaired. They laid low the Old Summer Palace whose glories can only be imagined from some forty paintings of it made just before the middle of the eighteenth century, which are now in the Bibliothèque Nationale in Paris. Forty years later, British troops were guilty of adding to the ruin, when out of revenge for the fiendish torture and murder of some British officers and men during the Boxer Rebellion in 1900, they burned and destroyed what was left of the Old Summer Palace.

The winds of change which under the inspiration of Sun Yat-Sen swept away the Manchu Dynasty in 1911–12 inevitably weakened a social system of immemorial antiquity. In the Communist China of today it is not known whether many Chinese are able to assuage that deep natural thirst for some personal, intimate communion with nature which the possession of a private garden can afford.

Occasional hints and oblique references indicate a force and quality in early Korean civilization and culture about which it would be interesting to know more. What Korea's ancient horticultural glories may have been, and how far they were native and independent, or whether they were entirely borrowed from the Chinese, is unknown. No great Korean gardens seem to have survived to the end of the nineteenth century. Mrs Bishop, whose *Korea and her Neighbours* was published in 1898, reported that there was no public garden in the capital of Seoul and the few illustrations of the country which she provided showed no signs of good private gardens either. In the cult of the dead however some faint relic may have survived of better things, for she describes how Korean cemeteries were to be found 'on a breezy hill slope with dignified and carefully-tended surroundings'. The living however had to be 'content with a mud hovel in a dingy alley'.

In earlier centuries the situation must have been different, for otherwise it would not have been possible for the Japanese to number the Koreans among those from whom they learned how to make and cultivate gardens. Their service as guides and transmitters of Chinese garden lore to Japan remains their main title to a place in gardening history.

It is difficult now to believe that less than one hundred years ago the government, social life, beliefs and practices of the Japanese were about as remote from those of Western Europe as were the ways of the Incas of Peru or the Aztecs of Mexico. It is also too easy to assume that all those differences have vanished now that Japan has taken a leading position among the industrial countries of the world.

Tradition has it that the first mention of gardens goes back to the time of the Empress Suiko (592–628), when a high court official, Soga-no-Umako, was said to have owned a beautiful garden. This was then a new development in Japan, said to have been inspired and largely undertaken by Korean gardeners who emigrated to Japan.

At that early stage of what seems in fact to have been the dawn of their cultural development, the Japanese were fortunate in coming under the influence of the glorious T'ang period of China's culture (618–906). Just as the Romans were able to draw lasting inspiration from Etruscan and especially from the examples of Greek culture at its best period of the sixth and fifth centuries BC, so the Japanese fell under the spell of the architects, sculptors, painters, craftsmen and gardeners of T'ang China. In the sixth century (552) Buddhist missionaries reached Japan from Korea to begin slowly to turn many Japanese away from their traditional, animistic worship (later called 'Shinto') of the sun-goddess, reputed ancestor of the imperial family, of certain trees and mountains.

Inspired by Chinese models, the Japanese began to adapt and adopt them to their native ways in accordance with their own taste. In Kyoto during the Heian period (794–1185) Japanese high society increasingly relished luxurious living, exquisite politeness and artistic refinement. In marked contrast was the military spirit of the fighting men in the service of their feudal chiefs. Specialized as a calling in the tenth century as *Samurai*, they obeyed a military code of harsh discipline and self-sacrifice; they despised money and all the means of getting it.

A special Sino-Japanese style of garden design, known as the Shinden-Zukuir, was developed in the Heian period. Houses of the richer Japanese were provided with gardens on their southern exposure. South of the open garden space was a long narrow pool of water fed by a stream which also supplied a waterfall. Beyond the pond, earth or stones were thrown up to symbolize a hill and at the same time to mask off the garden boundary. As in China, the whole was a carefully contrived composite landscape of trees, stones, rocks and water deeply symbolic of nature and of the mysterious forces by which the universe was supposed to be governed. The gods ruling the four quarters of the universe were ever present in thought and influence. Water had to flow from the east, the source of purity, into the west, whither all impurities were washed away. Such gardens seem to have been of a mixed, possibly idealist, type, attempting to harmonize the satisfaction of the senses, but at the same time reverencing traditional religious beliefs.

Cold from the high pressure area of Siberia gives Japan a severe winter with snow two to three metres in depth on the Japanese Sea side of the main island, Honshu. It is much milder on the eastern shores. Gardens are made with winter in mind, when moss, not grass, provides the only green from the end of November until March. There is more sun in winter, so oranges and camellias survive, although at night until the early morning, it is very cold.

Already by the beginning of the eleventh century high society in Japan had attained a remarkable degree of sophistication. At a time when Alfred the Great and others were striving to confer literacy upon his subjects, Japanese ladies were

producing chronicles and novels of great purity and refinement. The earliest piece of Japanese writing by a lady of the court, the *Book of Ancient Things* of 712, speaks of mandarin oranges as having been brought to Japan according to ancient tradition by order of a Japanese emperor during the first century AD. They found a ready welcome. Japanese poems and stories frequently invoke the scented glories of orange blossoms in May, and their romantic association as symbols of love.

Native Japanese wild flowers are also very numerous, but not as notable for their scent as were the narcissus plains of southern Persia. Japanese gardens are not distinguished by displays of flowers as are gardens in the West, neither have they splendid grass lawns, but there was an abundance of wild flowers, many acclimatized from the mainland since prehistoric times.

The long evolution of Japanese civilization and culture, relatively less disturbed than that of the countries on the mainland of Asia, enabled the rich and powerful to create some extraordinarily beautiful gardens. One such was the Byodo-in, or Summer Palace, built in 1051 by Japan's leading nobleman, Yorimichi, of the great feudal family, Fujiwara, whose descendants ruled Japan through the emperor from the ninth to the twelfth century. At his Summer Palace great gatherings were held of his elegant society friends to write music and poetry,

The enchanting lake and bridge at Shugaku-In, Kyoto

119

The Golden Pavilion, Kyoto, a replica of the original pavilion built in 1395 by the great Ashikaga Yoshimitsu, the supreme garden architect of the Japanese feudal period

OPPOSITE ABOVE Painting on silk of Wang Ch'uan Villa, after Wang Wei, the painter and poet of the great T'ang period. The love of the wilder aspects of nature, tumbling waterfalls and bare mountains, was a continual theme in Chinese gardens

OPPOSITE BELOW One of the fine bird-and-flower paintings (1126) of Emperor Sung Hui-tsung who was also responsible for enhancing the imperial gardens at K'ai Feng for which he ordered interesting rocks to be collected from all over his empire

OVERLEAF The Asakusa temple and gardens; print by Hiroshige, the 19th-century landscape painter

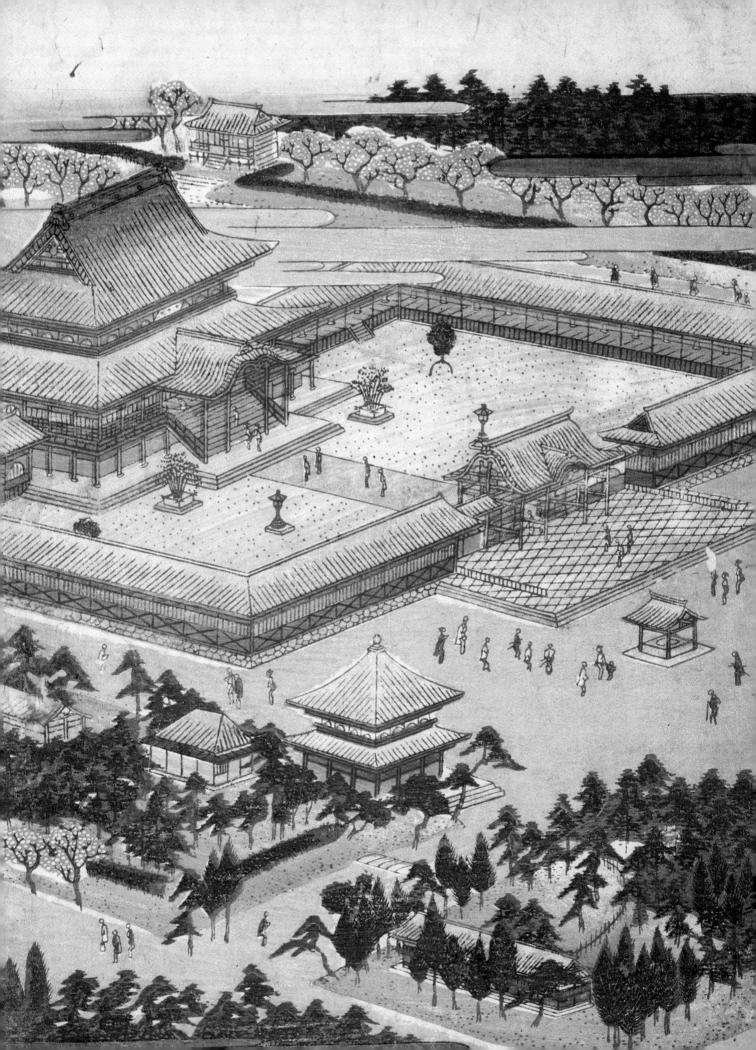

and to make perfumes and incense; they would sit up all night so as to witness the first opening of cherry blossom in the spring and would gaze from the terraces and pavilions at the glories of the moon. Some of these pavilions were full of grace in conception and execution, reminiscent no doubt of the earlier and now vanished pavilions of the best T'ang style. That Chinese and Korean influence in such a development of Japanese cultural life had been very strong may be imagined from the record that in 814 the nobility of Japanese birth numbered about 800 families, while nearly half as many were of Korean or Chinese origin. After 828 when the twelfth embassy went to the T'ang emperor of China, no more were sent.

By that time Buddhism had caused religious mania. Colossal bronze statues and seven of Japan's most magnificent temples were built in the eighth century, embellished by fine artists and equipped with huge bells. A new religious influence, also far-reaching and persistent, came to Japanese gardens in the thirteenth century during the Kamakura period (1185–1392) with the Zen Buddhists. Priests of this new sect brought with them an ascetic religious tradition and practice that had been matured for more than half a millenium. From the fourteenth century onwards a new note of austerity characterized some of their monastery gardens, although the softer and somewhat more sensate style beloved by the aristocracy continued, particularly in gardens inspired by those of Hangchow in southern China. The temple garden at Saihoji was of this type. It was said to have been made by a Buddhist abbot, Muso Kokushi (1275–1351), renowned as a garden designer. It still conveys an uncommonly fascinating impression thanks to a very skilful use of its natural features of hills and dells immersed in a soft impenetrable forest gloom, thick with moss and reflected in its still waters. On a greater or smaller scale such monastic interests spread in Japan and were copied by wealthy aristocrats.

For a thousand years, from the ninth to the nineteenth century, four great families in turn succeeded in ruling the country, using the mikado or emperor as their puppet. During and long after the twelfth century the country was cursed by civil war as rivals began a struggle for supremacy. Amid the poverty and ruin, Buddhism continued to flourish. During this feudal period under the Ashikaga Shoguns some splendid Japanese gardens were created, while garden architecture reached what was probably its finest and most glorious development. Something remains to indicate the magnificence then achieved, such as Kinkakuji, the Golden Pavilion, built in 1395, and so called because of its gilded roof. It became the temple of Rokuonji after the death of its creator Ashikaga Yoshimitsu. It was burnt down in 1950 but a replica of it was erected on the site five years later. Yet more famous is the later Silver Pavilion, about 1490, the crowning glory of Japanese garden design. It is still to be seen at Higashiyama, Kyoto, although it was never endowed with the silver sheeting intended for its roof. With its stream, lake, bays and islets, its tones, its green mossy banks and its tea-garden, the remains of which were discovered in 1933, it forms a vision of enchanting beauty.

Values of another kind, intuitional or intellectual instead of sensate, were sought under Zen inspiration. It is manifest in 'the flat garden' of some Buddhist temples. Such is the famous and still extant garden of Daisen-in of the Daitokuji Temple of Kyoto, commonly ascribed to the inspiration of the great painter Soami, who was also regarded as the greatest garden artist of his time. To Western eyes looking to gardens to minister directly to the pleasure and enjoyment of the senses, this 'flat garden' is not a garden but a sand-pit such as children might

OPPOSITE A typical Japanese garden with its charming use of water and stones, and its arched bridge set among trees

A Japanese flat garden, Kyoto; the placing of the stones and the patterning of the bare white sand is a skilled and much admired art, inspired by Buddhist spiritual values

love, for it is destitute of flowers, shrubs and often even of trees. Moreover, it is not a place in which to walk or to recline. It must be admired from a distance, from a veranda or a terrace. In essence it is nothing but a few large stones placed, it would seem, haphazardly in an ample rectangular bed of white sand which is kept free of weeds by being constantly furrowed into patterns with bamboo rakes. Its bare ascetic appearance conforms to Buddhist religious ideals, and the Yoga practices familiar to the Indian Buddhist missionaries to China and Japan.

Among the prohibitions of practical Yoga is the possession of property ministering to sensual pleasures. As the devout Buddhist sheds one human inclination after another, rising above bodily cares and the life of the mind as well, through to a stage of discernment in which all else seems vain, he has but one more stage to achieve, which is that of the ultimate bliss of dreamless sleep. Devout Japanese Buddhists were able to derive spiritual stimulus from the contemplation of a sand-garden. They prided themselves on their ability to discern the influence of a master-hand in the skill with which the shape, size and location of the various rocks or stones were chosen and disposed over the surface of the sand.

The Japanese 'flat gardens' owe their effects less to what they show the spectator than to what he is able to read or to project into them. In this respect they have a quality found also in Japanese poetry, painting, and flower arrangement, all of which aim at stimulating an attitude of mind and awakening thought, rather than at merely imparting the ideas of the artist, writer or their patrons.

LEFT Traditional Japanese use of stone and still water at Katsura Imperial Villa, a garden designed by the famed Kobosi Enshu (1579–1647)

BELOW Cleaning of the ceremonial tea-garden; c 1900

Today, when religious beliefs have largely fallen away and the nature and essence of culture is not generally understood, 'flat gardens', like so much modern abstract art, are unlikely to awaken a positive response but seem merely to contribute to the dry, dusty qualities of contemporary life. In ancient Buddhist Japan the situation was otherwise. The 'flat gardens' were so popular that they were re-created in miniature indoors by means of sand and small stones on black lacquered trays. Around temples and houses however, these large 'flat gardens' were not normally created without being brought into direct relation with surrounding trees, shrubs, moss and water, all of which served as their background and their foil and to which they cunningly served to lead or to introduce the eye. Such skilful combinations of the natural and the artificial were referred to as 'borrowed scenery'.

These striking developments in Japanese gardening were achieved despite desperate fighting between feudal chieftains from the early fourteenth to the beginning of the seventeenth century. When Hideyoshi (1536–1598), a rugged warrior of peasant stock, seized power in 1584, he also set an example in building and garden-making. By that time a few Jesuits had reached Japan and their influence has been seen in some of the new constructions. One of Hideyoshi's gardens, Sambo-in, survives as part of the monastery of Daigo near Kyoto. It was not begun until the year he died, 1598. The aim in these gardens was to ensure a succession of glorious blossoms, so there was a sequence of camellias, cherries, apricots, pears, wistaria, irises, lilies, peonies, and lotuses, while the long, genial Fall was enlivened by chrysanthemums, red maples, and other plants, trees and shrubs. They seem overtly sensate in comparison with the religiously inspired 'flat gardens'. The very best talent was brought in to make such gardens as beautiful as possible. Kobosi Enshu, who lived between 1579 and 1647, became a famous garden designer and he is supposed to have completed Sambo-in.

He was also a master of that ceremonial by which the Zen Buddhists had made tea-drinking into an art of religious significance. As it spread beyond the monastic sphere into the social world, the tea-ceremony was celebrated, with its own precise etiquette, in tea-gardens specially designed for the purpose. The essence of the tea-ceremony, as an expression of the normally serene and contemplative Japanese frame of mind, was subtly to induce modesty, restraint and a moral purpose in life. The tea-gardens, like the Zen 'flat gardens', had a reposeful tranquil quality, although, unlike the 'flat gardens', they were designed for an active community experience and not merely to be looked at from the outside. Water, stepping stones and a stone lantern were their regular features, as they soon became of other gardens also under the influence of the tea-garden style of garden design.

The long Edo period (1603–1867) under the Tokugawa which followed upon the death of Hideyoshi was a stern military dictatorship. In 1854 when Commodore M. C. Perry with ten ships of the United States Navy made the first considerable contact between Americans and Japanese, he found the Tokugawa system of government still in command. His curiosity about the country and its inhabitants was opposed by every device short of armed resistance. Every Japanese from the mikado down to the humblest peasant was watched by secret spies in the pay of the Tokugawa ruler of the day, the Shogun. All power was in the hands of the ruling Tokugawa Shogun acting nominally for the mikado or emperor whose descent from the sun-goddess of the Shinto religion could be traced back for over two thousand years. He was a prisoner, kept in seclusion,

upon whom the Japanese were forbidden to gaze if he ever was allowed to travel. A control almost as rigorous was exerted over the great feudal princes who might, it was feared, strive to supplant the Tokugawa family, as their ancestors had disputed the rule of previous dictators.

Noblemen and peasant alike were equally subject to the legal code, which was described in Commodore Perry's report as 'probably the bloodiest in the world'. Death was the punishment for most offences, carried out immediately after judgement. Very often the executioner was cheated of his employment by the suicide, *hara kari*, of the intended victim. In such a society, whose richer members were forced back upon their own resources, gardening, collecting and studying stones, flower arrangement and the tea-ceremony, along with art and music, could provide a blessed relief, and when the intelligent and educated Japanese were driven to seek aesthetic satisfactions from life, their sensibility, gaiety, good taste, and passionate attention to detail led to the creation of exquisite works of art. Their masters had been the Chinese and Koreans but they soon learned to go their own way. In painting, calligraphy, engraving, carving in wood and ivory, sculpture, metal-work, ceramics, enamels and lacquer they have for centuries produced miracles of beauty, many of them long antedating the work of the artists and craftsmen of Europe.

Such seem to be the main elements in the social and political background which help to explain for the West the acute aesthetic sensibility of the educated Japanese people in general and the form and nature of their gardens in particular. None but a Japanese historian would be able to say how much of Japanese art resulted from predominantly religious, traditional and ideational ideas about mankind, to what extent the strong sensate urges in Japan were reflected in art and how far a better integrated, idealistic blend of both gave harmony, order and beauty to it all. Gardens together with flower arrangements, which depend upon the product of gardening, seem predominantly idealistic in essence. Their form may have been strongly influenced not merely by idealistic attitudes arising from the contemplation of natural beauty but also from those which survived

Irises featured on a screen painted in the late 17th century, a period which saw the creation of numerous exquisite works of art

129

from past idealistic periods to serve as models for predominantly sensate owners, because the Japanese were deeply respectful of tradition, whether religious in origin or not.

Religious impulses, formerly supreme, as the myriad relics of Buddhism and Shintoism alone exist to testify, were already waning when Commodore Perry's expedition studied the matter in 1854. Any force that religion may have begun to lack in holding the Japanese to a traditional, if not to a pure ideational culture, was supplied by the stern rule of the dictatorship.

Under the Tokugawa domination gardens became larger. Aristocrats in their enforced leisure needed them more, so they were used for strolling about from one pleasant feature to another. To evoke thoughts which could not be roused by travel, little private worlds were created of islands, bays, bridges over meandering streams and irregular-shaped ponds representing the sea or a lake and all was set among glorious trees and adorned with a moss-grown lantern and old stones. The universal recurrence of all these features, however diversely they may be combined, is the special distinctive mark of a Japanese garden. In the West it is by no means unusual to find gardens without a pond, a stream, an island, a bridge, a waterfall, a fountain, a well, large ornamental stones, a stone lantern, a water basin, or paved walks. In Japan, however, a garden in the true sense of the word, apart from the 'flat gardens' of the temples, must possess not merely one or two such features, but all of them, as well as the trees, shrubs and fences. Flowers, being short-lived, were less in evidence because gardens in Japan, as in China, were designed to create that 'sense of permanence' which Lord Clark, in another context, stressed as an essential quality of civilization. Hence also the rocks, sand and old stones. Many of these fine gardens have been maintained down to our own days.

This brief survey cannot do more than try to point to some of the distinctive features which have contributed to the charm and fascination of the Japanese style of gardening. It was a style originally inspired by the gardens of China and it was profoundly influenced, as they were, by the Buddhist faith, including the later sect of Zen Buddhists.

In Japan, as in all other countries, well-cared for and magnificent gardens of the type described here were the privileged possession of the governing and wealthy classes of the feudal aristocracy who ruled Japan down to 1867. The Japanese upper classes had created over the centuries a traditional style of gardening that was undisturbed by foreign influences.

Apart from very small, very grudgingly permitted and very strictly controlled trading concessions to two or three Dutch ships each year, confined to one port, Nagasaki, Japan was virtually sealed against foreign contacts until the second half of the nineteenth century. Then Japan's rulers sought to modernize in the Western sense with all speed, but not without strong opposition. To overcome stubborn resistance to railways, the emperor himself had to inaugurate the first seventy miles of railway between Tokyo and Yokohama in 1872. Within no more than a hundred years the Japanese had changed course. They began to look less to tradition and more to future possibilities, as they made their country one of the leading powers in industry, commerce, and in naval, military and aerial transport. Such however was the force of tradition that the form and style of Japanese gardens have undergone little change as a result of amazing revolutions that have given strange new forms to all other aspects of Japanese life.

Flowers, although not prominent in Japanese gardens, were and are greatly prized in the daily life of the Japanese people. Japan, like China, is called the Flowery Land and its national emblem has long been the chrysanthemum. On the ninth of each September the chrysanthemum festival is observed as a national holiday. In cultured Japanese homes the flower is the object of an almost religious veneration. The flower ceremony, which is the most formal expression of the cult of the flower, can in fact be traced back, like so much in Japanese culture, to the Zen Buddhist monks from China who kept alive in the dark days of Japan's warring, feudal Middle Ages that regard for things not of this world that was to flourish more generally in Japan's cultural renaissance during the centuries of uninterrupted peace.

What exactly 'the Way of the Flower' fully portends is said to be part of those ineffable mysteries which none but the initiated can ever penetrate. Since feudal times it has been said that it was through flower arrangements that the silent, submissive Japanese wives communicated with their warrior husbands. It also enabled them to express their feminity. Japanese men admit that they do not understand the technique although they understand the meaning which Japanese ladies imply by their varying arrangements. It is the object of a professional cult to which skilled exponents devote their lives, to gain an honourable livelihood by imparting it to novices and students who enrol in their thousands all over Japan to receive, with due reverence, the instructions of a master. Japanese flower arrangement is an art altogether different from the lavish display of tastefully arranged and often exotic blooms massed in striking combinations at high cost on behalf of wealthy hostesses in Western lands. Its essence is simplicity. One sprig of pine, spruce, plum blossom, broom, camellia or peony, or two or three narcissi suffice for the decoration of a room. The whole art is in setting them forth in symbolic fashion, the essence of which is the Principle of Three. The topmost branch points straight upwards. It signifies heaven. The middle branch is shorter but it also aspires upwards. It stands for man. The third and lower branch is horizontal or pointing downwards to signify earth. This threefold form characterizes all traditional Japanese flower arrangements. Variations upon it are of course many and each has a significance of its own.

This seemingly simple act is simple in appearance only, for it is rendered amazingly complex by the refinement of a professional ritual governed by unexpressed and apparently inexpressible intuitions, canons of taste and no doubt of personal

Japanese women preparing for the annual chrysanthemum festival held on 9 September, a ceremony which dates back to the Zen Buddhist monks of the Japanese feudal period

idiosyncrasies and individual notions of the particular masters who happen to impart it. At their hands it becomes a guide to a whole way of life, for in the reverent atmosphere in which their flower lessons are given, the presumed nature of each flower is thought to inspire some moral guidance that seems to result from a somewhat diluted and secular form of the Zen ethical teaching. Devoted pupils may indeed be expected to acquire in this way an enhanced sensitivity; a delicacy of perception, a form of self-forgetfulness and of self-surrender, some awareness, however dim, of the majesty and unity of all living things in the world.

All such sentiments and feelings, if carried over into the affairs of daily life, may be expected greatly to improve the quality of human existence. It is certainly inexpensive in all but one respect, that of the time which the devotee must give up to it. A natural growth of peculiar social and political conditions where the great problem of elegant society ladies was apparently to find ways of appealing to or of influencing their uncommunicative husbands, if not merely to discover some honourable manner of occupying a long succession of vacant hours, the intricate, involved Zen art of flower arrangement would not be easy to transplant to the hectic West, where the bare idea of idle unoccupied moments has become for the great majority an ever-receding mirage. Flower arrangement, miniature trees, the exquisite 'Bonsai' exhibits now growing in popularity in the West, miniature 'flat gardens' of sand and stone together with the whole intricate appreciation of the size contours, surfaces, light and shade of large garden rocks and stones, are all examples of the infinite capacity of the human mind to derive aesthetic satisfaction from any specialism able to reveal unsuspected qualities in nature.

So swift has been Japan's advance to become a highly technological society, so great has been the population explosion there, that the question of how long these graceful arts with the equally refined tea-ceremony may continue to win devotees in Japan itself inevitably provokes pessimistic apprehension. Their long history as part of traditional Japanese culture suggests that they may continue as part of the Japanese way of life. As long as exhibitions of flower arrangements by well-known masters continue to draw greater crowds than normally flock in the West to view public exhibitions of pictures and sculpture, there is some hope that so special a feature of the life of Japan will not be suffered to perish from neglect.

The Japanese people would no doubt have created fine gardens under the stimulus of their own feeling for natural beauty, but the earlier achievement of the Chinese and Koreans was so striking and so impressive that no strong reason was seen to induce them to depart very far from it. If the gardening art of China was like a sun to illuminate the path of gardeners in other lands, that of Japan may be said to have been like a moon, for it also has lit up the way for many garden lovers elsewhere. The illustrations in these pages explain the profound attraction which oriental garden art can have for the West.

Some early beginnings of that contact which was later to enrich so notably the gardens of the Western world have been briefly mentioned above. As long as it was confined to land routes it was necessarily limited to a few seeds. It was not until the early modern period of European history and the late Ming period of China that the first sea-going vessels reached China from Europe. The Portuguese arrived in Canton in 1514; they are often said to have introduced the sweet orange into Europe from China, but as already recorded, oranges were grown in Mediterranean lands in Roman times. The Dutch came in 1622, after which they made a short-lived occupation of Formosa in 1624. The British followed in 1637. The Spaniards had stopped short in the Philippines in 1585, but a good deal of Chinese trade was carried on from there.

Some of these intrepid merchants brought back specimens of the vast floral and plant life they had admired during their brief encounters with China, a one-way traffic that was to be greatly expanded later. It was one thing to relish such remarkable novelties, but far more difficult for the average Westerner to comprehend the depth of feeling with which Chinese and Japanese viewed their gardens. They added new dimensions to garden art of a subtlety and refinement that has rarely found understanding and expression in the West, despite the poetic romantic delight that gardens began to evoke in England towards the nineteenth century. Gardens in China and Japan were a vital element in a civilization, culture or way of life that had attained a remarkable maturity many centuries before Europeans had once more raised themselves from the low standards of barbarous tribalism by which their Greek and Roman heritage had, for centuries, been submerged.

V

THE RISE OF RATIONALISM

During the 4500 years so far briefly surveyed in these pages, it is certain that pleasure gardens were made and cultivated in Egypt, the Middle East, Asia and Europe, but the amount of detailed knowledge of them is so small that generalizations by which they are usually dismissed in histories of gardens have very slender support. In the succeeding five hundred years generalizations about '*the* English garden', '*the* French garden' or '*the* American garden' are hazardous for the opposite reason. So many gardens have been made and described, that their variety upsets any easy classification. Nevertheless, without some grouping by periods or styles, the story would break down under its weight of detail. It is not an embarrassment affecting the history of gardens alone but all other aspects of the cultural life of so-called 'modern' times since the early Renaissance. English readers are accustomed to stylistic distinctions such as those denoted by 'Tudor', 'Stuart', 'Classical', 'Georgian', 'Regency' and 'Victorian', but useful as such descriptions can be in England, most of them cannot be applied in, say, France or Germany. The broader classification suggested in this study can have a wide application everywhere.

During those 'ideational' periods of rigid adherence to social and religious traditional ways of belief and conduct, gardens were small and utilitarian, to supply medicinal herbs, some vegetables, and fruit. When gardens began to be developed for pleasure in the later Middle Ages and the early Renaissance, the slow penetration of 'sensate', pleasure-seeking motives produced 'idealistic' gardens in Italy, France, the Netherlands and Germany. In England such 'idealistic' gardens were exemplified in 'Tudor' and 'Stuart' times down to the 'classical' period of Dryden, Addison and Pope in literature, Sir Christopher Wren and Vanbrugh in architecture. A similar evolution is to be observed elsewhere in Europe, where such labels as 'Tudor' and 'Stuart' are meaningless.

Such *jardins d'agrément* had their origin in Italy. Of the principal motives to create them, one was idealistic, the others more sensate. As men's thoughts began to range more freely, some wealthier men felt a need for agreeable, open-air settings in which they could talk to each other about their literary and philosophical interests. In the earlier ideational age of faith no such interest could arise among the laity while the clergy were often vowed to a silence that could be golden when eager debate might provoke condemnation for heresy. As wealth came to be valued for its own sake, a conspicuous display in a costly garden was a way of acquiring prestige. More sensate garden pleasures came later with the revival of romantic love stories. Classical antecedents thus stimulated these developments; the literary in the gardens of Plato's Academy, and the romantic in Hellenistic and late Roman pastoral romances.

Had the 'one world' of some philosophers' dreams been a possibility around 1400, the peoples of Europe might have been thought to have been able to profit from a rich storehouse of ideas to confer greater subtlety, complexity and artistry upon the small medieval gardens which were all they knew. But at that time not one European in a million had any knowledge of garden crafts, which other human beings in other lands had long since brought to high levels of artistic elegance. Had they been aware of them, they would probably not have copied them.

Survivors of the last Crusade had returned from the Middle East by 1300, as Marco Polo and his predecessors had returned from the Far East, without apparently having learned to appreciate any gardens they may have seen there and without bringing home any notable additions to the garden resources of Europe. The great age of exploration was still to come. There were no printed books and the few travellers' tales in circulation about other countries were usually provocative of little more than amazement or alarm, or both. Europeans had to find their own way in gardening as in other arts.

All memory of the way of life and the gardens of ancient Rome had vanished. Why it took so long to recover a sense of the past might seem to be one of the mysteries of history in the absence of the interpretative principle here adopted, which explains the break as the result of the exhaustion of sensate cultural values in ancient Rome and a turning towards the otherworldly, ideational culture of early Christian medieval Europe. Not until that, in turn, broke down was the European Renaissance a possibility. A great falling away from the wholly dedicated devotion of the early Christians was already evident in early fourteenth-century Rome. Ideational culture had declined to the point when two and, at one time, three rivals strove to become pope. Numbers of those faithful to the purer Christian tradition rallied to religious reformers such as John Wyclif in distant Britain, and Jan Hus (?1369–1415) and Jerome (?1360–1416) of Bohemia, both of whom had been profoundly influenced by Wyclif.

For the wretched inhabitants of Italy the troubles of the Church were of small account in comparison with the misery in which they struggled to survive. Theirs had been a troubled land for centuries and in the thirteenth and fourteenth centuries the situation was still chaotic. Divided into a great number of small towns, cities, dukedoms and kingdoms, Italy had few large areas of assured peace. All the centre of Italy from the Adriatic to the Mediterranean was owned by the Church, so it inevitably suffered from the struggles between rival popes and conflicts between ambitious cardinals. Southwards from Rome stretched perennially poverty-stricken lands; in 1300 they all were part of the kingdom of Sicily. There Arabs had brought a breath from the East, creating exotic gardens which freebooting, swashbuckling northern pirates had subsequently endeavoured to

PREVIOUS PAGES The garden of the Villa Lante at Bagnia, 1564, perhaps Giacomo da Vignola's finest achievement

maintain after a fashion, along with harems and other appurtenances of oriental overlordship. So poor and ruined was the land that it was not until the eighteenth century that it began to show some signs of recovery.

North of Rome the Patrimony of St Peter found its limits in the strongly forti-fied lairs of various local bosses, the *signori*, and in walled towns that sheltered an industrious, active, and growing population. Their urge to expand into the surrounding countryside involved them in conflicts with their neighbours reminiscent of the battles in olden times between Romans, Etruscans, Volscians and Samnites. None possessed the magic touch by which the Romans of the early Republic had doggedly fought their way to supremacy throughout centuries of war.

Everywhere strong men, lords or *signori*, were compelled to grasp the direction of public affairs. City communes were led by a few wealthy men, merchants and others, but they shrank from arming their poorer fellow-citizens for fear that the weapons would be used against themselves. For the same reason, it was dangerous to employ the mercenaries and the many marauding bands of cut-throats roaming the land. As a background to this chaotic scene there was the political rivalry between the popes and the head of the Holy Roman Empire.

While unrest, upheavals, and petty warfare kept Italians within their walled towns at night and whenever their fields were overrun, there could be little thought for gardens and the arts of peace. Yet here and there the very misery of the times provoked reaction. With monumental evidence of the earlier glories of imperial Rome all around them, sustained by dim memories and traditions, men began to look to the past for inspiration. Long-neglected manuscripts of great Roman classics were sought in the outhouses, cellars and hay lofts of old monastic buildings. Virgil was read with enthusiasm, as by Dante (1265-1321), who, however, gave no more account of gardens than many others of his day, much as he loved the few flowers, trees and shrubs often mentioned in his writings: the rose, violet, lily, daisy, narcissus, laurel, oak, olive, fig, apple, myrtle, vine, ivy and pine. Beyond the struggle for existence, deeper thoughts and aspirations in Dante's time were still directed above all else to otherworldly matters.

Despite the Black Death of 1348, despite senseless family feuds and the revolt of the masses against the rich in 1378, the city of Florence succeeded, in the fif-teenth century, thanks partly to the enlightened leadership of members of the Medici family, in gaining wealth and political influence. Then also came the first stirrings in men's minds that were to lead to a revival of art and learning.

No single man did more to provoke such progress than Petrarch (1304-1374). His father, like Dante, had been a political exile from Florence, but he had a French education, after which he joined the court of the Avignon popes from 1326 to 1337. Then he paid his first visit to Rome, drawn there as much by his passion for classical antiquity as by devotion to the Church in which he had assumed minor orders. He saw an almost dead city; its churches ruinous and neglected, and the vast remains of imperial Rome in hopeless decay. Grief-stricken, he retired to Vaucluse near Avignon where he called for a national re-vival which would create a Christian Italian republic. At the same time he was untiring in collecting and copying classical manuscripts, extolling Virgil, Cicero, Seneca and St Augustine. Striving to learn Greek, he glimpsed the idealism of Plato, whom he incited others to follow so that Greek scholars from Con-stantinople were eagerly welcomed in Florence.

From such beginnings came a new outlook on life. If men as joyously pagan as Petrarch's friend Boccaccio (1313-1375) had lived in the early Middle Ages,

The Villa Medici and its gardens amid the Tuscan landscape; detail from Benozzo Gozzoli's 'Journey of the Magi', 1459

they would certainly not have been widely-read authors. Both Boccaccio and Petrarch rejoiced in gardens as a setting for very human, earthly joys in a way that Dante did not. From his exile near Avignon Petrarch wrote in 1336 to a friend saying, 'I have made two gardens that please me wonderfully. I do not think they are to be equalled in all the world.' This was a new note in medieval times, just as Petrarch was one of the first men known to have climbed a mountain for the pleasure he got from the view from the top. From his activities in stirring interest and enthusiasm in humane learning and humanistic ways of life in Florence, the starting point of the Renaissance may plausibly be dated. Beginning as a literary, philosophical development in the fourteenth century, it soon became

138

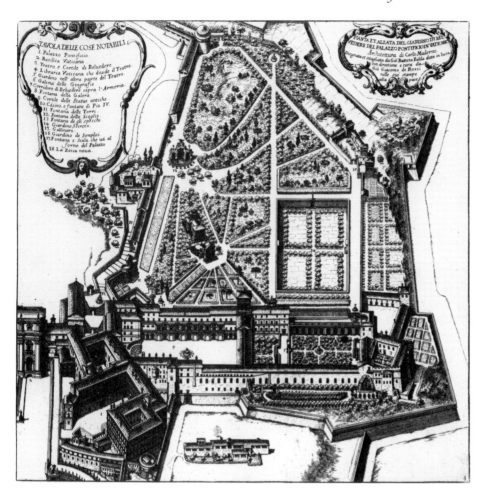

Plan of the Vatican gardens, from *The Gardens of Rome*, 1683

an artistic, architectural, and gardening advance also.

Cosimo de Medici (1389–1464) inherited a villa and garden at Careggi near Florence in 1457 which he employed the Florentine architect, sculptor and goldsmith, Michelozzo (1396–1472), to improve. He wanted an attractive setting for the gatherings of literary men and philosophers whom he assembled for discussions after the fashion of Plato's Academy. The humanist movement of the Renaissance began in this garden, which was likewise inspired by what was known or imagined about the gardens of ancient Rome. Classical bay, laurel, box, myrtle, cypress were planted, along no doubt with roses, violets, lavender and other fragrant flowers and herbs.

By 1419 over 200 of the letters of the younger Pliny had been discovered. They were unknown to Petrarch but by 1460 garden lore from Pliny's account of his Laurentian villa was being quoted by Alberti (1404–1472) and Pagello of Vicenza in their architectural writings.

Cosimo de Medici had also commissioned Michelozzo to build a villa and garden at Cafaggiolo in 1451 and it was there that Cosimo's grandson, Lorenzo (1449–1492), got his boyhood enthusiasm for flowers and gardening. Florence was later to rise to the height of its magnificence and fame under his firm rule. Merchant princes and humanists copied the pleasant practice of the Medici family who had made gardens fashionable. Yet they looked to the past for inspiration – not to the immediately preceding centuries from which there was nothing to learn – but to the spacious days of the Roman Empire of the first and second centuries.

While Florence was achieving a respectable degree of peace and prosperity in the fifteenth century, life in Rome, the Eternal City, was miserable by comparison. When the election of Pope Martin V, of a Roman family, in 1417, ended the hundred years conflict between rival popes, he spent nearly two years among the artists and humanists of Florence before it was possible to return to Rome. In September 1420 he returned to find little but poverty and ruin. Long before there could be any thought for gardens, an immense work of reconstruction had to begin. The next pope, Eugenius IV (1431–1437), had more austere ideas but he went ahead with the task until 1434, when invasion and revolt forced him to flee to Florence, where for ten years he experienced the full force of Renaissance humanism. There he and the papal court, including the cardinals who were to succeed him, were impressed by the work of the famous artists, sculptors and craftsmen of Florence.

From that marvellous city on the Arno came the men who, by creating the Renaissance, gave to the world the first impetus towards the restoration of cultural life, including, of course, gardens as a form of art. Not merely did several popes spend some years there but practically all the humanists on the staff of the popes as secretaries or counsellors were Florentine.

Against so sombre a background the achievement of the men who made the gardens of Rome stands out all the more brilliantly. The story has often been told how, during the sixteenth century, a handful of men in and around Rome suddenly lifted the whole idea of what a European garden might be to new and undreamt heights of elegance and magnificence. Their achievement was all a part of what they and other Italians were doing for art and learning generally at that time.

The new-style Italian garden was no mere indiscriminate enlargement of the little medieval European garden with its few beds of herbs, a flower or two, one or two figured parterres, perhaps a flowery mead and a small orchard as a private pleasaunce fenced round with wooden rails, trellises or hedges. Medieval Italians had no better cultural heritage than other countries, except the ever-present reminders of the imperial Roman past. But this had existed in greater magnificence for centuries without provoking any reaction save that of loot.

Gardens then for the first time began to be planned on a generous scale and elaborated with all the thought, care and discriminating sureness of touch that Italian painters were putting into their pictures or architects were devoting to their buildings and palaces. Garden design was in fact taken over by architects and painters. Before long their achievements aroused astonishment, admiration and envy among similarly minded men, who were becoming more numerous in other countries. It was not merely a gardening development, for it was not the work of practical gardeners.

The inspiration which changed the garden world came at first from the studies of a few bookish men who began to wonder what life had been like in ancient Greece and more especially in ancient Rome, nearly 1500 years before their day. It was one of those great creative periods in cultural life that seemed to take Western Europe almost in one bound from the cramped ways of medieval life to a fresher, clearer atmosphere with vastly wider cultural horizons.

The enjoyments of the senses which had been slighted and even rejected in medieval times were no longer so much despised. Absolution for committing the Seven Deadly Sins gradually ceased to be regarded as a merciful boon, although, unlike today, people knew very well what they were. Envy, intemperance, lust and avarice were all incidental to the great business of getting

OPPOSITE Gardeners pruning a tree; manuscript illustration, *c* 1460, from Pliny the Elder's *Natural History*, an encyclopaedic collection of Roman gardening lore written in the 1st century AD

OVERLEAF LEFT The chateau of Villandry and its elaborate parterre; the garden has been reconstructed to reflect as closely as possible du Cerceau's original intentions and is unique in showing the plan of a great garden of the early 17th century

OVERLEAF RIGHT The cherub fountain at the Villa Taranto, Lake Maggiore; the beautiful gardens in their superb setting of water and mountains were in fact created in this century

rich, while sloth and pride were often the natural consequences of riches. Such a weakening of the stern principles of traditional morality gradually affected more and more people in all walks of life, not merely the humblest of the laity but even some bishops, cardinals and popes.

In the sixteenth century idealistic impulses shaped the form and style of grand, architect-designed Roman gardens for the popes and the princes of the Church, who alone were then able to pay for them. Pope Alexander VI (1492–1503), the Borgia of evil repute, more thoroughly sensate than his predecessor Innocent VIII, created no gardens. Julius II (1503–1513), who had been exiled by Alexander VI, gave the first impetus. He summoned Bramante (1444–1514) to improve the papal residence, the Vatican, with a large courtyard and garden, the Belvedere Court. Combining architecture and garden design in one master-plan, Bramante revolutionized old-style gardening by creating the beginnings of landscape art. His design is supposed to have been inspired by the ruins of Hadrian's Roman imperial palace and by the Temple of Fortune at Praeneste. Bramante cut three levels of gardens into the Vatican Hill, looking down upon a large courtyard. As it was used for tournaments and other public attractions, the first level had a series of ramps forming an auditorium. Steps led from there to the upper garden proper with its intricately designed parterres. Later the Vatican Library was built across the site, destroying the whole scheme. But a beginning had been made with a new style which involved imposing architectural order, symmetry, perspective and proportion upon a garden site in order not only to create a pleasant retreat but above all to relate it to the house and other buildings in one comprehensive plan.

Upon this new principle the greatest triumphs of planned garden design were to be achieved during the following two centuries. Energies were henceforth directed to devising a central perspective point reinforced by short horizontal right-angled or diagonal adjuncts to lead the eye towards and to focus upon the culminating, crowning vista. Here, too, for the first time, antique statues representing the Tiber and the Nile were used as garden fountains to provide sheets of water as well as garden ornaments. Poggio Bracciolini (1380–1459), the energetic discoverer of lost Latin classics, had to endure a lot of sarcasm when, like Cicero before him, he began the practice of putting ancient statuary in his garden in Florence. Then began that lavish use of stonework in garden design which some thoughtful garden-lovers, such as Karl Foerster, came to regard as possessing 'an unique power of transmitting joy in, and feeling for garden pleasures', even going to the length of declaring that it is indispensable if gardens are to attain their greatest worth.

A great era of building began. Rome had been sufficiently restored to attract artists and craftsmen. In a relatively very small population, a marvellous generation had been born between 1470 and 1483; Michelangelo, Raphael, Bembo, Peruzzi, Castiglione and others. Florence, Urbino and Naples, once centres of cultural and intellectual life, had lost their great patrons and leaders. Pope Julius II was succeeded by Leo X (1513–1522), a son of Lorenzo de Medici, friend of Marsilio Ficino, whose translation of Plato's *Dialogues* had appeared in 1484. In 1523 another Medici became Pope Clement VII (1523–1534), but the sack of Rome by the French in 1527 grimly arrested artistic progress.

Meanwhile others had begun to follow the lead given by the pope. The genius of Raphael has been said to have been engaged by Cardinal Giuliano de Medici, father of Clement VII, to help to create his splendid Villa Madama between 1516 and 1520. It was designed less as a house than as a suite of garden rooms. It was

OPPOSITE Hampton Court. The gardens date back to King Henry VIII but their present form is owed to King William III and Queen Mary who modelled them on Dutch and Continental gardens. Tulips and hyacinths provide blazes of colour in the formal layout of paths and flower-beds.

never completed but sufficient had been finished to make it a show place to impress and to stimulate others. Later in the sixteenth century the developments foreshadowed in the Belvedere Court and in the Villa Madama carried garden art far beyond earlier simplicity. Architects improved their design by incorporating a garden layout as part of their plan of the house, as Bramante had done in Rome. Other brilliant architects struck out boldly in resolutely imposing gardens upon the site according to their own notion of what the whole situation required in order to form a unified, satisfying design.

Prominent among these creators of Renaissance gardens was Pirro Ligorio (1493–1580), a Neapolitan painter and architect, for ever famous for his work at Tivoli, where, as the personal antiquarian of Cardinal Ippolito d'Este, he planned the gardens and the Villa d'Este. Begun after 1550, the work went on until the death of the Cardinal in 1573. Painters have ever since striven to recapture something of the magic of these gardens, but much of it depends upon its amazing waterfalls and fountains. They were terraced down the hillside below the house with many spectacular, surprising features. A walk of one hundred fountains, a symbolic architectural presentation of ancient Rome, fish ponds and water stairs were among the show pieces. Unlike the still pools of Persian invention and imitation, the crash and constant splashing of water at the Villa d'Este assails the ears and astonishes the eye.

In a more restricted area, Ligorio built a charming casino with a secluded garden, the Villa Pia, as a private retreat for Pope Pius IV in 1562. His spendid achievement was rivalled and almost eclipsed by the work of Giacomo da Vignola (1507–1573), the man who succeeded Michelangelo as chief architect of St Peter's in Rome in 1564. With fresh inspiration and a grace in execution, he astonished visitors drawn by the fame of his creative handling of buildings and gardens. He is said to have had a hand in designing the gardens of the villa built by Peruzzi on the Palatine Hill sloping down to a loggia on the banks of the Tiber which Raphael decorated with frescoes, to which Giovanni de Udine added garlands of roses, jasmine, lilies, violets, iris, poppies, daisies, cyclamen, clematis, convolvulus, periwinkle, wallflowers and anemones, and others. This Villa Farnese was later destroyed, as Dorchester House, London, modelled upon it has also disappeared.

Vignola's greatest achievements were undoubtedly at the Villa Giulia, the pleasure villa of Pope Julius III (1550–1555) outside Rome, and especially at the Villa Lante at Bagnia (1564). Perhaps his most renowned creation was the Villa Farnese at Caprarola, Viterbo, the gardens of which he planned but did not live to complete, although the north garden there was finished in the year of his death, 1573. The two lower gardens were not begun until 1577, at the expense of the community of Caprarola.

With these gardens a new insistence upon symmetry and harmony in the design of the land around a dwelling gave a fresh impetus to that intellectual planning for artistic effect to which the idealistic Renaissance gave priority over and above the cultivation of herbs, flowers and fruits, upon which medieval gardeners had concentrated. Among the merits of Italian Renaissance architect-gardeners was their advance beyond the notion that one level stretch of land alone was best suited for gardens. Instead, bold use was made of different planes and altitudes, often with a waterfall cascading down as a unifying link. Both at the Villa Lante and at Caprarola water rushes noisily downwards over a series of upturned shells. These Italians 'played with water', said Sir George Sitwell, 'as a Sultan with his jewels'. Vignola's architectural garden features, the massive stonework of ter-

OPPOSITE One of the spectacular terraced waterfalls of the Villa d'Este at Tivoli, a wonderful garden of fountains and pools, created by the Neapolitan Pirro Ligorio over a period of 23 years

Water flowing from a fountain bordered by two bearded giants into a cascade ending in an upturned shell, at the Villa Farnese, Caprarola; the garden was planned by Vignola who died before it was finally completed in 1587

races, walls, fountains, pavilions, the stone allegoric figures, the nymphs, satyrs, gods and goddesses, the balustrades, stairways, large urns and other garden ornaments, were more notable features than the box hedges, the parterres, the evergreens, the flowers and occasional tree had been in the older gardens.

Making free use of such new adornments, garden architects transformed the clear, open, classic gardens of the Renaissance into the larger, more complicated and more mannered parks which spread throughout northern Italy during the later sixteenth and seventeenth centuries. Then came the vogue of the massed trees and tall hedges, trimmed to flat surfaces to provide walls of green defining open circles around the house as well as to give endless vistas down the long alleys leading from it into the country beyond. The Villa Mattei on the Caelian Hill at Rome, the great Boboli Gardens of Florence (1550), and Vignola's designs for the Villa Mondragone at Frascati (1572) were distinguished by their splendid avenues of cypresses.

Because of the need for protection from the burning sun and for coolness during the hot Italian summer, such shaded walks and such shelter were naturally

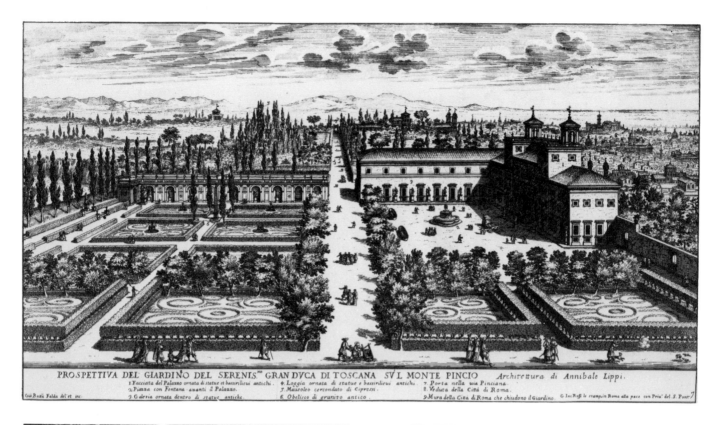

PROSPETTIVA DEL GIARDINO DEL SERENIS.^{mo} GRAN DVCA DI TOSCANA SVL MONTE PINCIO   Architettura di Annibale Lippi.

1 Facciata del Palazzo ornata di statue et bassirilievi antichi .   4 Loggia ornata di statue e bassirilievi antichi .   7 Porta nella via Pinciana .
2 Piazza con Fontana avanti il Palazzo .   5 Mausoleo cercondato di Cipressi .   8 Veduta della Città di Roma .
3 Galeria ornata dentro di statue antiche .   6 Obelisco di granito antico .   9 Mura della Città di Roma che chiudono il Giardino .

Giò Batà Falda del' et inc.   G.IacRossi le stampi in Roma alla pace con Priu' del S. Pont 7

ABOVE View of the gardens and Villa
Medici on the Pincian Hill, enlarged by
the Grand Duke of Tuscany after 1576

An avenue in the garden of the Villa
Medici, which featured the Grand Duke
of Tuscany's collection of antique
statuary

149

relished as they had been in Roman times. Flowers were of less account because relief was sought by contrasting green and grey in the search for cool tones, because brilliant colours accentuate the heat of the sun. Instead great lines of trees were developed to provide groves, such as the pine grove at the Villa Doria Pamphili at Rome, the work of Giacomo della Porta (1541–1604), a pupil of Vignola's and the creator of the Villa Aldobrandini near Frascati as well as several of the magnificent fountains of Rome.

Notable, both on account of its architecture and the many splendid antique sculptures collected within its walls, was the Villa Medici on the Pincian Hill, the site of the famous gardens of Lucullus in the days of ancient Rome. It was bought in 1576 and subsequently enlarged by Ferdinando de Medici, then twenty-six years old, already a cardinal, who in 1587 became Grand Duke of Tuscany. He was a great collector of antique statuary and busts, some of which he had inset in niches in the walls of the house. Others, together with fountains, decorated the gardens. The first garden was a formal set of rectangular flower-beds planned to be admired for their design from the house rather than as a garden of delight. But they were flanked by a grove of trees under which it would have been pleasant to escape the full force of the Italian sun. Fifty years later many of the smaller plots hedged with box had been thrown together in changes to which all gardens are subject with the passage of time.

Beyond Rome to the north, in Tuscany and on the mainland territory of the republic of Venice, there was also an outburst of garden-making. Roman examples were not very useful on the flat northern plain where the winters were colder and the rainfall heavier. Great as was the wealth of many Venetians and magnificent as were their villas, their estates could not be treated in the grand architectural manner. Often their gardens were smaller, more conventional, with patterned parterres in the style of embroidery.

In Siena, Verona, Lucca and Genoa the impulse to create gardens had an uneven response. Their grander gardens were mostly made later in the seventeenth and eighteenth centuries, but by then new influences, again largely inspired by Roman initiatives, determined their form and style. They were not, as were the Roman Renaissance gardens, examples of a new direction in garden art but rather felicitous variations upon established themes.

That all these architected gardens were intended for the satisfaction and enjoyment of their owners may be assumed, but it was an intellectual rather than a sensuous satisfaction like that derived from the architecture of the buildings to which the gardens were an integral part. They were gardens for display as well as for living, meeting, and conversing in a fresh, agreeable natural setting. Among the more socially inclined, such gardens were also devised as means of impressing spectators by the good taste, wealth and importance of their owners. Yet already a century earlier, around 1467, a Dominican friar Francesco Colonna had shown the way the cultural wind was blowing by his strange romance *Hypnerotomachia*.

Pagan rather than Christian in inspiration, it gave minute descriptions of flowers and the design of a garden as 'a place of hearts' desires'; all of which were sensuous in their appeal. A large flat space enclosed by a hedge of cypress and myrtle, clipped and fashioned, was divided into many concentric sections, separately planted with all manner of vegetables, fruit trees, herbs, woods and delightful shrubs. These were interspersed with meadows or flowery meads protected by trellis on which sweet-scented creepers, honeysuckle, jasmine, convolvulus and others were trained. In the centre of some of these enclosures there were fountains and marble baths around which joyous maidens with lutes, lyres, and violins ministered to the fortunate lover of the story. A dream picture it was, compounded out of every kind of classical memory, but not without a very considerable knowledge and love of a wide range of garden plants, many sorts of rose, lavender, hyacinths, narcissus, gladioli, iris, orchids, pansies, forget-me-nots as well as many trees, shrubs, and herbs, including oaks, pines, cypress, rose-mary, juniper, nut trees, marjoram, and mint. A more formal feature was an island garden set out with small scented herbs in the form of 'knots' and specific designs such as coats-of-arms, human figures and so forth.

Here was a garden feature, in 1467 already, that was to have a lasting vogue in France and one to be temporarily fashionable in England. When the labour of tending and replanting such living patterns became too onerous, the plants were replaced by coloured stones and bricks similarly patterned. Colonna's reveries were probably on too large and too ambitious a scale to be adopted, but something of the spirit by which he was inspired was to be found in the small private retreat, the *giardino segreto* of medieval times, which was often per-petuated along with the formal, semi-public gardens designed by architects. The perpetuation of this more sensuous type of garden reflects the rising tide of sensate urges and sensual values in the general way of life. Gradually it was to be given more overt recognition in gardens as elsewhere.

Italy, which had led the way in reviving gardens as works of art, was once more responsible for the new style which increasingly characterized gardens, archi-tecture and art generally during the seventeenth century. More ostentatious, flamboyant and theatrical than anything that had been created earlier, this new style is described as baroque. Many explanations have been suggested of its origin and motivation. A British traveller, Lord Chandos, in 1620, started the idea that it owed its origin to the Jesuits of Rome: an attempt by the Catholic Church to regain lost ground and to win converts. Like the Jesuits themselves, the new baroque style in architecture, painting and gardens arose during the Counter-Reformation, in reaction to the greater austerity of the reformed and puritan churches.

Plausible as such a Jesuitical origin may seem and true though it is that Bernini (1598–1680), the principal exponent of the new style, was in close contact with the General of the Jesuits, Oliva, it leaves the main problem unexplained. Why should the new style be developed and why should it be so popular? Such a question can be answered only by taking account of the trend of the whole system of cultural values which was steadily moving away from the earlier traditional, religious inflexibility; away from Michelangelo's Platonic reverence for beauty in the abstract, and forward into a new age that would make the gratification of the senses the new standard by which all values would be determined.

Bernini's whole life work illustrates the change. His great fountains in Rome, such as the Fountain of Four Rivers in the Piazza Navona, and his many highly decorative, highly realistic, emotional sculptures in a markedly sensate style, whether secular or religious, became instantly popular and were widely imitated.

They were not the only influence upon garden decoration. Gardens tended to become larger, more heavily planted with trees and shrubs to create great walls of greenery. Matching the large scale on which baroque Italian gardens were planned, along with a great development of masonry work, went the lavish use of water in fountains, cascades and pools. The single jet of water of the early Renaissance period was soon replaced by more lavish and more noisy displays.

Ordinary folk delighted in the bold, decisive designs of the baroque artists, the brave and often lavish ornamentation, the crash and splash of high waterfalls, cascades and elaborate fountains, the large pools under dark shade, the massing of trees and high hedges, the cultivation of aromatic trees, shrubs, the orange and lemon trees, the rosemary, bay and laurel and brightly coloured flowers, all of which provided so many instant gratifications of the senses which medieval and early Renaissance austerity would have thought unnecessary, and no doubt improper. Men were beginning to assert themselves in God's world, to impose ideas of their own upon nature which were directed, not as in the Middle Ages, to the greater glory of God and his saints but to very personal and very earthly satisfactions.

It was not of course a transition which came at once to transform radically all that had gone before. Loyalty to the old ideals often diluted the new tendencies and delayed their victory. The planned order devised by architects restrained the 'painterly' exuberance that would have been more akin to that later 'longing for a return to nature untouched by man'.

After the classic Renaissance emphasis upon qualities of form, design, proportion and symmetry, an effort was made at first to realize a more idealistic perfection. An appeal predominantly intellectual was balanced and enhanced by multiplying satisfactions for the senses through scents, colour, light and shade and the noise of falling water. But concessions to sensual gratifications were still restrained by an austere idea of the objectivity and impersonality of the artist's aim and ideal. Michelangelo (1475–1564) gave the keynote to this inherited frame of mind in a madrigal in which he declared:

> Rash is the thought and vain
> That maketh beauty from the senses grow.

It was not until a century after Michelangelo that Bernini's free and frank expression of sensate emotion appeared in architecture and sculpture. Because it was a trend so much in conformity with the later development of art elsewhere, it was not regarded with disfavour. On the contrary some of the later baroque gardens have retained their strong appeal.

No visit to Florence is complete without a sight of the Boboli Gardens, or to Lake Maggiore without a trip to the Borromeo Gardens of Isola Bella (1630–1670), already proclaimed in the seventeenth century to be 'one of the loveliest spots of ground in the world, a place worthy of fairies who have transported here a portion of the ancient gardens of Hesperides'. Where it has been possible in northern Europe to create a resemblance of an Italian garden, as at Hever Castle in Kent, visitors throng to see it when it is open to the public. A curious feature of many baroque gardens which has fortunately vanished may be noted by way of an artistic anti-climax. There was a childish delight in devices by which water power was used, as in Hellenistic and Byzantine times, to give movement to mechanical toys such as birds, water organs, moving statues and so forth. Immense hilarity seems to have been generated by cunning water-traps which would suddenly deluge unsuspecting visitors as they made the rounds of the garden. Crudity and immaturity lay very near the surface of society to threaten idealistic refinement. But before any such a decline had made much progress, news about the wonderful gardens of Italy was soon carried to France, England and other countries, for the stream of travellers to the Eternal City was again becoming a flood. There was something for everyone according to their taste and it is interesting to see what they made of it. At first baroque novelties made

The glorious baroque Borromeo Gardens of Isola Bella (1630–1670), 'one of the loveliest spots of ground in the world'

little appeal. When they began to influence more people they were modified in the interest of intellectual qualities characteristic of the earlier Renaissance gardens. Much later, in the eighteenth century, the more sensate qualities of Italian garden craft found a ready response.

Before Italian gardens had been endowed with any great splendour and long before those of France became famous, a grand park and garden had been created by the dukes of Burgundy at Hesdin. During the first half of the fifteenth century no European country could rival the wealth and prosperity of their dukedom. Philip the Good, duke for nearly half a century (1419–1467), ruled over territories which stretched from Burgundy to the North Sea, including the Low Countries and Luxembourg. In alliance with England he met Louis XI of France on equal terms. At his court a brilliant array of artists flourished, including Hubert and Jan Van Eyck. In gardening as in art the Burgundians attained an excellence which may be regarded either as a great culmination of ideational medieval art or as the dawn of an exquisite new idealistic era. Before their line expired in 1477 with the death of Charles the Bold (1467–1477), they and an earlier Capetian line had ruled continuously since 1032.

Under Philip the Good, Hesdin, its great park and gardens, attained a splendour greater than that of which any contemporary monarch could boast, befitting the centre of European diplomatic intrigue that Hesdin had become. When Louis XI sent his Queen and her maids of honour there on a diplomatic mission in

1464, they were regaled with a succession of feasts, dances and hunts of such splendour that the Queen prolonged her stay despite an order to return.

A century before Hesdin was obliterated by Charles V (1553), a succession of the famous miniaturists at the Burgundian Court had depicted scenes giving some idea of the nature of its famous gardens. They adorned manuscripts made for the Ducal Library by the first artists and calligraphers of the day. Parks and *préaux*, the enclosed gardens of late medieval times, appear in a number of texts made for the instruction or for the diversion of the duke and those of his court who could read.

A man who perhaps did more than Philip the Good of Burgundy to mediate the transition from such essentially medieval, ideational attitudes towards a garden to the larger, freer, secular expanses of idealistic Renaissance gardens was René of Anjou (1409–1480). In his domains, first in Anjou and later near Aix in Provence, he took immense trouble to create gardens and to enrich them with new plants. He brought roses and other plants from Provence to Anjou, strove to improve cherry trees and almond trees and to spread the cultivation of the mulberry. Foiled by Alfonso of Aragon and his son in his attempts to convert into actual possession his empty title of king of Naples, he gave his energies to patronizing the arts. Among his enthusiasms was that of creating great parks as menageries or zoos in which he collected lions, elephants, camels and other beasts, strangers to Europe. Some of his ambitions outran the technical competence of the age. Such was the installation and management of fountains, a task in which he is said to have failed in spite of his engagement of foreign, so-called experts.

At Hesdin the dukes of Burgundy seem to have been better served with fountains, though in the form also of ingenious but unpleasant water-traps. There were three figures there who could suddenly vomit water over passers-by. In another path water would suddenly be squirted up the legs of ladies as they traversed it. A rainstorm could be made to soak visitors entering the hermit's cave to the accompaniment of mock thunder and lightning.

Despite these earlier gardens of Burgundy and Anjou, it was from the expedition of Charles VIII (1483–1498) to Italy in 1495–1496, in a vain attempt to wrest the kingdom of Naples, the Anjou heritage, from Spain, that the origin of the Renaissance in France is commonly dated. Among the great cultural achievements of the Italians, their gardens attracted the King's attention. 'You would never believe the beautiful gardens I have seen in Naples,' he wrote to his brother-in-law in 1495. So deep an impression did the gardens make upon him that he brought an Italian back to France whom he set to work to dignify with gardens in the Italian style the royal domain of Blois and Amboise.

Some progress was made in garden design under François I (1515–1547). His royal residence at Fontainebleau was then endowed with small flower-beds, hedges and statuary. Italian influence is also usually regarded as the explanation of that development which was hastened by the Italian gardeners who had been brought to France. A new enthusiasm for gardens then began to grow. It was to transform completely the small, ideational 'Gothic' garden of the late Middle Ages and to carry the idealistic Italian Renaissance idea of a garden to a development on a more extensive scale than the Italians had ever attempted.

This early royal initiative had little immediate impact. During the sixteenth century France was embroiled at first with Spain until the peace of Cateau-Cambrésis of 1559 and then, almost immediately, with the disastrous Wars of Religion which caused immense suffering until the victory of Henry IV (1589–1610) and his Edict of Nantes of 1598. However, despite wars, persecution and massacres

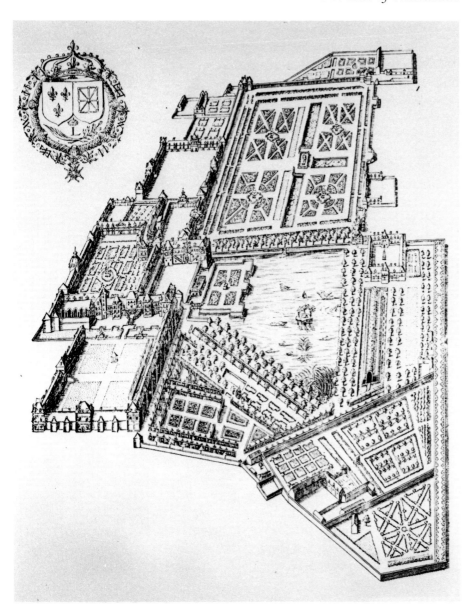

in the name of a religion of peace and charity, some Frenchmen were beginning, in the sixteenth century, to take a new interest in rural pleasures.

In the seventeenth century wealthy Frenchmen began to alter, adapt, expand and, as they thought, to improve upon the early Italian models. For all their striking originality and magnificence, the great gardens of Italy had been relatively few in number, mainly around Rome and to the north of Italy. To the French aristocracy belongs the credit of having raised the art of magnificent large-scale gardening to a more nation-wide artistic development.

Beginning in a modest fashion by enlarging and extending the medieval pleasure garden and with imitations of Italian grottoes, French gardeners were directed by architects, as in Italy a generation or two earlier, so that by the end of the seventeenth century an entirely new idea of what an elegant garden should be began to spread throughout France and from there to other countries. Like all forms of cultural change, it was a gradual, by no means uniform progress. In 1636 an engraving of the old royal palace in Paris shows a large medieval mound in an enclosed garden alongside a much larger garden set out with parterres in embroidery design and extensive plantations of fruit and other trees, as well as a special tulip garden.

A gardening literature began to increase and to become popular reading. An early manual, which long retained its popularity, was *La Maison Rustique*. Written originally in Latin as *Praedium Rusticum* in 1554, its vogue began with two French translations in 1564 and in an improved, expanded version in 1583. It was almost equally successful in England after it had been translated in 1600.

Despite Charles VIII's enthusiasm, it was not until a century after his day that many notable gardens were developed in France. Garden joys held out for French admiration by Charles Estienne in *La Maison Rustique* were at first simple.

> It is a commendable and seemly thing to behold out of a window many acres of ground well-tilled and husbanded ... yet it is much more to behold fair and comely proportions, handsome and pleasant arbours, and, as it were, closets, delightful borders of lavender, rosemary, box and other such like; to hear the ravishing music of an infinite number of small, pretty birds ...

Towards the end of the sixteenth century the French embarked upon that strenuous improvement of the land around their houses which was to make theirs model gardens for the wealthier landowners of Europe. By the first half of the sixteenth century many large houses had formal gardens which represented a considerable advance upon the small garden plots of late medieval times. Some, such as the semicircular garden outside the moat and half-surrounding the château of Montargis, seem to have been mainly for vegetables and fruit, but it also had its small rectangular and circular parterres, some in the form of a maze.

Such medieval features long remained a striking feature of French gardens and they were more in evidence in the plans of other gardens, such as the châteaux of Bury, of Valeri, of Fontainebleau, of Gaillon (Eure) and Blois. It was therefore upon no mean foundations that succeeding gardeners were able to build. With the stimulus of Italian inspiration and improving social and economic conditions, further great progress became possible. In France there was greater scope for the creation of gardens. 'There are more than four thousand noble houses in France,' said Bernard Palissy (1510–1589), Huguenot metal worker and author of a treatise on waterworks and fountains.

Henry of Navarre, who had become Henry IV in 1594, faced a tremendous task of reconstruction and religious reconciliation coupled with the need to reduce the political power of the feudal factions. The French monarchy, already set upon the road of increasingly autocratic and centralized rule, was powerfully aided by his skilled and patient work. Then also were laid the foundations of those great royal gardens that were to become the admiration and the envy of the world. Henry IV was well served at Fontainebleau, at Saint-Germain-en-Laye nearer Paris and around the royal palace of the Tuileries inside the capital city by some able garden designers, whose craft was already regarded as a profession requiring a long apprenticeship and journeyman service.

His wife, Marie de Medicis, brought from her native Florence girlhood memories of the glories of the Boboli Gardens. She is remembered for the Jardin du Luxembourg, which she adorned between 1611 and 1620 while acting as Regent for her young son Louis XIII after the assassination of Henry IV in 1610. John Evelyn on a visit in 1644 said that the high walls by which it was enclosed were a good mile in circumference. He greatly admired the pattern of the parterre seen from the windows, although it was executed in nothing but box. There were four divisions, each with a marble fountain nine metres (thirty feet) across.

Elms, limes and other trees flanked the many alleys. Despite the encroaching streets and houses which in the nineteenth century lopped off whole areas, notably a charming nursery garden, the Jardin du Luxembourg has continuously refreshed and stimulated poets, artists, students and writers; Watteau, Diderot, Bernadin de Saint-Pierre, l'Abbé Prévost, Rousseau, Rilke among them. Today it is more frequented than ever, a charming playground for children. Marie de Medicis's memorial fountain may still be seen there, although no longer on its original site.

This new impetus to gardening on the grand scale was able to gain force and momentum thanks to the political and social changes brought about by the succession of able men who guided the destinies of France after the brilliant career of Henry of Navarre had been suddenly closed by the murderous dagger of Ravillac in 1610. The great Richelieu guided the kingdom from 1624 to 1642. He nominated Mazarin to succeed him. Mazarin, before he died in 1661, recommended the young King Louis XIV to rely upon Colbert, a man who, had he been able to restrain his headstrong young monarch, might have made France the prosperous land it was destined by nature to become.

By this time many of the aristocracy and some of the more successful business and professional Frenchmen were becoming wealthy. The bulk of the people were still very poor, destined by the ruinous folly of the King to become poorer still. Nevertheless a fortunate few were able to prosper and they spent their wealth in flamboyant profusion on great private houses, and huge gardens. The new châteaux of the aristocrats were more magnificent than the palaces of earlier kings and their gardens matched their architecture in splendour and spacious design. Tens of thousands of visitors to France and hundreds of thousands of readers all over the world who may never have been to Europe, are familiar with the pictured glories of many of these châteaux which still remain to attest to the grandeur of scale and conception upon which their seventeenth-century designers proceeded. The gardens they had to improve still retained pronounced late-medieval and Renaissance qualities.

Indeed it was not until the seventeenth century was well advanced that the tide of innovation began to sweep away the forms and styles prescribed by tradition. Features borrowed from Italian revivals in the classical manner – grottoes, fountains, automata, topiary work, classical figures and busts – had been combined with medieval mounds and figured parterres, all however on a larger scale than was common in previous centuries. The transition had begun already in Burgundy and Anjou and it was resumed during the reign of Henry IV. His terraced riverside garden at Saint-Germain-en-Laye was in the Italian Renaissance manner, whereas the parterres around the Luxembourg Palais, despite Marie de Medicis, were French. They were the work of Jacques Boyceau de la Barauderie. He was the first of a long succession of highly skilled garden designers during the seventeenth century who were responsible for creating the new French style that dominated large-scale garden planning everywhere for several generations. It may be shortly described as a strictly disciplined, ordered rearrangement of the land around the house.

After Boyceau, later in the seventeenth century, two families of royal gardeners won special renown. Jacques Mollet was the founder of the first such dynasty. His son Claude, who succeeded his father as royal gardener at the Tuileries in 1630, had served a long apprenticeship. In the introduction to his excellent collection of reproductions of paintings and engravings, *Les Jardins de France* (1913), M. Henri Stein quotes significant passages from Claude Mollet's own manuscript

The small parterre of Marie de Medici's Luxembourg garden, from *Traite du Jardinage* by Jacques Boyceau, 1638

account of the changes which he was able to boast, it seems with justice, that
he himself had brought about.

Mollet recalled how forty or fifty years earlier gardens were no more than
small rectangular beds each containing different plants of the sort then still represented in the illustrations of *La Maison Rustique* of Estienne, and he explained
that mere gardeners had no idea of altering such a traditional arrangement. This
is hardly surprising, for their job was to grow things on their employer's ground,
not to air their ideas about its shape or size, still less to tell their masters how
it all ought to be swept away and rearranged. Mollet himself, however, was fortunate enough to be instructed about this new art of garden design by someone
he calls 'a very illustrious person', the late 'Sieu du Perat', chief architect of King
Henry IV.

Étienne Dupeyrac (sometimes spelled du Perat) (?1525–1604) had been in Italy
until 1582. The Duc d'Aumale put him in charge of all his châteaux among which
was that of d'Ennet (Anet), where Claude's father had been the gardener. It was,
said Mollet, the most beautiful château in the whole of France. Dupeyrac himself
had drawn up the designs for the garden. He swept away all the little rectangular
plots and dealt imaginatively with the whole garden space as a unit, laying it
out in parterres designed after the manner of a comprehensive all-over embroidery pattern. Mollet said that they were the first parterres and compartments
en broderie that had ever been made in France. Not long before the year 1600,
therefore, the first step in the new style had been taken. It was due not to a
gardener but again to an architect who had been greatly influenced by what he
had seen in Italy. In the same year that he had returned from Italy, 1582, Dupeyrac
published his *Vues perspectives des Jardins de Tivoli*.

Mollet records that at first he had some difficulty about maintaining his embroidery designs. The green plants he used were not hardy perennials and he
says that they would not stand up to the summer heat and winter cold of France,
so he had the great labour and expense of replanting the whole garden every two
or three years. Some way had to be found of making the figured designs with
a plant that would survive in the French climate. Mollet chose box, and this,
he said, was a novelty, because very few persons of quality liked to have box
planted in their gardens. The idea soon caught on, for Henry IV in 1595 commissioned Mollet to plant out the garden around his new palace of Saint-Germain-
en-Laye (since destroyed), the garden at Monceau and the small garden by the
pool at Fontainebleau. Mollet records that all these gardens were planted with
box in the same year and that it was still in very good shape as he was writing,
about thirty years later.

Thanks in part no doubt to royal patronage but mainly as a result of having
hit upon a pleasant artistic innovation, Claude Mollet was regarded as the first
gardener in France and he soon found imitators among the rising generation.
His own son, André, set out the basic idea of the new style of gardening in the
book he wrote for his employer Queen Christina of Sweden, *Jardin de Plaisir*,
published in 1651 in Stockholm. It was the first such book to appear in Sweden
and as the text was in Swedish and German as well as in French, it was able
to exercise a great influence in the Gothic north. There was an English translation
also, almost all copies of which have disappeared.

The first thing to be done, he said, was to plant a noble avenue of elm or
lime trees in double or treble rows perpendicular to the front of the mansion,
leaving, however, a broad semicircular or square sweep bare before the house
itself. At the back, the embroidered parterres should begin, clear of all trees or

The south view of Vaux-le-Vicomte, the
first triumph of André Le Nôtre, built for
Louis XIV's minister, Fouquet

fences so that an uninterrupted view of their design could be had from the windows of the house. Beyond them should be lawns, shrubberies, alleys, hedges, avenues or espaliers each with a statue or a fountain at the end. He also makes the strange recommendation, reminiscent of ancient Rome, that a pleasant perspective painted on canvas should be placed at the end of such avenues, provided that due care be taken to protect it from the weather. The garden should be raised in terraces to suit the lie of the land and to provide fountains, jets of water, canals, aviaries and all other suitable embellishments. Waterworks began to be more skilfully devised after Torricelli (1608–1647) and others began the science of hydrostatics around the middle of the seventeenth century. All the main elements of the new style of gardening which the world was to learn from France in the late seventeenth and early eighteenth century are here in essence. As in Italy earlier, flowers, fruit, herbs and vegetables get little attention.

In 1613 Claude Mollet's wife had stood as godmother to André, the infant son of Jean Le Nôtre who had worked under Jacques Mollet's direction as a royal gardener in the Tuileries, the royal palace in Paris. André Le Nôtre was fortunate in his ancestry, in his talents, his remarkable opportunities, and in his happy equable disposition. The story of his achievements has often been told and many accounts have been given of his first triumph, the famous garden he created for the unfortunate Fouquet at Vaux-le-Vicomte. It brought him to the notice of Louis XIV, whose despicable conduct in ruining, robbing and imprisoning Fouquet for life was an early dark spot on the supposedly shining glory of the 'Sun King'.

André Le Nôtre, 1613–1700, son of the famous gardener, Jean; the sheer grandeur of his conception and his magnificent achievement at Versailles, the supreme example of his style, continues to inspire awe

OPPOSITE ABOVE Le Nôtre's plan of the immense estate at Versailles

OPPOSITE BELOW The Tapis Vert, Versailles, lined with marble vases and leading on to distant prospects

Le Nôtre, to whom Vaux-le-Vicomte was a heaven-sent opportunity, was then set upon the road to fame. Other aristocrats asked him to create gardens for them. His royal master was the first with a task probably more formidable than that any gardener has had to face before or since. It was to create the gardens at Versailles. The territory upon which Le Nôtre had to work was a rather small traditional garden bounded by a vast swamp amid dull country. Out of it he was somehow to design plans for a great garden that should not merely match the huge scale upon which the vast new royal palace was to be built but should enhance and set off its grandeur. The difficulties of the site were enormous. Fever raged in the marshy land where workmen, over 36,000 of whom were put to work in 1685, died like flies from fever which Louis XIV himself did not entirely escape. Vast resources were lavished on the work. Over forty sculptors were employed on ornamental work and thousands of soldiers reinforced the workmen. Millions of seeds, countless plants and thousands of trees were planted, only to need new supplies as many perished. Hardly one quarter of the forest trees transported at vast expense survived in their new setting. There was never enough water. Resolutely and confidently the work was pressed forward throughout years of exhausting toil.

Over a territory so vast, flowers naturally had to be subordinated, so they were concentrated in special areas of the park, notably at the Trianon (built and rebuilt by Louis XIV), the 'Parterre de Latone' and the 'Midi'. Even so, a colossal cultivation was undertaken. To assure a massive display of blooms at the height of their glory so that the King never saw a spent or faded flower, they were moved in pots and equally swiftly removed. Le Nôtre was said to have a stock of two million flower pots at his disposal to effect these very rapid shifts of scene, but they presumably served all the other royal gardens also, not only those of Versailles. He was able to command the resources of the nation. Colbert personally instructed the admiral in command in the Mediterranean to institute a search for 'all the strange flowers which you think would help to decorate the palaces and send them soon'. Jonquils and tuberoses were specially mentioned.

It was as though a magician's wand had suddenly produced flowers, trees, bushes, fountains, alleys, garden statuary, enclosures and buildings. Nothing as vast had ever been seen before. Small wonder therefore that casual visitors to Versailles today can hardly fail to be impressed by the grandeur of the scale and conception of the great gardens that stretch out before them. How much of the general design of the original gardens, which have largely disappeared or been changed, were due to the architects Le Vau and Hardouin-Mansart, and how much to Le Nôtre will probably never be sorted out satisfactorily. Tradition credits Le Nôtre with the work.

Developing the new conception of landscape gardening, first tried out on a somewhat small scale by Dupeyrac and Claude Mollet, Le Nôtre transformed it at Vaux-le-Vicomte and again later at Versailles into a great crescendo of garden 'grand opera'. The grandeur of his plans would stand out all the more clearly if today's tourists could have seen the site before Le Nôtre set to work. Then wonder would quickly turn into amazement.

It was a resounding aesthetic triumph. It carried forward the Italian style inasmuch as it also was an architectural as much as a horticultural victory, a designer's rather than a gardener's adventure, appealing more to the intellect by its design and proportion than to the heart by satisfying emotions with sensuous curves, moulded contours, subtle colourings or alluring scents. The world had never seen anything to excel the sheer magnificence of conception and execution

of the great French garden designers; the scope and amplitude they were able to accord to every feature – the symmetrical parterres of variegated pattern to be seen from the windows; the avenues radiating in goose-claw pattern and opening on far-distant prospects; the long alleys, shaped trees, gushing fountains, still pools and canals, reflecting the rays of the setting sun on the house; terraces on different levels; the stairways, balustrades, statuary and other ornaments. Master hands orchestrated with consummate skill all these varied elements into a complex, theatrical yet satisfyingly intelligible aesthetic unity. The gardens they produced, like the buildings they adorned, were classic of their kind, meriting renown because they responded so well to the social and artistic standards of their day. Excellence in creating such a grandiose style remains a title to distinction in cultural history which deserves to survive even when the conditions shaping it have vanished.

Versailles as the supreme example of Le Nôtre's style was an outstanding European, as well as a French event, constantly described, visited and to some extent copied. Royal and aristocratic luxury eclipsed the smaller gardens of less renowned owners of the substantial houses that the rising commercial and professional men were adding to the French capital. Turgot's renowned great plan of the whole city of 1739 shows many small gardens all over Paris. In the faubourgs beyond the then built-up area of the city were gardens and market gardens of vast extent which have since all been covered by streets and buildings.

French garden art, as distinct from the horticultural operations upon which most of the French were engaged, had reached its peak with André Le Nôtre. When his style has been understood and assimilated, there is little more to be said about a distinctive French style of gardening. Some murmurs against it can be detected in France early in the eighteenth century, as when Marivaux (1688–1763) contrasted two gardens. One was symmetrical, magnificent, grand, superb, beautiful according to the most approved aesthetic standards. The other had been the work of happy chance directed by good taste but without matching up to the theoretical definition of beauty as thoroughly as the first. Yet, said Marivaux, it made an instant appeal, despite its apparent disorder; it had an indefinable charm, an ability to stir the emotions and to lay hold of the hearts of all beholders. Already such a profound need to recognize the urge of the human spirit to penetrate the surface of reality and to enlarge the range of reason and thought can be seen in the canvases of Claude Lorrain and Poussin to encourage a more intuitive approach to reality. Here was one of the first hints of a complete change in attitudes towards natural beauty in general and to garden art in particular.

What was the lasting influence of the great classic French gardens? They were the wonder and the admiration of the world in the seventeenth and early eighteenth centuries. Gardeners brought up in the tradition created by the master craftsmen of the seventeenth century, the Mollets and the Le Nôtres, went forth to serve the aristocracy of Europe who learned the sort of effects they should order them to produce from the increasing number of books being published about gardens.

Gardens imitating the new French style, small or large, began to be created in many parts of Europe. Le Nôtre was in demand. Charles II of England, who had come to know France well in his ten years of exile, asked for him when he wanted to redesign the royal garden at Greenwich. No proof has yet been found that Le Nôtre ever came to England, although he has been credited with designing St James's Park, or at least of sending plans for it.

In Spain the gardens of Philip V at Aranjuez and Granja; in Italy those of his

son, Charles III of Naples, at Caserta; in Portugal at Queluz; in Russia where Peter the Great sought to rival Versailles with his Peterhof; in Hungary at Esterhazy; in Hanover at Herrenhausen; in Austria, the Netherlands and Sweden, the inspiration of the French garden style was evident. Grand as they all were, they had no Louis XIV or Le Nôtre to form them with a fresh inspiration. Le Nôtre's great and immediate influence was exerted solely by example, for he published nothing to explain his art.

The nobility and gentry of England, when they did not make it a point of honour to reject French ways, were not very eager to admit to learning from them, but so striking was the achievement of France that it imposed itself upon the world. To estimate the extent of this French influence, it is sufficient to look through the many plans of the seats of the English nobility in the *Nouveau Théâtre de la Grande Bretagne* by two Dutch artists, Knyff and Kip, a large illustrated volume (1708). Amid much that was clearly traditional, there was much also that was new, particularly in a striving for grandeur through mere size and repetition rather than with any inspired design. But soon some of the English were to allow their hearts to dictate to their heads what their gardeners' hands should do. Marivaux shows that in France, despite its long tradition of rational, formal gardens, new notions allowing more freedom to fancy and the imagination were making a subtle appeal.

The story of gardening in England has been told and retold, often in fascinating detail, so no more will be attempted here than to show how, in the changing

18th-century drawing of Peterhof, Peter the Great's attempt to rival Versailles; the designs were considerably influenced, not with total success, by those of Le Nôtre

THE SECOND PART OF THE
Gardeners Labyrinth, vttering such skilfull experience, and worthie secrets, about the particular sowing and remoouing of the most Kitchin Hearbes, with the wittie ordering of other daintie Hearbes, delectable Floures, pleasant Fruites, and fine Roots, as the like hath not heretofore been vttered of anie. Besides the Phisicke benefits of each Hearbe annexed, with the commoditie of waters distilled out of them, right necessarie to be knowen.

A characteristic Tudor garden with its raised flower-beds, 'wall-herber' and sparse planting; from *The Gardeners Labyrinth*, 1586

cultural climate, medieval gardens were gradually enlarged and then more quickly expanded in the seventeenth century until in the following century revolutionary changes were made to respond to the new ideas about the satisfactions which gardens should provide.

Unlike the people of Europe, the English were not confined so long in their history to houses within walled towns. Nevertheless most English gardens down to the sixteenth and seventeenth centuries remained small. As they were enlarged, they gradually became more elaborate, enclosed by hedges or walls of stone, brick or mud, with wooden palings and lattice-work rails. These often divided a small pleasure garden, the *hortus inclusus*, from a larger area of fruit trees or vegetables. Sometimes these fences were gaily painted in colour or gilded. When Henry VIII took Hampton Court from Cardinal Wolsey he had the wooden railings there painted Tudor white and green at a cost of £24, which then represented two years' wages for the head gardener. Heraldic 'beasts' were also set up on poles along the garden paths. For carving and erecting these lions, leopards, dragons, greyhounds, bulls, antelopes and griffons, 159 in all, he paid one pound apiece, then a very large total expenditure. Later they were all painted and gilded, again at great expense.

Flower-beds were sometimes raised as much as half a metre (two feet) above the level ground, perhaps with a turf border in which flowers also would be grown. Similar raised turf-covered banks were also made as garden seats on which ladies sat among the flowers. This was a medieval feature. As late as 1626 such raised turfed seats with camomile, pennyroyal, daisies and violets were described by W. Lawson in his *Country House Garden* as both 'seemly and comfortable', but by the end of the century they were not surprisingly denounced as 'apt to impair your health'.

In addition to turf seats, artificial mounds or mounts were also thrown up, to be turfed and perhaps planted with flowers. Fountains and springs of water were naturally popular and more decorative features such as arbours, pergolas, topiary work, labyrinths and mazes, flowers and trees in pots began to multiply during the Renaissance. 'Knots' or plants set in arabesque and other decorative patterns or merely strips of coloured soil similarly designed were also a popular feature. The lack of sufficient ornamental flowers meant that many of these 'knots' were merely patterned with some greenery. Out of them the parterre in French style was developed in the seventeenth and eighteenth centuries. Fanciful designs in flower-beds, persistently employed down to the nineteenth century and sometimes with poor taste, may be regarded as survivals of these late-medieval and Renaissance knots.

By the end of the sixteenth century a new spirit becomes evident. William Harrison in his 'Description of England', as a preface to Holinshed's *Chronicle* of 1577, said 'in comparison with this present, the ancient gardens were but dunghills and laistowes [rubbish dumps] to such as did possess them'. It was not, therefore, until the traditional, ideational culture had already given way to the dawn of more sensate 'modern' times that a real beginning can be said to have been made in England with those improvements which, within 300 years, were utterly to transform gardening, not in England alone, but generally round the world.

Voyages of discovery had begun:

See how many strange herbs, plants and annual fruits are daily brought unto us from the Indies, Americas, Taprobane [Ceylon], Canary Isles and all parts of the world. . . . There is not almost one noble gentleman or merchant that hath not great store of these

flowers which now also begin to wax so well acquainted with our soils that we may almost account them as parcels of our own commodities ... inasmuch as I have seen in some one garden to the number of three or four hundred of them, if not more, the half of those names within forty years we had no manner of knowledge.

Elizabethan embroidered valance featuring scenes of Adonis in a typical garden of the period

The face of England and of its gardens, like much else, was undergoing rapid transformation in the hundred years that followed upon the accession to the throne of Queen Elizabeth I. The 'modern' cultural age had begun. New plants were being brought back by traders from North Africa, Spain, North America and the Far East to attract an admiration not then generally bestowed upon garden architecture and design, in which the Italians had by then successfully pioneered. In time, that influence reached England after the French had taken up and modified the style.

During the seventeenth century the English were moving towards a better integration of the powers of reason, of sensory awareness and response with their traditional faith in values of a purely transcendental order. In literature, in art, in architecture, in natural science, in philosophy, in manners and behaviour, developments then occurred which, by adding new meanings and values to life, gave the whole world of culture and civilization new and rewarding directions. It is not surprising therefore that gardening arts, and the attitude men and women began to take towards gardens and their place in social life, also began to change.

Gardening benefited indirectly from the more vigorous quest for new herbs and plants useful in medicine, which stirred a new, scientific interest in plants. Traders and explorers were encouraged to bring back specimens and seeds as they enlarged the bounds of the known world for men of the West. Nicholas Leete, John Tradescant, John Goodyer, John Ray, John Watson, are among the handful of hardy pioneers celebrated in English gardening history for their labours in enlarging the resources of English gardeners.

A simple, humble, pious joy pervades many of the old English garden books. It was the spirit in which Izaak Walton walked through the country air of Tottenham to find peace along the banks of his trout stream. French literature has nothing to show of similar quality. With greater eloquence and more deeply pondered wisdom, Francis Bacon had turned his reflective gaze upon the new enthusiasm for gardening in his celebrated *Essay* of 1625, declaring that a garden affords 'the purest of human pleasures. It is the greatest refreshment to the spirits of man without which buildings and palaces are but gross handiworks.' He was the first to observe that garden art reached a greater perfection than fine architecture.

Progress at first was slow, although in 1691 John Aubrey affirmed that 'there is now, 1691, ten times as much gardening about London as there was in 1660'.

In the same year John Gibson said that the royal gardens of Hampton Court and Kensington Palace were both poor. That of the Palace of Lambeth was also undistinguished, 'the late Archbishop [Sancroft] not delighting in one'. While the upkeep and cultivation of smaller gardens by successive owners and occupiers went on in England throughout the reigns of Queen Anne and the Hanoverian Georges during the eighteenth century, mainly for use and partly for pleasure, some new ideas about the satisfactions to be had from the contemplation of gardens and landscape began to be aired not long after the death of King William III in 1702.

The prestige of French gardens was then high among the English. Lord Burghley had employed French gardeners at Hatfield under the direction of John Tradescant at the beginning of the seventeenth century. Charles II asked advice from André Le Nôtre and also appointed André and Gabriel Mollet as royal gardeners. Pictures of many seats of the nobility and gentry drawn by Knyff and engraved by Kip, which were published in 1708, show many English large estates already set out in formal French fashion with long leafy avenues. A little later Stephen Switzer (c 1682–1745) deplored 'the misfortune most of my profession is under in not having been abroad' and he referred admiringly to 'that noble taste with which gardens in France and other countries abound'. Just how strong French influence was is difficult, if not impossible now, to estimate.

French examples were not the only foreign influence. Many Englishmen, including Charles II, had been refugees in the Netherlands during the Commonwealth. Before the arrival of William III in England in 1688, trim, well-tended formal gardens such as the Dutch cultivated, were already to be seen in England. However, to pick upon some phenomenon in gardening such as a 'French style' or a 'Dutch style' and to assert, as so often is done, that they 'triggered off' a similar change in England is to overlook a question more serious than 'who pulled the trigger?' The real question is 'who loaded the gun?'

A well-tended Dutch garden with its neat flower-beds; from *Hortus Floridus*, 1614

Queen Anne's garden at Kensington Palace; engraving by Kip after Knyff, 1708

VI

THE ENGLISH REACTION

The first stirrings of revolt against the predominant French formality in garden design came at a time when traditional ideas in philosophy had been assailed in France by Descartes in the name of sceptical reason and in England by John Locke, who published his famous *Essay concerning Human Understanding* in 1690 to vindicate his belief that there was nothing in the mind that had not reached it through the senses. These philosophers are mentioned here not because they had any direct influence upon garden design but because their work showed that a new spirit, a new attitude and a new way of thought was coming about which was soon manifested in garden design as in other aspects of cultural life.

Arguments then began about styles of gardening which were to continue, not without considerable bitterness and rancour, throughout the eighteenth century. The story is of the first importance in the history of civilization and culture, because it was in the garden that evidence was to be seen of that turning towards a greater delight in natural beauty mediated through the pleasures of the senses, then becoming paramount, from which the romantic movement in literature, art and music was later to emerge.

Joseph Addison (1672–1719) and Alexander Pope (1688–1744) were able to express the new spirit, then stirring, more successfully than others, so they exercised an influence upon taste and opinion greater than that of any other men of the age. Addison through his graceful, good-humoured essays in *The Spectator* and *The Tatler*, and Pope through his skilful, pointed and often witty couplets, won audiences for their ideas about natural beauty and helped to turn men's thoughts upon gardening. Addison was the pioneer. It was a new idea to many Englishmen in 1712 that they should cultivate 'the pleasures of the imagination' and that 'a man of polite imagination' was to be envied. In a much-quoted passage in his *Spectator* No. 411 of 21 June 1712, Addison told his readers that such a man 'is let into a great many pleasures that the vulgar are not capable of receiving'.

William Kent, 1684–1748, the first of the landscape architects who reacted against the artificiality of 17th-century gardening

He 'often feels a greater satisfaction in the prospect of fields and meadows, than another does in their possession'. Imagination gives him 'a kind of property in everything he sees, and makes the most rude uncultivated parts of nature administer to his pleasure: so that he looks upon the world, as it were in another light'.

Addison followed it by further thoughts on the subject. In *Spectator* No. 414 of 25 June he said:

there is generally in nature something more grand and august, than what we meet with in the curiosities of art . . . On this account our English gardens are not so entertaining to the fancy as those of France and Italy, where we see a large extent of ground covered over with an agreeable mixture of garden and forest, which represent everywhere an artificial rudeness, much more charming than that neatness and elegancy we meet with in those of our own country.

Edition after edition of *The Spectator* poured from the presses and no periodical essays have been more frequently reprinted, even down to our own times. Yet the type of garden in which Addison rejoiced was soon to be swept away in all houses of any pretension, although thousands like it on a small scale no doubt continued to flourish and to defy the fashionable army of 'improvers' who were shortly to ruin many of the larger and finer gardens.

Addison and Pope made the old ideas about garden plans unfashionable even if they did not invent new styles. Change, as always in cultural life, was 'in the wind'. Many histories of gardening have described in detail the aspects of the revolutionary effects which new ideas were to have on the English landscape, and have given some account of the men thought to have been mainly responsible for them. Addison was in the English tradition that Bacon had voiced with his desire for a 'heath or wilderness' and Robert Herrick had commended

a wild civility
Doth more bewitch me than when art
Is too precise in every part.

Stephen Switzer followed Addison in the three volumes of his *Ichnographia Rustica* in 1718 with his condemnation of 'the Dutch taste' and his belief that 'those who were most capable of art were always most fond of nature'. He believed that gardening required 'so noble and sublime a taste, beyond any one art, I might say the collective body of arts'. Batty Langley's *New Principles of Gardening* in 1728 also condemned 'that regular, stiff and stuft up manner' of the French formal style in favour of something 'truly grand and noble after nature's own manner'.

Addison and others spoke of 'greatness' in relation to the wild, awe-inspiring and stupendous aspects of natural scenery. Edmund Burke's famous essay on the *Origin of our Ideas of the Sublime and Beautiful* of 1757 included 'terror' in the notion, not without being sharply criticized for doing so. Awareness of that attitude makes it easier to understand the great fame achieved by garden planners such as Thomas Bridgeman, who helped Queen Caroline to replan royal gardens at Richmond and in Kensington. He was later praised by Horace Walpole for 'the capital stroke, the leading step to all that followed . . . the invention of fosses . . . that the common people called Ha! Ha's!'. They were ditches sustained by a brick or stone wall which kept cattle needed to crop the wide area of grass from the vicinity of the house.

What followed was begun by a minor artist, William Kent (1684–1748), who

PREVIOUS PAGES Rousham, Oxfordshire, the creation of William Kent and according to Horace Walpole 'the most engaging of all Kent's works'

possessed, according to Horace Walpole, 'a genius to strike out a great system from the twilight of imperfect essays. He leaped the fence and saw that all Nature was a garden ... the pencil of his imagination bestowed all the arts of landscape on the scenes he handled.' None of his gardens remain, so it is largely to Walpole that he is indebted for his fame as 'the father of modern gardening'. Others were also enthusiastic, such as John Gwynn in 1766 with his opinion that 'the best designed pleasure grounds, parks etc., in this kingdom were designed by the late Mr Kent'. Gwynn lamented 'a want of taste among persons of distinction', a particularly wounding accusation that all wished to avoid. One line of escape was tried by Aaron Hill (1685–1750), who made a Moral Garden in Petty France, Westminster, in 1734. It had a vault, cave, fountain, and was pitted by grottoes, all symbolizing moral qualities. Four large grotto passages, of Riches, Power, Honour and Learning, led to eight small winding paths adorned by statues of virtues and vices. The whole was surmounted by a Temple of Happiness approached by but a single path, although many seemed to lead to it. Satisfaction for the senses had not yet eclipsed traditional ideational and idealistic values.

Lancelot Brown, 1715–1783, better known as 'Capability' Brown, the best known of the English landscape gardeners

What was later described as 'the first modern, English, irregular, natural, or landscape style' in the design of parks and gardens was carried to its greatest lengths not so much by Kent but by Lancelot Brown (1715–1783). 'One Brown', wrote Horace Walpole in 1751, 'has set up on a few ideas from Mr Kent.' He used them with good effect to become one of the best-known names in British garden history. His fame owes something to his nickname 'Capability' Brown, acquired through his habit of assuring prospective clients that their grounds 'had great capabilities'. He began as a gardener's boy in Northumberland, moving after his seven years' apprenticeship to Stowe, the seat of Sir Richard Temple, Viscount Cobham, but he first began to be noticed after he had become head gardener to the third Duke of Grafton at Euston Hall, Suffolk, where he had been allowed to put some of his ideas into practice. Leaving the Duke, he went to Blenheim, where his innovations made him famous. Retaining Vanbrugh's bridge, he created two lakes, out of the small stream it spanned. So small had Vanbrugh's little stream appeared in relation to the bridge, that it inspired Pope's sarcastic lines

> The minnows, as under this vast arch they pass,
> Murmur, "How like whales we look, thanks to your Grace."

Throughout the eighteenth century the aristocracy and gentry of Britain were frequently journeying up and down the country, visiting friends and their often numerous relatives, getting introductions to view houses and gardens, striking up acquaintances and stimulating those they met with new ideas as well as gathering many themselves. Such contacts and conversations were prolonged by letters, by the loan of books and by later meetings. By such means the spirit of the age was fortified, standards of taste were formed and consolidated in food, drink, dress, building, decorating, furnishing and, not least, in gardening.

Throughout that time the English countryside wore an appearance that would startle anyone able to see it today. Glimpses of it afforded by chance references and travellers' accounts testify to the courage and fortitude of those undertaking any considerable journey, particularly in winter, when many roads were impassable. Celia Fiennes, that indefatigable horsewoman, whose delight was to traverse the land at the end of the seventeenth and at the beginning of the eighteenth centuries, leaves no doubt about either the hazards or the frequently wild state of the country. Journeying from Huntingdon to Stilton in 1697 she saw Whittlesey

OVERLEAF The lake created by Brown for Vanbrugh's bridge at Blenheim; his innovations here were to make him famous

Kent's drawing of Venus' vale, Rousham with its fountains and cascades; his aim was to create delight and surprise in a series of garden scenes

Mere, six miles long and three miles wide. It 'looked like some sea' and in a hurricane was as dangerous. It was not drained until 1851. Examples could be multiplied in order to fill in the now forgotten background against which the early landscape gardeners had to work.

Great was the renown of anyone who was able to tame part of the wilderness and to redeem the ragged appearance of the communal open-field cultivation still evident wherever agricultural enclosures and improvements had not already been undertaken. Such was the achievement of many eighteenth-century land-owners, some of whom evicted cottagers in the process. Henry Hoare at Stour-head, south-west of Salisbury Plain, in Wiltshire, was able to create around 1740 a splendid scenic effect without upsetting his humble neighbours. Stourhead still draws immense numbers of visitors but it is now far more richly planted with trees and shrubs unknown to Henry Hoare, such as catalpa, Atlantic cedars, cotoneaster, magnolia, rhododendron, sequoia and others.

In July 1764 'Capability' Brown became royal gardener at Hampton Court with £2000 a year to maintain it and other royal gardens. Like Le Nôtre at Versailles, he was treated on familiar terms by his royal master, who allowed him to advise wealthy landowners up and down the country who wished to redesign their estates. He, too, is credited with many more achievements than he himself planned. Those he undertook left an enduring monument.

If Kent and Brown did not transform 'the face of this beautiful country', as Walpole described England, they radically changed the appearance of many of its fields, woods and uncultivated wasteland by creating scores of parks and grounds for the English nobility and gentry. It was a task involving back-breaking work for thousands. Rivers and streams were dammed to create lakes in ground that had first to be excavated with pick, shovel and wheelbarrow. Millions of trees – oak, beech, ash and others – were planted and transplanted. If willingness to spend is a measure of devotion, the arts of gardening and land-scaping ranked with architecture in the eighteenth century, for large sums were readily forthcoming for 'improvements'. Horace Walpole reported in 1755 that the garden at Wanstead cost £100,000 (in gold), 'as much as the house'.

Brown, although he improved wild land to create pleasant views, was a great destroyer of gardens immediately around the mansions of his employers, and his effects were achieved at a cost of the destruction of much old familiar charm and beauty around houses. Ignoring Batty Langley's warning, he hacked down grand old avenues, demolished walls and hedges, swept away 'old world gardens' with their box-lined paths, mazes, labyrinths, flower-beds, and parterres, including that of Wise at Blenheim; abolished orchards and vegetable gardens; cleared away stone steps, terraces and garden ornaments. Ponds or pools he either drained to become meadows or linked together to form a great lake with smooth grassy banks cut to follow the fashionable 'serpentine line', usually ascribed to Hogarth as his 'line of beauty' but which Lord Bathurst (1714–1794) told Daines Barrington he had been the first to use in transforming the straight lines of ornamental canals and waterways. Earlier precedents than this have however been cited by some writers.

Brown's entire art lay in combining the attractions of stretches of water with undulating grassy meadows over which clumps and belts of trees were distributed at strategic points to give a pleasant picture from their position and their light and shade effects. He enclosed the whole scene with a belt of trees to ensure privacy. His clumps were among Brown's borrowings from Kent, who had spread them around, said Walpole in 1743 'till the lawns look like the ten of spades'. Even more than Le Nôtre and the French garden designers did he forgo flowers, and for the same reason. Their plans were on so vast a scale that flower-beds to match would have required far too much labour and expense, even if Brown had known where to put them.

Illustration from Batty Langley's *New Principles of Gardening*, 1728; an example of the call to include romantic scenery and exotic settings when considering garden planning

To those who had grown fond of an old familiar garden of grass, flowers, arbours, trees all set somewhat haphazardly, 'Capability' Brown was a disaster, while some of his less perceptive imitators were even more so. Yet there were still those who wholeheartedly applauded his achievements. These could best be appreciated by his contemporaries, who had known the often wild and ragged nature of the eighteenth-century countryside lying beyond but within sight of the great houses in England whose environment he was the first to tame.

With the passage of time, his improvements, his lakes and streams, their well-trimmed banks, his clumps of trees, his vast expanses of grass; the 'belt' which screened the whole from inquisitive eyes, all seemed so natural that they were taken for granted as though they had always been there. Then they could appear too simple, too rational, too emotionless. Horace Walpole, who remembered rough scenery that Brown had improved, remained grateful to him. 'We have discovered the point of perfection, we have given the model of gardening to the world.'

In fact, Kent, Brown and their followers had taken only the first, merely tentative step. When Brown died in 1783, Walpole lamented the loss of 'Lady Nature's second husband and the second monarch of landscape', Kent having been the first. Others began to lament Brown's wholesale slaughter, which began to seem a predominantly negative reaction, later described as being 'distinctly marked by the absence of everything having the appearance of a terrace, or of architectural forms, or lines, immediately adjoining the house'. Buildings 'in short, rose abruptly from the lawn; and the general surface of the ground was characterized by smoothness and bareness'. Many engravings and paintings of English mansions of the mid-eighteenth century show well enough what had happened and how barren were the sites on which they were placed.

Notable at the time was the so-called 'garden' or grounds of Leasowes, the estate in Shropshire, which the versifier William Shenstone (1714–1763) inherited and sought to beautify between 1745 and 1763. Its fame spread throughout the land and visitors from far and wide came to see it. Dr Johnson and his faithful Boswell were among them in 1774, so it was still a show place after Shenstone's death. He had, said Johnson, begun 'to point his prospects, to diversify his surface, to entangle his walks, and to wind his waters, which he did with such judgement and fancy as made his little domain the envy of the great and the admiration of the skilful; a place to be visited by travellers and copied by designers'. Johnson, whose short sight deprived him of real power to appreciate landscape, who once said that 'one green field is very much like another green field and water is the same everywhere', had doubts whether Shenstone's thought and care 'demands any great powers of mind' adding that 'perhaps a sullen and surly speculator may think such performances rather the sport than the business of human reason'. Leasowes was one example of the reaction against Le Nôtre, which became exaggerated in its virulence.

The clash of opinions upon the strongly contrasted natural landscapes of 'Capability' Brown and the earlier architected, geometrical designs inherited from Italy, France and the Netherlands provoked a more general discussion of the aesthetic elements that make up the art of designing gardens. Viewed more generally, the debate can be seen as but one aspect of a movement of thought which was manifest in literature, art and philosophy. In Germany Alexander Baumgarten (1714–1762) founded modern aesthetics as the special study which Leibniz had foreseen a generation earlier, at about the same time as another German, Johann Winckelmann (1717–1768), aroused the learned world by his reflections upon the art of ancient Greece and Rome. Lessing (1729–1781) raised the whole subject to a higher plane, especially in his *Laokoon* (1766), a masterly analysis of the aesthetics of poetry and sculpture. In England the portrait painter Jonathan Richardson (1655–1745) had earlier published two works, *An Essay on the Theory of Painting* (1715) and *An Essay on the Whole Art of Criticism in Relation to Painting* (1719), which for many years remained the only printed discussion of art to set besides the (3rd) Earl of Shaftesbury's *Characteristicks of Men, Manners, Opinions, Times* (1711).

Probably of greater significance than any printed books were the animated debates ranging over the whole world of ideas in which men and women in 'polite society' increasingly delighted as the eighteenth century advanced. Social life had been rapidly enlarged and for the first time an aristocracy of intellect regularly associated with the hereditary aristocracy upon more or less equal terms. Sir Joshua Reynolds wrote on 'Connoisseurship', on the 'Imitation of Nature' and on 'Beauty' for Samuel Johnson's *Idler* in 1759, but he impressed far more people more often with his ideas on art while they were sitting for their portraits, or during evening discussions over dinner at his house in Leicester Square or at the Literary Club, the Thursday Night Club, the Devonshire, the Dilettanti Society or in casual conversations at Almacks, Ranelagh, Vauxhall and elsewhere. At the same time, in a different circle, Thomas Gainsborough (1727–1788) was opening many eyes to the splendours of nature through his glorious landscapes.

One of the first successful attempts to arrive at an awareness of the aesthetic problems involved in the art of designing the grounds of estates and gardens was *Observations on Modern Gardening* by an active politician, Thomas Whately (d. 1772), published anonymously in 1770. He claimed 'a place of considerable rank among the liberal arts' for gardening, saying that it is 'as superior to landskip

OPPOSITE The view across the lake at Stourhead, Wiltshire, the landscape garden created by Henry Hoare in the early 18th century

OVERLEAF Sheffield Park, Sussex. Capability Brown's basic design of 1775 combined trees, sward and serpentine waters but much of the splendour of these gardens lies in its variety of trees and shrubs

Pl. 8.

1. Aquilegia Skinneri. _ 2. Aquilegia glandulosa. _ 3 Aquilegia glauca
4. Aquilegia fragrans. _ 5. Aquilegia Sibirica _ 6. Aquilegia Garneriana.
7. Aquilegia Canadensis. _ 8. Aquilegia atropurpurea.

Day & Haghe Lith? to the Queen

painting as a reality to a representation; it is an exertion of fancy, a subject for taste and being relaxed now from the restraints of regularity and enlarged beyond the purposes of domestic convenience, the most beautiful, the most simple, the most noble scenes of nature are all within its province'. Such aesthetic landscape effects were to be had, Whately said, by understanding and applying simple natural elements from which every garden must necessarily arise. These obviously are the ground or site; next wood, that is, trees, shrubs, groves and clumps; then water in lakes, rivers, bridges, rills and cascades; and finally rocks and buildings. Flowers were conspicuously absent from this survey which shows that 'gardens' were still predominantly 'landscape'.

Without referring to Kent or 'Capability' Brown by name, he stoutly rejected some of their ideas although he approved of Stowe and of Brown's lake at Blenheim. He pointed to the difference between a farm, a garden, a park and a riding, correctly relegating Shenstone's famous Leasowes in Shropshire to the first class, aware however of the care with which the trees had been planted and the paths planned. Indeed, he observed that 'many gardens are nothing more than ... a walk round a field', adding that 'this species of garden, therefore, reduces almost to a sameness all the places it is applied to; the subject seems exhausted ... the fine scenery of a garden is wanting'.

Whately lifted the whole subject of garden art beyond 'Capability' Brown's notions to a higher, more inclusive, aesthetic level. The Italians, French and Dutch readiness to allow architectural principles priority in garden design repudiated by 'Capability' Brown then found a new advocate. Whately harked back to

Leasowes, the great Shropshire estate bought and remodelled by William Shenstone between 1745 and 1763. A reaction against Le Nôtre, it attracted numerous admiring visitors including Johnson and Boswell

OPPOSITE Illustration from Jane Loudon's *The Ladies Flower Garden*, first published in 1841. Its success underlined women's increasing interest and involvement in gardening

The view to the south-east at Stowe, the garden originally planned by Charles Bridgeman and taken over by Kent and which was the greatest and most famed garden in England in the 18th century. It was here that Brown began his career

earlier times as when Switzer confessed that ''tis to architects and builders that I owe a great part of that knowledge I have in the designing part of gardening, their taste being, generally speaking, greater than gardeners'.

One edition after another of Whately's slim volume was printed, and his views were popularized in France by the clever versifier, the Abbé Delille (1738–1813). And no wonder, for there had not previously been any such penetrating study. Whately however did not question the basic aims of Brown, which indeed were generally accepted, although it seemed to be sensed that he lacked the genius to carry his sound instinct to a rich fulfilment, as Daines Barrington perceived when he wrote in 1782, 'I could wish Gainsborough gave the design and Brown executed'.

Tempting as it is to discover supposed 'influences' in largely forgotten, little-known books and articles, the tendency must be resisted. All these suggested 'influences' may more correctly be regarded as spontaneous manifestations of the same spirit as that which provoked change in art and literature. What is clear is that new kinds of gardens were devised to provide more obvious elements of sensuous enjoyment than either French and Dutch formality or the studied, mannered indifference of plain English landscape effects could then provide.

The three men who most successfully expressed the new attitude to the garden world were William Gilpin (1724–1804), Sir Uvedale Price (1747–1829) and Humphry Repton (1752–1818). The first two sought to influence through their

182

writings while Repton, although he wrote on the subject also, was a professional landscape designer, the first, he claimed, so to describe himself, although the term 'landskip gardening' had been used by Shenstone somewhat earlier.

Capability Brown's landscape park at Petworth, Sussex, which proved such an inspiration to Turner

Gilpin was a clergyman of the Church of England who diversified his teaching and parochial duties by travelling up and down England and Wales, sketching the scenery and writing descriptions of the more striking views he enjoyed. He sought 'the picturesque', a term he claimed to have invented. Many of his essays were illustrated by somewhat lugubrious aquatints of his own composition. A series of volumes in succession from 1770 to 1807 called attention to the scenic beauties of the river Wye and South Wales; the mountains and lakes of Cumberland and Westmorland; the New Forest and the Isle of Wight; the coasts of Hampshire, Sussex and Kent; and the Highlands of Scotland. For the first time they taught people who rarely saw paintings to look at the natural beauties of their homeland untouched by man, with a more discerning gaze and with deeper appreciation.

In 1791 and again in 1794, Gilpin published *Three Essays on Picturesque Beauty, on Picturesque Travel and on Sketching Landscape*. In the second of them he declared that 'the more refined our taste grows from the *study of nature*, the more insipid are the *works of art*'. Among offending 'works of art', gardens were prominent. 'How flat and insipid is often the garden scene!' he exclaimed. 'How puerile and absurd! the banks of the river how smooth, and parallel! the lawn, and its boundaries, how unlike nature!' He had the gardens of Kent and 'Capability' Brown in mind.

Uvedale Price had not read these remarks when he wrote his first *Essay on the Picturesque* in 1794 but he was in agreement with much of them. Like Gilpin he was an amateur. In his *Dialogues on Various Subjects* (1807) he continued to assert that 'we should make the scenes of nature our model for our artificial improvements in gardening'. He was already lamenting 'depredations' deforming 'the mountainous parts of Cumberland and Westmorland and the Lakeland scene'. Price's *Essay on the Picturesque* was 'a direct and undisguised attack upon modern gardening'. Despite the high opinion entertained by many of his contemporaries, including Horace Walpole, of 'Capability' Brown, Price mounted a sustained attack upon him and more particularly upon his followers, 'the Brownists'. They were, he said, 'universally and professedly, smoothers, shavers, clearers, levellers and dealers in distinct serpentine lines and edges'. Although they called themselves 'improvers', beauty withered before them. All that Brown was good for was elegant gravel paths.

Gilpin and Price wanted landscape scenes to be beautiful as the paintings of renowned artists were beautiful. They entered into long disquisitions about the meaning of the then new word 'picturesque', to distinguish it from two other ideas then much debated as a result of the celebrated essay by Edmund Burke on the *Sublime and Beautiful*. 'Picturesque' was generally used, said Price, to refer 'to every object, and every kind of scenery which has been, or might be represented with good effect in painting', that is to say in a picture but which sculpture cannot express. Price himself was at pains to separate 'picturesqueness', a word he also claimed to have coined, from any necessary connection with painting and to distinguish it clearly from either the sublime or beautiful. In Part II of his *Essay on the Picturesque* he applied his ideas to gardening.

In the considerable controversy which Price stirred up, Richard Payne Knight (1750–1824), although he disagreed with him on some points, supported him in his poem *The Landscape* (1794) and his *Analytical Inquiry into the Principles of Taste* (1805). He said that he 'did not know a more melancholy object' than a large square house in the country 'midst spacious lawns interspersed with irregular clumps or masses of wood and sheets of water'. It was a sad contrast with 'the old system' when houses had been surrounded by gardens, even if many of those earlier gardens seemed too fussy. Nevertheless the 'picturesque' school of Price did not succeed in creating a new gardening style. Beauty, Price said, is characterized by smoothness, the picturesque by roughness which needed mixing with beauty 'as lemon does with sugar'. Knight soon criticized this curious distinction.

Horace Walpole defended both Kent and Brown to the extent of stimulating the very indifferent poet William Mason to attack Price and Payne Knight in a 'Sonnet occasioned by a late attack upon the present taste of English Gardens'. Mason declaimed that 'Taste from his polish'd lawn indignant rose' to scorn the 'two Arcadian Squires' who 'in rhyme and prose' had dared 'to prate of Picturesqueness'. Price and Knight had little to fear. 'Capability' Brown and his imitators had gone too far in their rejection of 'formality' and their ignorant scorn of Le Nôtre. Brown's talent was modest enough and it soon degenerated into mannerism, while his followers had nothing but mannerism to offer. The time had come for a change, and not in gardening alone. In poetry William Wordsworth (1770–1850) and Samuel Taylor Coleridge (1772–1834), in painting Samuel Palmer (1741–1813), Joseph Turner (1775–1851), John Constable (1776–

1837) are among the artists who very powerfully illustrated the changing world of aesthetics on similar lines.

When 'beauty, animation, variety, mystery' are, according to John D. Sedding, the qualities that gardens should possess, it is easy to accept Wordsworth's opinion that 'laying out grounds may be considered a liberal art in some sort like poetry and painting and its object is or ought to be, to move the affections under the control of reason'. That is precisely the 'idealistic' style of cultural life.

Humphry Repton, 1752–1818, the influential landscape gardener and writer who modified the ideas of Brown and his followers and introduced variety into garden design

Humphry Repton was a landowning gentleman who had expected to be able to lead a life of leisure. As a boy of fourteen he had been sent to school in Holland for two years. The small formal 'gardens' he saw there were mostly parterres filled with different coloured material, red brick dust, yellow sand, charcoal, broken china, green glass – anything except plants. Many were surrounded by an edging of box. Where there were trees, in larger gardens, they were relentlessly cut and trimmed. 'All has neatness; the effect of incessant labour. A Dutch merchant's accounts and his garden were kept with the same degree of accuracy and attention.'

When the loss of his income drove Repton to take up landscape gardening he began to follow 'Capability' Brown's ideas, which he defended in print, only to be answered by Price. The cumulative effect of Price's arguments was so overwhelming that Repton, although continuing to resist them in print, nevertheless changed his ways in practice. He set forth his own ideas in *Sketches and Hints on Landscape Gardening* (1795), *Observations on the Theory and Practice of Landscape Gardening* (1803), *An Inquiry into the Changes of Taste in Landscape Gardening* (1806), *Designs for the Pavilion at Brighton* (1808) and finally *Fragments on the Theory and Practice of Landscape Gardening* (1816). All, except the *Inquiry*, were illustrated in colour from the neat sketches he provided for his prospective clients, showing the house and grounds as they were with similar sketches on the same scale giving his suggested improvements. These were his little 'red books'.

Repton's good sense and ability to learn from experience enabled him to correct many mistakes and to leave many estates with agreeable surroundings. Regarding a garden 'not as a landscape but a work of art using the materials of nature' he lamented in 1816 that 'the pleasures of a garden have, of late, been much neglected'. Instead 'a taste, almost a rage for farming had superseded the delights of a garden'. He did not have much to say about flower gardens but he did restore many. Consequently he ended by reacting sharply against Brown and 'the Brownists', condemning 'baldness and nakedness round the house' because 'a large lawn, like a large room, when unfurnished, displeases more than a small one'.

Repton expanded Whately's recommendation by advocating a pleasure ground or 'artificial garden, richly clothed with flowers and decorated with statues and works of art' to be either visible from the windows or very near the house, as 'the rich frame of the landscape'. When cost was no obstacle, his ideas were certainly expansive. He applauded the magnificence of Woburn where he proposed 'a series of different gardens under the following heads:

The terrace and parterre near the house.
The private garden used only by the family.
The rosary or dressed flower garden.
The American garden for plants of that country only.
The Chinese garden, surrounding a pool in front of the great Chinese pavilion, to be decorated with plants from China.

The botanic garden for scientific classing of plants.
The animated garden or menagerie.
And, lastly, the English garden or shrubbery walk connecting the whole.

So much debate and controversy about the best way of laying out grounds and gardens round a house in England during the nineteenth century would be excessive if it were not for the number of 'English gardens' that were created on what was supposed to be the English style in Europe. Often the result was not very happy – 'the unhallowed Giardino Inglese', said Sir George Sitwell.

That controversy also marks a turning point in gardening and cultural history. After Repton's considerable modification of the ideas of Brown and 'the Brownists', no single 'school' or fashion of garden design became generally predominant. Variety in garden design undoubtedly existed in the eighteenth century, despite Kent, Brown and the Brownists. Addison testified to it at the beginning of that century when he said that there were as many styles of gardening as there are of poetry. Thereafter variety became the rule. Repton led the way, so encouraging others to try to devise yet more different garden designs.

As the nineteenth century advanced, sensate culture was steadily being debased by the growing desire to enjoy the greatest possible satisfaction from purely personal impulses. Examples of this freedom and licence multiplied to affect garden design, sometimes in startling ways.

One rich man of outstanding ability, William Beckford, spent a princely income on innumerable follies and lavished a fortune on his house, Fonthill, and its grounds. Novelties and unusual gardens became more numerous and they attracted increasing attention. A more sober style than Beckford's, but still markedly individualistic, was that of the wealthy collector and patron, Thomas Hope (1769–1831), at Deepdene, near Dorking, a wild and romantic spot. Hope

Alton Towers, the wildly fantastic garden made for the wealthy Earl of Shrewsbury, an enthusiastic lover of gardens and architecture 'with much more fancy than judgement'

spent lavishly in his efforts to revive ancient Egyptian, Greek and Roman classical styles in decoration, architecture, furniture and dress. His great house and grounds were later described as an example of the 'ecstatic' style.

Enthusiastic amateurs who formed the Society of Dilettanti in 1732 subscribed to send artists to the Mediterranean lands to collect antique sculpture and to publish their reports. A new impetus was given to the study of ancient civilization to inspire painters as well as historians and to revive interest in the gardens of Lucullus and Pliny.

Wildly eccentric was the wealthy 16th Earl of Shrewsbury, who, rejecting the plans of all the many landscape gardeners he had called in to advise him, resolved upon schemes of his own and set about executing them between 1814 and 1827 at Alton Towers near Cheadle in Staffordshire. The result in the restrained language of John Loudon who saw the place in October 1826, was 'one of the most singular anomalies to be met with among the country residences of Britain and perhaps in any part of the world'. Ponds and lakes on the tops of hills; bridges below without water; vast exotic conservatories; a Chinese pagoda spouting water from each storey; a pseudo-megalith to outdo Stonehenge, were all among the Earl's achievements, which Loudon said 'defied all criticism'. He rightly assessed the cultural climate of his day by adding the reflection 'how far it may be commendable for a man of wealth to gratify a peculiar taste, rather than one which is generally approved by the intelligence of the country in which he lives, is not, in these days, perhaps a question of much consequence'.

It was not a question many people thought of asking. So, as wealth accumulated in the nineteenth century, more people were able to indulge in whims only less bizarre than those of the 16th Earl of Shrewsbury because they lacked his resources. Fanciful houses and gardens were created for retired traders, manufacturers and others who had not succeeded in acquiring good taste as speedily as they had gained riches, and who moreover usually saw no reason for preferring the ideas of others upon art, architecture, gardens or morals to their own.

At the end of the eighteenth century, garden artists faced new tasks. The first was to vindicate Schiller's prediction in 1795 that 'a middle way will in all probability be found between the formality of the French gardening taste and the lawless freedom of the so-called English style'. Secondly, an artist's discernment was needed to devise and popularize pleasant small gardens. A third task, of which the British were then barely conscious, was to create public gardens, which had been a reality in ancient Rome and which had a longer history on the continent of Europe.

A few eccentrics and great magnates might astonish the world by magnificent or strange constructions, but all the time men of lesser but substantial wealth were becoming more numerous, building their villas, and creating gardens. In England some of them did not hesitate to seek the professional advice of the foremost expert in garden design of the day. In the early nineteenth century Repton, who had begun his career as a landscape gardener in 1788 on the broad acres of the nobility, lived to report that 'in the neighbourhood of every city or manufacturing town, new places, as villas, are daily springing up; and these, with a few acres, require all the conveniences, comforts and appendages, of larger and more sumptuous, if not more expensive places. . . . These have of late had the greatest claim on my attention.' There had of course always been private gardens, but on nothing like that scale.

Villas in the then country air of Streatham, Ealing and Epping Forest were

687

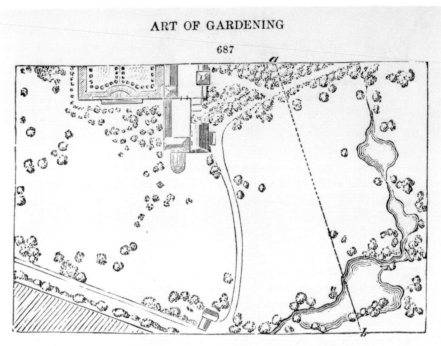

be laid on with reference to some medium elevation, referred to or illustrated by sections, taken in the direction of indicated lines (*a...b*), it will give an equally correct idea of the variations of the ground. In short, it is the best mode for most purposes, and is now coming into general use.

2340. *A very complete method* of giving the plan of an estate, is to adopt the profile manner, and include such a portion of the plans of the adjoining estates or country as shall be contained within a circle of moderate extent (*fig.* 688.), the centre of which may

688

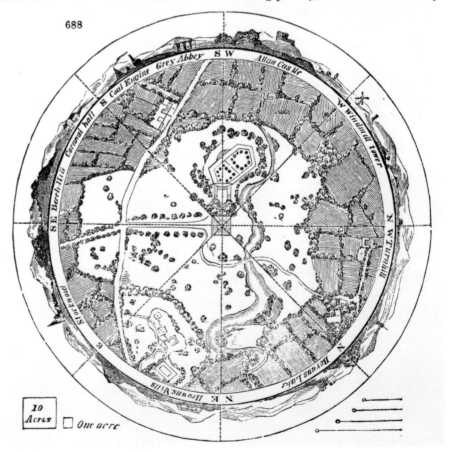

among those for which Repton devised plans. Over the country as a whole, such garden plots became of vaster extent than that of the large, landscaped parks. Most of these villas and their large gardens near London, such as that belonging to the Thornton family on the side of Clapham Common, have long since been eaten up by houses.

Repton's plans for these villas were something of a novelty. He sought to make the most of their very limited possibilities. Where the view from the garden was 'disfigured by a redundance of obtrusive houses', he tried to protect it by putting trees and shrubs in the way. Where trees and shrubs shut out pleasant glimpses of surrounding landscape, he cut them down, perhaps bounding the estate with a ha-ha. He laid out flower-beds near the house and filled them with crocuses, snowdrops and other spring flowers; roses and fruits for summer and autumn. He 'set the winter at defiance' by providing heated glass-houses for grapes and flowers.

Repton was not a romantic by nature and his career gives the impression of a man intelligent enough to learn by experience how to adopt and develop emerging trends. If the romantic garden was not his creation, he gave an impulse towards its development. There could be no sudden reversal to the formality of seventeenth-century gardens despite some nostalgic backward glances. A continuing admiration for the paintings of Poussin, who 'combined in such full measure the ideal and the real', surprisingly a favourite painter of André Le Nôtre, pointed to another style.

Eighteenth-century common sense continued to resist romantic innovation, although the prevailing mood was for greater sensuous satisfactions than either the classicism of seventeenth-century styles or the plain, bluff stuff of 'Capability' Brown's landscapes could provide. A delight in plain natural effects never died away among the English, most of whom did not need artists to convince them about the beauty of 'a good view'.

Repton, disabled by a fall from his horse in 1811, died in 1818. Already a young Scotsman from Lanarkshire, John Claudius Loudon (1783–1843), was beginning to make a name for himself as a gardener. Accustomed early to a life of unremitting hard work and largely self-taught in arithmetic, botany, chemistry, Latin, French and Italian, he travelled, planned gardens, and with the help of his equally energetic wife, published enough for the life work of ten other men. In 1822 his huge *Encyclopedia of Gardening* appeared, scoring a success which shows that practical interest in making successful gardens was rapidly growing. Three years later came his massive *Encyclopedia of Agriculture* (1825), followed in 1829 by an *Encyclopedia of Plants*. From 1826 until his death, his *Gardeners' Magazine* appeared each month, although it lost circulation after 1831 to Paxton's *Horticultural Register*.

Loudon's health was never good. In 1820 he lost the use of his right arm which had to be amputated in 1825 after five years of chronic pain. Nevertheless he struggled on. In 1830 he married Jane Webb, who had attracted his notice by her strange novel *The Mummy* (1827), an early effort at 'science fiction' in the manner of H. G. Wells. Before long they could show on their quarter of an acre in the Bayswater Road, London, more than 2000 plants, all grown by their own efforts with the aid of a jobbing gardener at a cost of about £25 a year. Their exertions were herculean. The success of Loudon's *Encyclopedia of Cottage Farm and Villa Architecture* in 1832 led him to embark upon his most scholarly and extensive *Arboretum et Fruticetum Britannicum*, which ruined him financially. He was threatened with bankruptcy and arrest for debt, but on 14 December

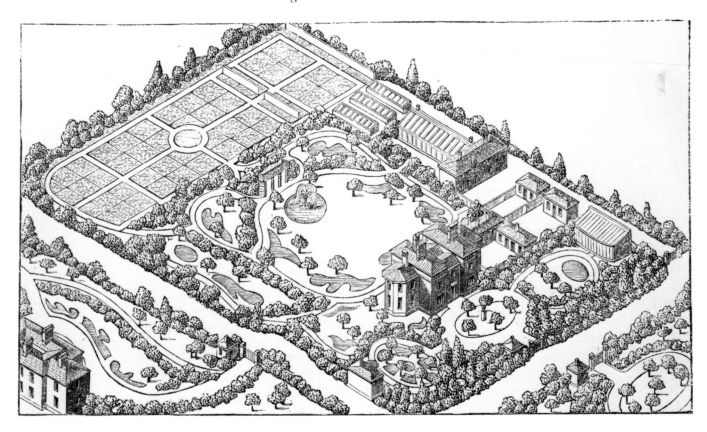

Loudon devised numerous designs and styles for the increasing number of devoted suburban gardeners; this plan of a 3-acre estate is from Loudon's *The Suburban Gardener*

1843 he died at midnight while at work with his loyal and hard-working wife.

No other pair laboured so assiduously, so continuously to aid British gardening as Loudon and his wife. He was one of the giants of scholarship and industry of the nineteenth century, the like of which are no longer seen. His publications are by no means exhausted by the few titles so far mentioned. In practical garden planning and advice his commissions included the Botanical Garden at Birmingham, an arboretum at Derby, cemeteries at Southampton and elsewhere, as well as many private gardens.

His wife, Jane Loudon (1807–1858), had been his staunch supporter. After his death she continued to struggle for a livelihood with her pen, scoring a considerable success through her series on *The Ladies Flower Garden*, of which the *Ladies Companion to the Flower Garden* appeared in 1841. Nine editions of it had been published by 1879. Some two dozen printed works, all but half a dozen on gardens or allied topics, stand to her credit between 1846 and 1855. They afford early evidence in social history of a widening scope for feminine energy and skill in a field in which men alone had previously been active.

Surveying the varied garden styles of the past towards the end of his life, Loudon tried to see the comparative merits of the main conflicting styles of garden design of earlier times. Each had been, he said in 1839, 'in different stages of society, equally congenial to the human mind'. The first, 'the Ancient Roman, geometric, regular or architectural style' was, he thought, 'most striking and pleasing and most obviously displayed wealth and taste in an early stage of society and in countries where the general scenery was wild, irregular and natural'. Such a description would not be applied to the Netherlands, but the geometric style was equally suitable there because the country was 'perfectly flat, distinguished by long, straight canals and grassy terraces'.

This 'geometric style' characterizing the Italian, French and Dutch schools,

was rejected by 'the modern, English, irregular, natural or landscape style ...
Kent's school'. That reaction had been successful, for classicism had lost its earlier
vitality and not only in gardening art. In painting also classicism had suffered
a somewhat similar fate. All styles work themselves out, and in garden art the
English reaction to classicism had been a reversion to naturalism of a singularly
plain and unadorned fashion in the open space of grass, trees and water of 'Capability' Brown and William Shenstone. In England, as Loudon pointed out, the
reaction came sooner than elsewhere because the enclosure of former open agricultural land into separate fields by hedges had introduced a new note of formality
into the countryside. Informality in English parks and gardens therefore often
provided a greater contrast to natural landscape than it would have done on the
continent of Europe.

There were probably deeper reasons for the difference. Lord Clark's comment
upon the evolution of English painting in the eighteenth and early-nineteenth
centuries – 'the idea that an appreciation of nature can be combined with a desire
for intellectual order has never been acceptable in England' – has additional con-
firmation in the new development of garden art. At length, said Loudon, 'the
rage for destroying avenues and terraces having subsided and the propriety of
uniting a country house with the surrounding scenery by architectural appendages having been pointed out in a masterly manner by Uvedale Price, Kent's
school gave way ... to what may be called Repton's school'.

Loudon thought that there were three sorts of English natural garden. The
'picturesque' was 'particularly suitable for being represented by painting' because
of 'its strongly marked features'. The 'gardenesque', his own not very original
contribution to the problem, aimed at 'displaying the art of the gardener – the
individual beauty of trees, shrubs and plants in a state of culture, the smoothness
and greenness of lawns and the smooth surfaces, curved directions, dryness and
firmness of gravel walks'. The third, the 'rustic style' was that 'commonly found
accompanying the rudest description of labourers' cottages in the country'. All
stood in marked contrast to 'the geometrical style of landscape-gardening, the
ancient or architectural style', which however had been perfectly reasonable as
a necessary contrast to the wild irregularity of the surrounding country. 'An enlightened mind,' he wrote, 'will derive pleasure from any style.'

Loudon did not pitch his hopes or claims for the art of landscape gardening
too high; he said indeed that 'it must rank much lower in the scale of imitative
art than landscape painting'. The advantage it had over painting was that 'which
architecture had over sculpture; viz., that of combining the useful with the agreeable'. Indeed his practical mind knew very well that utility had to be the keynote
where small suburban gardens were concerned. He claimed that his 'gardenesque'
style was 'particularly adapted for laying out the grounds of small villas'. He
had not included the conscious pursuit of 'the beautiful' or of 'art' among the
suburban gardeners' aims, but the care and effort he put into devising and record-
ing a great number of designs and styles for small gardens of all kinds had no
other motive than to ensure that the results should be both efficient and as artistically satisfying as possible.

VII

GARDENS IN
MODERN TIMES

I n their stalwart efforts to advance and diffuse botanical and horticultural knowledge, the Loudons created and bequeathed a series of scholarly publications superior to anything hitherto available. Loudon caught up and dealt systematically and thoroughly with trends that had long been evident. His 'gardenesque school' was stimulated by 'the introduction, from other countries, of many new plants which thrive in the open air in our climate' and its aim was 'to display these new plants to a greater advantage than hitherto. . . . All trees and shrubs are planted and arranged in regard to their kinds and dimensions, and they are . . . thinned out to such distances apart as may best display the natural form and habit of each: while at the same time, in a general point of view, unity of expression and character are aimed at.' When Loudon wrote, the immense floral wealth of China had not been fully revealed but enough was becoming known for him to predict in 1838 that 'many species of trees and shrubs in China now wholly unknown to us will at some future time be added to the British arboretum'.

New energies were exerted to set out exciting novelties to the best advantage in flower-beds, rockeries, conservatories and hothouses. Botanical knowledge expanded with the general advance of scientific investigation and mechanical invention. New chemical fertilizers, weedkillers, insecticides, machinery and tools began to lighten and to make more effective the hand labour still essential if ground was to be prepared, seeds sown, plants tended and their flowers and fruits duly harvested. Horticultural societies, beginning with the Horticultural Society of London in 1804, now the Royal Horticultural Society, brought enthusiasts together whose subscriptions provided resources which could be used to advance gardening knowledge by organizing shows of plants, flowers, vegetables and fruits, by publishing magazines and by occasionally financing plant-hunting expeditions.

No single country and no single style henceforth provided the dominant ideas by which gardening work was done, in the way that Italian ideas were foremost until the mid-seventeenth century and French ideas during the remainder of that century. Just as in industry, trade, commerce and the exploration of the globe, the British then took the lead in gardening. In 1829 already, George Johnson could record some 300 varieties of hyacinth compared with the fifty known to Parkinson about 200 years earlier, and 350 kinds of heath against the three of the early-seventeenth century.

In 1843 Robert Fortune began what were to be several journeys to the Far East for the Horticultural Society of London, sending back seeds and plants that caused a sensation among European gardeners. Among them was the male plant of the *Aucuba japonica*. All the many plants in Europe had been female, so the berries had been unknown. Other botanists followed in the next hundred years and penetrated further into the Far East, notably A. E. Pratt, E. H. Wilson, G. Forrest, R. Farrer, Fathers J. M. Delavay and P. Farges and Mr F. Kingdon Ward, who was active until the Second World War. The new worlds of the Americas, Australasia and Africa also yielded some astonishing discoveries. Not all was positive gain because along with many treasures came also pestilential weeds, destructive small mammals and insects by which many gardeners are still plagued.

Many of these findings were improved by European plant breeders who were already busily cultivating varieties of European trees, shrubs and flowers. Their amazing achievements in revolutionizing modern gardens call for special appreciation as a contribution to civilization and culture. The English cabbage rose, *Rosa centifolia*, for instance, was already known in the sixteenth century; *Rosa damascena* was earlier, brought home according to a vague and dubious tradition by a crusader. The white rose of York and red of Lancaster in the fifteenth century are said to have been of this variety. *Rosa chinensis* and the related *Rosa odorata* were the source of the tea and hybrid roses; these were not however fully and successfully developed until the period 1873–1890. Then, too, other varieties, noisette and dwarf hybrid polyantha roses, added to the astonishing variety.

The main sources of the new plants which revolutionized the gardens of Europe, apart from India and East China, according to the eminent authority Dr W. T. Stearn, were:

Near East 1560–1630
Canada and Virginia 1620–1686 (mainly herbaceous plants)
Cape of Good Hope 1687–1772
North America trees and shrubs 1687–1772
Australia 1772–1882
Japan and North America 1820–1900 (mainly glass-house and hardy plants)
West China 1900–1930
Hybrids bred in Europe 1930 onwards.

The story has often been told of the tulip and of 'tulipomania' in early-seventeenth-century Holland when rare bulbs were said to have been exchanged for a sumptuous carriage and two fully-harnessed horses, or a small holding of twelve acres, or a mill. The tulip never lost favour.

Many if not most popular garden flowers – hyacinths, roses, narcissi, gladioli, peonies, carnations and chrysanthemums – have been transformed by being greatly improved in size, colour, hardiness and fertility but not always, it would seem, in scent, by the skill and devotion of generations of nurserymen and plant-breeders. Never have the palettes of garden artists been more richly charged;

Rosa centifolia, the cabbage rose; painting by Pierre Joseph Redouté, the celebrated 19th-century rose artist

The 19th century saw an immense increase in the number and variety of plants available to gardeners; the exotic *Victoria regia* caused a sensation when it was introduced to Britain from South America in the 1840s

Tulips and hyacinths at Keukenhof, Holland, the greatest bulb-garden in the world and particularly noted for the numerous varieties of Holland's tulips

opposite The water garden at Cliveden, Buckinghamshire, with a 'Japanese' pagoda bought at the Great Exhibition of 1851

overleaf left Longwood Gardens, near Philadelphia, the magnificent estate endowed by the du Pont family, which cultivates ornamental plants from all over the world

overleaf right White azaleas blossoming in the glorious woodland of Winterthur, Delaware

never therefore have greater demands been made upon their skill and their ability to choose, combine and arrange the content, form, tone and colours of their gardens so as to satisfy both their plant-collecting and plant-growing enthusiasms as well as the eye of taste. A large volume would be needed to record their triumphs. A smaller appendix would suffice to record the objections which may have been made by those overwhelmed by this *embarras de richesses* which some purists deplore. Their regrets at the exotics, such as rhododendrons added to gardens such as Stourhead, Bodnant and Sheffield Park, do not diminish the enjoyment of the vast majority of visitors.

Less spectacular but none the less real progress has also been achieved by the introduction of new vegetable and root crops and by the improvement of old stocks of traditional vegetables such as cabbage, carrots, parsnips, turnips, lettuces, beans, onions, cucumbers, leeks and globe artichokes. Vegetable plots and herb gardens rarely come into the discussion of garden aesthetics because, no doubt, their appeal is utilitarian rather than artistic. Yet they formed the first gardens from the dawn of time and, together with orchards, they have undoubtedly yielded aesthetic satisfaction as they contributed to the well-being of their owners. A well-weeded, well-arranged kitchen garden, as at Villandry, is a gratifying sight able to give pleasure to more beholders than the gardener or owner by whom or on whose behalf it has all been planted.

In spite of pessimists and reformers, enthusiasm for gardening began to be shared by more people during the nineteenth century than ever before. There was progress all along the line, evident in the immense increase in new plants and flowers at the disposal of European gardeners; the improvements in 'utilitarian' gardening producing better fruit and vegetables; the well-tended lawns;

The interior of the huge conservatory at Chatsworth, built in 1844 for the Duke of Devonshire

the vast increase in books and periodicals devoted to garden cultivation; the foundation and expansion of voluntary horticultural societies; and the growing popularity of flower shows and horticultural exhibitions. Large sums of money continued to be lavished upon gardens and their equipment. Loudon lived to see the first lawn-mowing machine. Paxton began his huge green-houses and hothouses for the Duke of Devonshire at Chatsworth, which inspired his vast structure for the Great Exhibition of 1851 which became the Crystal Palace.

Inevitably a livelier awareness of the aesthetic side of gardening was engendered by so much technical activity, to spread slowly from the leisured reflective classes to a vastly greater public. Progress was slow. 'The prevalence of bad taste that accompanies wealth suddenly acquired' made life difficult for Repton before 1816, and like garden weeds, it is always with us. The more artistic

OPPOSITE The famous white garden of Sissinghurst Castle, Kent, with the Tudor castle tower in the background. The gardens are the creation of Victoria Sackville-West and Harold Nicolson

early Victorians strove to blend everything in their gardens into a pleasing harmonious whole. How to succeed in so difficult a task in small gardens, satisfying good taste by unpretentious simplicity, avoiding dullness and tameness, and how at the same time to provide pleasure arising from some intricacy yielding elements of mystery and surprise is a general aesthetic problem with which poets, painters and other artists, as well as gardeners, are forced to strive in order to avoid the boredom that arises whenever an art fails to evoke more than a single set of associations.

Among the more obvious defects already condemned by 1850 were such adjuncts to gardens as mock 'ruins', purposeless bridges, wells, model birds and animals, little gnomes, fairies and other shams, eccentricities and surprise effects that only surprise once and thereafter seem silly. Artificial rockeries too near the house using large shells, broken pottery and other debris were condemned, along with sham grottoes and arbours with bits of mirror-glass, cork bark and so on. The exciting annual increase in newly-imported plants of all kinds together with the remarkable new varieties produced by plant-breeders powerfully stimulated the temptation to cram small plots too tightly and to scatter too many little flower-beds, often in geometric designs, all over lawns, as well as incongruous, brightly-coloured flowers and trees in tubs. In winter and when the plants died, the plots lay bare and were a bore.

An effort to reintroduce more harmony and attraction led to more 'bedding-out', the rapid replacement of spent plants by a succession of others of later maturity, and some gardeners became skilled 'quick-change' artists. However, such displays were beyond the ambitions or resources of the average small householder who usually had to be content with a small grass plot surrounded by flower-beds and a few trees and bushes. Where more space was available it was not always successfully used. Despite good advice given before 1830, bizarre striving for novelty through over-lavish ornament and decoration was naturally extended to the garden, where it became a further provocation to those who spoke with scorn of the achievements of the Victorian era. Loudon's 'garden-esque' style became their target when it was not maintained with the care and knowledge which he and Jane devoted to every inch of their botanical treasure-house.

Much ingenuity went into making a small garden appear larger by wide expanses of lawn while yet inviting the eye to explore recesses, leading it on, as Repton had done, by sinking the boundary in a ditch or ha-ha whenever in country districts an open space lay beyond, taking away sufficient trees or bushes to reveal glimpses of agreeable distant prospects. Where this could not be had, other devices were recommended, such as concealing some of the garden paths from the house, masking their turns and bends with bushes and shrubs; obscuring unsightly neighbouring obstacles as far as possible by trees, evergreens or small garden-houses; a green-house or summerhouse.

Within the garden itself the Victorians were urged to try to arouse interest without eccentricity or feeble-mindedness, by elements of mystery and surprise, luring the eye onwards with a hint of something over and beyond, yet to be explored. Such aims recall those of the earlier gardeners of China. Graceful and flowing outlines and contours of paths, borders and mounds were recommended, leading by easy stages to the garden's best or most striking element.

As cities grew in size and squalor, as the demands of an increasingly complex, competitive industry and commerce became more exacting, there was a growing urge to seek that calmness, serenity and repose which a true garden retreat pro-

OPPOSITE Hush Heath, Kent, a garden which successfully blends English and Italian styles

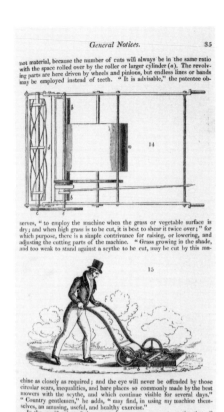

not material, because the number of cuts will always be in the same ratio with the space rolled over by the roller or larger cylinder (*a*). The revolving parts are here driven by wheels and pinions, but endless lines or bands may be employed instead of teeth. "It is advisable," the patentee ob-

serves, "to employ the machine when the grass or vegetable surface is dry; and when high grass is to be cut, it is best to shear it twice over;" for which purpose, there is a simple contrivance for raising, or lowering, and adjusting the cutting parts of the machine. "Grass growing in the shade, and too weak to stand against a scythe to be cut, may be cut by this ma-

chine as closely as required; and the eye will never be offended by those circular scars, inequalities, and bare places so commonly made by the best mowers with the scythe, and which continue visible for several days." "Country gentlemen," he adds, "may find, in using my machine themselves, an amusing, useful, and healthy exercise."

In the specification of the patent, it was unnecessary to notice that all the grass cut off may be collected in a box (*fig.* 15.); but this we consider a valuable addition, as saving sweeping, and as completing the oper-
n 2

The first mowing-machine, illustrated in *The Gardeners Magazine*, 1832; the vast increase in gardening literature was but one aspect of the 19th-century enthusiasm for gardening on every scale

vides from the burdens and fatigues of life, from jarring human relationships and the fears and anxieties of an environment too constantly evoking defensive or aggressive reactions. 'O let me escape thither,' wrote Abraham Cowley of the garden of his dreams, 'and my soul shall live.'

Loudon's matter-of-fact eight motives for gardening did not include satisfactions of this kind if only because he wrote before such psychological and cultural matters had begun to get the emphasis now put upon them. Matthew Arnold in the following generation did as much as any man, apart from John Ruskin, to expose the often appalling social evils and the relatively low cultural level of mid-Victorian England. It was, he complained, a country of 'Barbarians, Philistines and Raw Populace' and he called urgently for 'more sweetness and light'. He did not mention gardens, but he might well have done so, for William Robinson was then lamenting that 'the art of garden design is yet in a very barbarous state'. Poverty and the lack of education seemed to bar all hopes of much progress among the mass of the people. Yet, from conditions that now can barely be imagined, the scene began to change before the end of the nineteenth century.

In countless suburban streets at weekends or on summer evenings, men might be seen trimming hedges of privet or laurel that threatened to block the windows of their small front parlours. They and their wives had no more than a few pennies to spare for a few cheap plants from the costermongers' barrows in the innumerable street markets, such as the popular mignonette, marigolds, pansies, calceolarias, London pride, forget-me-nots, petunias, lobelias, and so forth, with perhaps some geraniums or standard roses as luxuries. Many of these plants were set out in array with sharp contrasts of vivid colours, a splendid symbol of defiance, matching the readiness to endure intense and constant hard work, the optimism, gusto and bravado of the Victorians.

Then also mid-Victorian parlours, drawing rooms and perhaps small conservatories, began to be decorated with ferns and plants with variegated leaves, not, however, without complaints that 'the rooms are infected with the smell of earth'. Poorer householders shared the cult of *Aspidistra lurida fol. var.* and long maintained it, despite the jibes of music-hall comedians and of suburban wits trying to raise a cheap laugh at the expense of the Victorians. Loudon in 1830 recorded two varieties as having been brought to England from China in 1822. It was described in Lowe's *Beautiful Leaved Plants* of 1861 as 'a hardy herbaceous perennial from Japan, more curious than ornamental'. In the 1860s it was often seen in Paris also as an indoor plant. Paxton's revised *Botanical Dictionary* in 1868 recorded half a dozen varieties of these 'curious plants remarkable for producing their flowers under the surface of the earth'.

Within a generation or two many people began to look upon the gardening styles which had been popular in and around London in the 1830s as unbearably stuffy, fussy and over-elaborated, with their many little flower-beds puncturing the trim lawns, their shrubs and trees in ornamental tubs, their rustic arches, deplorably ugly 'rock-work', miscellaneous stone urns, statuary and other mannerisms. If they were tired of 'gardenesque', what novelty could be found? There seemed little scope in England for a revival of the geometrical designs or the vast ambitious garden-parks of the French and Dutch classical traditions. Landscape gardening on Brown's or Repton's scale was beyond most people's resources. Around many large houses a solution to the difficulty was 'so simple' in the words of the *Quarterly Review* of 1855 'that it seems incredible our grandfathers did not hit on it. Instead of destroying the architectural garden, how much more agreeable to good sense and good taste does it seem to surround it with

Design for a summer house, illustration of 1874, characteristic of the Victorian enthusiasm for the 'rustic' style and elaborate garden novelties

grounds of a more natural though still highly dressed character, and to permit these again gradually to melt into the bolder and wider scenery of the wood or park!' But there was another idea.

Loudon had mentioned 'rustic' gardens, the simple cottage gardens of agricultural labourers in the country with their few plants massed together. A generation or two later, especially in some towns, many humble folk, as Loudon pointed out, 'took a great delight in their gardens' and gave patient hours to their few brightly-coloured, old-fashioned flowers, their tulips and one or two florists' flowers'. Particularly was this true in Norwich, Lancashire, Cheshire, Paisley and Glasgow, and in London at Spitalfields.

To convert the English to a new love of their own native flowers was the ambition in the 1880s of William Robinson, a self-taught, quarrelsome Irish gardener's boy with ideas of his own acquired as an eager journalist in his travels in Switzerland and France. His discovery of the glory of Swiss alpine flowers thrilled him also, and he was a pioneer in contriving more natural rock gardens than those which his predecessors had devised to look, as one critic said in 1855, like 'larded chickens'. In *The Wild Garden or our Groves and Shrubberies made Beautiful by the Naturalization of Hardy Exotic Flowers, with a chapter on the Garden of British Wild Flowers* in 1870, Robinson deplored the 'great mistake in destroying all our sweet old border flowers from tall lilies to dwarf Hepaticas' and denounced the bedding system as 'base and frightfully opposed to every law of nature's own arrangement of living things'. Nearly half his small book however was devoted to foreign exotic plants.

By his writings and example, he popularized the 'wild garden', a style which had some faint affinities with 'rustic' cottage gardens, in so far as hardy native plants such as primroses massed together were among its features. A generation earlier, Mr Edward Hussey had created a wild garden and a rock garden, both great novelties, at Scotney Castle in Kent but unlike Robinson he did not actively seek converts. His example indicates that the time had arrived for a change from the somewhat chaotic, ragged 'gardenesque' style.

Shortly after publication of his small book, Robinson began a magazine, *The Garden*, in 1871. It published articles by several well-known garden enthusiasts in sympathy with his ideas. Among them were Dean Reynolds Hole (1819–1904)

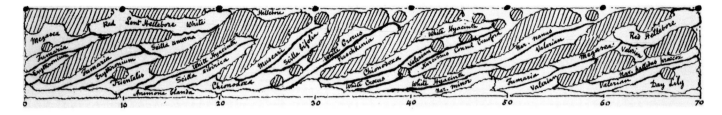

Plan for an early bulb garden; illustration from Gertrude Jekyll's *Colour in the Flower Garden*, 1908

of Rochester, who probably did more than anybody to popularize rose-growing in England, Canon Ellacombe (1822–1916) of Bitton, Gloucestershire, John Ruskin and others. Soon Robinson had attracted a new contributor, Miss Gertrude Jekyll (1843–1932), a high-spirited, cultivated young lady of independent means who, after two years as an art student, was using her aesthetic talents as an interior decorator for the Duke of Westminster and others.

She had early developed a passionate interest in gardening, in which she was able to indulge when she went in 1876 to live near Godalming in Surrey on Munstead Heath after the death of her father. There she created a garden out of heathland, a task which she accomplished with such success that she began to attract visitors, drawn by its growing reputation and by her numerous articles on gardening subjects. Soon she became a professional designer of gardens, a career in which she was greatly aided by her friendship with a young architect whom she met by chance in 1889 who became Sir Edwin Lutyens (1869–1944). They proved congenial and sympathetic partners. Her naturalistic gardens, planned in the light of Robinson's ideas, however, hardly seem easy to combine very well with the Lutyens style of architecture.

Soon launched upon a professional career, she became a leading personality in the garden world. Two books in which she collected her periodical articles spread her fame. Her *Wood and Garden* went through six printings in a year of its publication (1899). It was followed by *Home and Garden* (1900). These two books and especially her *Colour in the Flower Garden* (1908) set forth the essence of her wisdom on garden art. Myopia arrested her career as a painter and deprived her of many pleasures, for which she found compensation in gardening. She retained a keen sense of colour from her days as an art student and from her lifelong association with artists, notably Ruskin, William Morris and Hercules Brabazon (1821–1906). She experimented with flowers and plants massed in blocks of colour: blue, gold, grey, orange and green gardens. She found that no colour would long stand alone so she took immense trouble to hit upon pleasing contrasts, such as a bed of white tulips in a patch of the silver-grey, velvet leaves of *Stachys lanata* (now *Stachys byzantina*), or lilies amid rhododendrons. Few artists have laboured so extensively, so long, and so successfully as Miss Jekyll at a task which she herself said, had taken her 'half a lifetime merely to find out what is best worth doing and a good slice of another half to puzzle out the ways of doing it'. She described it as 'painting with living plants'.

Within a few months of her death in 1932 in her eighty-ninth year she could truthfully claim: 'If my books have any merit it is because I have never written a word that was not a record of work actually done and because I have had some early training in the fine arts.' Miss Jekyll transformed Robinson's 'wild garden'. It might be called 'wild', but it had to be 'well planned', an inherent contradiction which its critics did not miss.

As Miss Jekyll was at the height of her fame and popularity, an architect, Sir Reginald Blomfield, took a diametrically opposite line to the wild garden of Robinson. In his little book, *The Formal Garden in England* (1902), he trenchantly

The charming modern English garden of Daneway in Gloucestershire with its lawn, yew trees, herbaceous borders and background of varied trees

advocated old Renaissance styles and delivered a resolute attack upon the landscape gardeners and all their works. 'People with a feeling for design and order', he wrote, 'will prefer the formal garden, while the landscape system, as it requires no knowledge of design, appeals to the average person who knows what he likes if he does not know anything else.' He scorned 'the vaunted naturalness of landscape gardening' as 'a sham'.

At the end of the nineteenth century there were very few old formal gardens left in England but some survived in Scotland, described by H. Inigo Triggs in *The Formal Gardens of England and Scotland* in 1902. The many links with Italy, with Italian art and literature, notably through their study of Dante, which the English aristocracy and intellectually inclined people preserved, ensured a continuing lively interest in Renaissance-style gardens. Triggs' larger book on *The Art of Garden Design in Italy* in 1906 stressed the architectural aspect of garden design, the stonework, foundations, terraces and garden ornaments. Nobody

gave more passionate devotion and energy to the effort to recapture and to impart the spirit and inspiration of Italian formal gardens than Sir George Sitwell, who condensed his strong opinions into an excellent small volume *On the Making of Gardens* (1909), which had a wide influence.

The upshot of the long story of change and development in garden styles has thus been a mixed medley of styles with every kind of revival and adaptation from the past. In this respect it shares common qualities with painting, music, architecture, dancing, poetry, drama, literature and generally with every kind of aesthetic activity. What the development of gardens signifies in the rise of civilization and culture must be included within the whole panorama of human history, an immense task beyond the scope of any single volume. Many of its aspects that have had to be omitted here can merely be mentioned as eminently deserving of inclusion. There is the story of the later creation of public gardens and open spaces in London and other great cities, a theme closely allied to the contribution of gardens to individual physical and mental health. Herb gardens, 'physic gardens', have a longer story with which that of gardens and gastronomic delights should be linked in modern pleasure-seeking societies. Gardens everywhere prosper or fail according to the degree of knowledge and skill possessed by their creators, their owners and those entrusted with their maintenance. No better source of such wisdom exists than that offered at relatively trifling cost to anyone willing to pay the small annual subscription that sustains great garden societies, notably the Royal Horticultural Society, England, and their allied specialized societies devoted to the culture of single flowers such as roses, carnations, delphiniums, orchids, chrysanthemums, fuchsias, dahlias and others.

These and many other topics deserve fuller treatment. Garden art in France after Le Nôtre, for example, was affected by the vogue of the 'English garden' for a time before the catastrophe of the French Revolution. In recent years there have been noteworthy revivals of the classic French style perfected by Le Nôtre. In Germany and Austria, where gardens developed later than in France or the Netherlands, a considerable scientific interest became evident from the seventeenth century onwards.

In Russia, Eastern Europe and North America human ingenuity grapples skilfully and with good taste with the stern task of minimizing the severe restrictions by which harsh climatic conditions limit gardening. In such countries, where trees are bare over the long winters, gardening art is displayed by selecting and blending evergreens and trees whose bark varies in colour and tone, to make an aesthetically satisfying spectacle. European immigrants brought memories of already developed, traditional garden styles with them to North America, South Africa, Australia, Tasmania and New Zealand. Specimens of such early English domestic gardens have been painstakingly and lovingly recreated in Williamsburg, Virginia, to contrast with the immense gardens lavishly created elsewhere in that great North American continent in more recent times.

Over many areas of the globe fine gardens have been made, notably in the South American continent, hardly known in Western Europe apart from casual references in travellers' tales. It can only be guessed therefore, how far the distinction between small ideational gardens of bare utility, larger architecturally planned, idealist, formal gardens, and the colourful, romantic, 'wild' gardens of sensuous delight exist or may have existed in their history. It seems more likely that today's eclectic mixture of styles is everywhere predominant. All, everywhere, are aided by the great botanic gardens, of which that at Kew, near London, is one of the earliest and most famous.

OPPOSITE The gentle climate of Logan, on the west coast of Scotland, has enabled exotic plants to flourish in this beautiful formally designed garden

The Americas became a hunting ground for new plants for Europe very soon after their discovery. 'North America,' said Loudon writing in 1834, before Europe was able to draw freely upon the vast plant wealth of China and the Far East, 'has supplied more valuable materials for ornamental gardening than all the rest of the world put together.' Not that the ancient civilizations of Central and South America had lacked all interest in gardening. The Aztecs lavished upon flowers a passion and a devotion which still shine forth in the few remaining scraps of their literature. The fine gardens they had created in Mexico amazed their Spanish conquerors, who, however, had no more interest in them than they had shown towards the splendid gardens of the Moors in their own land.

Nothing like the ancient Mexican gardens had ever existed further north where the British first came as settlers. Unlike the Spaniards, they brought with them that love of gardens which some generations of their forebears had begun to foster in England and which they were to pass on as an enduring force in the cultural life of their new home. Their immediate need was to grow food in order to survive, so the production of vegetables, herbs and fruits was their first objective. All around them were splendid flowers, trees and shrubs. Magnolias, tulip trees, dogwood, rhododendrons and others lent glory to the spring while the long, sunlit Fall was ablaze for weeks with glorious colours more vivid and more lasting than anything they had known at home. Virginia seemed a veritable Garden of Eden.

Yet, as the emigrants gazed in wonder and delight at the scarlet, lemon-yellow, orange and brown of the maples, beech, dogwood, oaks and chestnut, many hearts still lay over the waste of waters. So roses, hollyhocks, honeysuckle, primroses, cowslips and violets were soon brought to grace a few seventeenth-century gardens on the eastern seaboard. There also came Dutch and Germans bringing tulips, a keen garden sense and a yet greater capacity for unremitting work on the land, as anyone who has been through Lancaster County, Pennsylvania, is unlikely to forget. The French settlers in Montreal long continued to astonish travellers in the depth of the fierce Canadian winter by the roses, carnations and pelargoniums glowing with colour against the snow as they shone forth from front parlour windows, where they were kept alive by the strong heat of stoves and by constant tending.

By the end of the eighteenth century, American gardens were becoming more numerous, more extensive and more elaborately planned. Yet progress was slow, for in the early-nineteenth century not more than four or five nursery gardeners existed in New England. Their livelihood depended upon the exports they were able to send to Europe rather than upon the domestic market. If there were to be gardens, a much greater effort was essential than was necessary in England. Plants that survive the coldest English winters, such as box, laurel, ivy and roses, must be defended by elaborate precautions in the frozen ground of winter in New England, where also the swift, hot spring can suddenly be blighted by a renewal of arctic blasts from the north-west.

Pleasure gardening slowly made headway. The estate of Dr David Hosack (1769–1835), Hyde Park, on the Hudson river, a pioneer botanic garden, drew rapturous praise from Mrs Frances Trollope in 1832. She was also struck by 'the pretty villas and stately mansions' on Manhattan Island with their lawns running down to the North and East rivers. Cottage gardens were never developed generally as in England. After three years in the United States, another traveller described them in 1833 as 'universally of the most slovenly description and full of weeds'.

OPPOSITE The hanging terraces of Powis Castle in Wales offer superb views; this spectacular early 18th-century garden with its numerous statues, and wide variety of plants and shrubs is one of the few to survive almost unchanged to modern times

A view of the fruit garden, with its espaliered apple and pear trees, of the Governor's Palace at Williamsburg, Virginia, lovingly restored to its original colonial appearance

None but resolute gardeners would have accepted the challenge of the New England climate. It led to a somewhat greater formality in garden design which was favoured also by tradition and by the need to provide a contrast with the wild, unkempt scenery of the vast open spaces. Native evergreens had to be given a large place if the garden was not to look bare and barren in the winter.

Devoted efforts in our own times have been put into the reconstruction of some of the old gardens of colonial days, nowhere with more conspicuous results than in Williamsburg, the ancient capital of Virginia. George Washington's garden at Mount Vernon has been restored by the Ladies Association of Mount Vernon; the Pennsylvania Society of Colonial Dames has undertaken the gardens at Stenton, while individual enthusiasts have been active, such as Mr and Mrs Stephen Pell, who re-made the King's Garden at Fort Ticonderoga.

Gardening in the grand manner was less difficult in the South and on the Pacific coast after the opening of the Oregon trail and the settlement of the North-Western States. The luxuriant plant growth of the Carolinas, Georgia and Florida is often used with immense effect. After the wreckage and chaos of the Civil War were slowly overcome, gardens of breathtaking splendour were re-created in these Southern States. Native and exotic flowering trees and shrubs provide wondrous scenes. For many years past any traveller without an advance reservation would be lucky to find a bed in any hotel when the resplendent glories of

the Japanese cherries foam over Potomac Park in Washington; when the blazing furnaces of azaleas and the magnolia gardens of Charleston subdue in wonder all who see them, banishing all thoughts and memories of winter's gloom and chill. Then, as the visitors depart, after too short a spring, huge chestnut and other trees are quickly in full leaf and flower, creating black caverns of shade beneath, a welcome refuge from the brilliance and heat of the sun.

Where rewards can be so great, it is not surprising that an upsurge of gardening enthusiasm, in more affluent times, has matched the expansion of the United States. The Pennsylvania Horticultural Society had been founded in 1827 and two years later the Massachusetts Horticultural Society began, both pioneers in a movement which had begun in 1790 and was to spread slowly throughout the North American continent. Andrew Jackson Downing (1815–1852) was working as America's first landscape designer between 1825 and 1852. Two years before his tragic death in a fire at sea, he had taken into partnership Calvert Vaux, a young architect he had met in England. Together they designed many houses and gardens in Long Island and along the Hudson River. Landscape gardening in the Middle West had a doughty champion in H. W. S. Cleveland (1814–1900), whose *Landscape Architecture as applied to the wants of the West* (1873) was as remarkable for its far-sighted vision of future greatness as for its trenchant denunciation of the tragically missed opportunities of the past.

Geraniums fill the urns on the terrace and steps of the garden at Old Westbury, Long Island; an endowment by the J. S. Phipps Foundation has enabled the beauty and charm of this early 20th-century garden to be preserved for future generations

OVERLEAF Middleton Place, Charleston, South Carolina, the first garden in America to have been landscaped, in 1741. Spanish moss, a feature of most Southern gardens, trails from the trees around the lakes in front of the rice-mill which dates to pre-revolutionary days

213

The great name in later-nineteenth-century American park and garden design was Olmsted. The firm of Olmsted Brothers, formed in 1898, was founded on the reputation gained by Frederick Law Olmsted, who had known Downing. After a varied career, which had included foreign travel and authorship, he joined forces with Vaux and in 1857–1858 was appointed architect-in-chief for the new Central Park in New York. His great garden at Biltmore, North Carolina, made for Cornelius Vanderbilt, still remains. When he died in 1903, the firm was continued by his nephew and stepson, John Charles Olmsted (1852–1920). Many public parks, public fairs and private gardens were designed by them and their example stimulated others to become landscape gardeners.

A larger book than this would be necessary to attempt merely to describe some of the gardens of the United States and the many activities centred upon them. Community garden clubs and societies following the examples of Pennsylvania and Massachusetts now exist in every State of the Union. They often federate many county and specialist clubs and societies, so bringing together tens of thousands of garden enthusiasts. As in Great Britain, there are many societies enrolling gardeners who are specially devoted to a particular plant, flower, shrub or tree. Such is the huge extent of the United States and so varied is its climate that these specialist clubs and societies range from Amaryllis, Begonia, African Violet, Cactus and Succulent Societies in New Mexico, Arizona, California, Colorado and other Southern States, to Chrysanthemum, Gladioli, Daffodil and Dahlia societies in Northern States. Most States have Orchid Societies, Camellia Societies and there are Hibiscus Societies also; all of which testify to the existence of many private glass-houses and conservatories.

In addition to these general and specialized groups of garden and plant lovers there are many scientific, botanical societies, concentrating upon research and the growth and development of knowledge rather than in spreading and sharing it as garden clubs mostly concentrate upon doing. So there is a wide range of magazines, journals, bulletins, as well as books, on all aspects of garden interest, work and knowledge. Then there are many trade and commercial organizations of garden suppliers such as nurserymen, seedsmen, florists and so forth. A special resource which few other countries possess upon a comparable scale are the 'All-America Selections' to which camellias, gladioli, chrysanthemums, roses and other flowers and vegetables may be sent for testing, comparing and assessing. In this way standards can be determined of the qualities of the vast number of varieties grown in any part of the country.

Realization of the direct and potentially immense contribution of gardens to cultural life may not be very explicit, but that it exists, whether subconsciously or intuitively, is evident in the zeal with which energies in every State of the great American Union, almost in every county, are currently put into the cultivation, maintenance and creation of splendid gardens. The boldness, energy and efficiency with which gardens are designed, created and transformed in the United States continues to impress European visitors, who are amazed, for example, when they see huge trees being transported often over long distances, to confer an air of established maturity upon many a new North American garden. Blending influences from Europe generally, the landscape gardeners were able, in the varied climatic zones of the vast American continent, to create many glorious gardens. Their most successful achievements still predominantly reflect European precedents in garden design but they often succeed in achieving richer effects. Their success is in part due to the more than princely resources which are lavished upon some favoured sites, such as the gardens of the Du Pont family

in Delaware, notably Longwood, which was constructed and endowed with a magnificence that Louis XIV might envy.

Admirable gardens on a smaller scale in countless townships, suburbs or country estates have been created, enjoyed and subsequently transformed as they are acquired by new owners. Such was the splendid azalea garden in Worcester, Massachusetts, made by the late Professor Pitirim A. Sorokin, founder and first Director of the Department of Sociology at Harvard University. It is mentioned here not only because for years it has drawn admiring visitors, some of whom have been stimulated to make such gardens themselves, but also because in his great study of development and change in social and cultural life Professor Sorokin defined the three great classes of values, the 'ideational', 'idealistic' and 'sensate', that have been dominant at various periods in cultural history.

In Canada where the climatic range is greatest between East and West, gardens often seem to be English gardens transported to North America. Particularly was this true of some towns such as Victoria, British Columbia, which the guidebooks used to assert with great plausibility to be 'more British than Basingstoke'. Its Butchart Gardens, with a formal Italian garden, a Japanese garden, and its splendid displays of roses, are justly renowned. In the extreme east in Labrador, Nova Scotia and the Province of Quebec, cold climatic conditions in winter

The site of The Huntingdon Botanical Gardens, California, in 1880; these gardens, among the most important of the many American botanical gardens, specialize in rare and precious plants including cacti and water lilies

naturally limit gardening, but the area is notable for its wild flowers. In Montreal and its suburbs, however, there are many large houses and gardens. The Botanic Garden there is relatively recent, having been created between 1932 and 1936. Earlier botanic gardens are at Hamilton, Ontario (1930–1941), and Vancouver, British Columbia (1912).

If visitors from Europe feel the lack in some North American cities of the numerous public gardens to which they are accustomed at home, all must be struck by the care and skill devoted to many miles of motor-roads around large towns which have been converted by clever planting and design into veritable landscaped parkways. Such effects, combined with the superlative welcome and hospitality of many an American and Canadian garden-lover, make the American continent seem the last stronghold of gardening in the grand manner.

Much of what has so briefly been said above in a general way about the gardens of North America could be repeated about the gardens of the South American continent. In more detail, however, the situation is very different. There are fewer private gardens. Public gardens added dignity and charm to Buenos Aires where they were generously provided, as in the Plaza Mayo, Plaza Libertad and others, to give them their names, at the end of the nineteenth century. Many of their cities and streets and avenues were tree-lined as New York used to be. The Botanical Garden 'Carlos Thays' in Buenos Aires was founded in 1912.

Garden literature is the poorer for the lack of a full history and description of the gardens in Latin America, where climate and vegetation are often more favourable than in the North. From Mexico to the Argentine, flower markets offer gorgeous spectacles in many a town and city, where flowers are a great joy. Gardens there were already capturing the eyes of tourists in the latter half of the nineteenth century. 'What a lovely flowery land Chile is,' wrote Mrs Brassey in October 1876. 'The whole air is perfumed with roses ... they formed hedgerows on either side of the road, in many places producing the effect of a wall of pink.' To the south, climatic conditions were harsher and the natives were almost savages. Chile also suffered severely from earthquakes. Towards the end of the nineteenth century large areas of Valparaiso were in ruins. Not until the twentieth century has much advance been registered in the gardens of private houses. In Brazil a botanical garden was opened in 1808, since when it worthily sustains its reputation. That of Mexico City in Chapultepec Park was established in 1923. When South America's gardens are given the recognition they merit, the claim for a greater place for gardens in social and cultural history will be very effectively reinforced.

Then also the power and influence of the cultural creativity of Renaissance Europe would become as apparent in many gardens in remote parts of the world, whose very existence was unknown to Petrarch or Michelangelo, as it is in all other manifestations of aesthetic and intellectual life. Europe was certainly not the only continent in which garden art flourished, but it was from Europe, and very largely from the British Isles, that many other lands first learned what needs to be done if mankind, in the words of Francis Bacon, is 'to garden finely'.

The nineteenth century witnessed that tremendous increase in population and the concentration of more and more people in or near large towns, which has been a major factor in the economic revolution of modern times. Generations of city-dwellers grew up with little or no direct, personal experience of garden art.

A massive increase in the number of people demanding housing, roads and

OPPOSITE 'Paul's Lemon Pillar', one of the most beautiful of all climbing roses, blossoming on an arched doorway at Sissinghurst Castle, Kent

other land-consuming facilities threatens to make town-planners' dreams completely unrealizable. It will be ominous for future generations if solutions to the tough problem faced by the town-planner obscure the scope for personal effort and expression which garden art affords. Indeed in this respect gardening ranks high among cultural activities, many of which tend in modern times to be receptive rather than active and creative. Garden art can and should elicit active endeavour rather than passive receptivity. Not of course that passive delight in gardens and their products is in any way to be decried. The sight of a tree through the window, or a crocus, hyacinth or rose in a pot can be intense, and a splendid garden or park such as Wisley, Bodnant, Sissinghurst, Sheffield Park, Vaux-le-Vicomte, Villandry or Versailles, will provide constructive inspiration as well as memories for a lifetime.

Another contemplative and rewarding aesthetic experience arising from garden art, involving also personal activity, is the enthusiasm for the art of floral arrangement. Bearing no resemblance to the esoteric, quasi-mystical attitudes of Japanese flower ceremonies, formal flower arrangement has an aesthetic of its own giving scope for a personal style of which the late Miss Constance Spry was for some years probably the best internationally known exponent. Equally significant is the increasingly vast number of flowers and pot plants bought annually without any such conscious striving for specially artistic display.

Because gardening is a form of art, a demand has been heard that it too should now conform with fashionable trends. One critic who called for radical change, roundly declared that all styles of gardening 'should be thrown out like old clothes' and that with them should go all ideas about pattern, colour, decoration and ornament. 'The garden is dead' was his message, referring presumably to conventional lawns, flower-beds and herbaceous borders and to the gardens of Robinson and Miss Jekyll as well as of Le Nôtre and Loudon. Gardens, it was proclaimed, must become 'functional' and 'expressive of our times'.

There is only one way in which gardens can be 'functional' and that is by making the best possible use of the materials of nature, to produce flowers, lawns, shrubs, trees, fruits and vegetables so as to yield pleasure and recreation as well as general mental and psychological satisfactions. Fundamentally, 'functional' is not a cultural value but a utilitarian concept always subordinate to some end or purpose, some true value which utility should serve. Gardeners today as in the past, make the most of what opportunities they have and introduce, as they always have done, modifications in traditional patterns according to their own ideas of what an artistically contrived garden should be. As John Parkinson said about garden design in a period of rising sensate culture during the seventeenth century 'to prescribe one form for every man to follow were too great presumption and folly: for every man will please his own fancy'. Such an opinion could never be proclaimed in an 'ideational' culture.

Pessimistic fears for the future of gardening as it has been traditionally cultivated in free societies clearly are not without ample foundation. Nevertheless the fact and the strength of tradition exists to encourage optimists to persevere in their support for it. Their faith will be fortified when it is realized that gardening is, or should be, prominent among the arts without which civilization would not endure.

Garden art is far more vulnerable than painting, architecture, music, literature, to the ravages of time. After even a few years the growth, decay and replacement of its original living contents can greatly change its original conception. The ele-

220

ments of garden art are everywhere the same. They include the shape, proportion and design of the garden; the disposition of trees, shrubs, flowers and herbs to allow for their time of flowering, rate of growth, their length of life, their colour, shape and height at various seasons, their scents, their suitability for different soils, their need for fertilizers, their protection from insects, birds, disease and premature decay. Change over time demands felicity in their arrangement, in conjunction with static elements such as lawns, paths and water; not forgetting the question of possible fountains, stone ornaments, pavilions or other garden buildings.

To construct a garden worthy of the name clearly makes great demands upon memory, foresight, imagination, taste and discernment. An almost infinite number of potential variables are involved. All living things have so many distinct qualities that the limited number of notes of music or of colours of the spectrum and on the artist's palette seem, in comparison, to be of an almost elemental simplicity.

Through their beauty and charm gardens, like painting, music and other arts, find their place in general aesthetics. Those with philosophical interests will seek to penetrate yet further by enquiring into the nature and essence of 'beauty' and 'charm'. When Ogden, Richards and Wood in their *Foundations of Aesthetics* in 1922 surveyed sixteen attempts which had been made to track down the source of that elusive quality of beauty, they found that only two theories gave up the enquiry as hopeless by declaring that beauty is an intrinsic, unanalysable 'something'. Seven of the other theories tried to find beauty in some objective factor such as the imitation of nature, the exploitation of a medium, the production of some utility or illusion. Or they said that beauty is a revelation either of truth, of the spirit of nature, of an ideal or merely of the typical. The other seven theories about the source of beauty concentrated not upon these impersonal realities but upon personal, subjective and psychological explanations, such as the experience of pleasure, of emotion, or empathy or of heightened vitality. Finally 'synaesthesis' was proposed by the authors, which seems too near explaining beauty or aesthetic value by its own term. However, the authors gave most weight to just that experience of harmony and equilibrium to be achieved through 'synaesthesis'.

As a spectator's theory or explanation of beauty, 'synaesthesis' has much to commend it, but is it able to explain the devotion of a gardener or of any other practising artist to his craft? W. P. Wright had already said in 1903 that 'a sense of the beautiful springs out of love. Taste in gardening is educated love. Affection gives the impulse, knowledge the guidance. Love is the road, education is the lamp that lights it.'

In whatever cultural epoch he may chance to live, the gardener can achieve the often intense satisfaction of an artist as he devotes himself to his trees, shrubs, flowers, and lawns in wholehearted absorption in the work in hand, forgetful of his personal worries and concerns. As an art form, gardening has a continuity and a stability which changing cultural patterns cannot shatter. Amid the diversity of cultures for which it provides a connecting link, with its flowers, fruits and other delights, gardening has less need of interpreters and translators than many other art forms. As an art of peace it speaks a universal language. On a more exalted plane, Sir George Sitwell's praise should make everyone long for a garden: 'Gardens have coloured every dream of future life, every hope of happiness in this, and he who can make them more beautiful has helped to exalt the sentiment of religion, poetry and love.' Any art that can enhance life

OPPOSITE The canal bordered with beds of herbaceous plants leads to the gabled Pin Mill at Bodnant, north Wales, a beautifully designed garden full of colour and splendid views

with meaning and value of that order has an assured and honoured position in cultural life.

Inevitably incomplete, as any summary survey must remain of the nature of the aesthetic satisfactions mankind has derived from gardens down the ages, speculative and hypothetical as any attempt to account for their changing nature and its motives must be, still more hazardous any attempt to predict their future, this rapid, cursory glance may have been worth taking if it is able to evoke some recognition of the reality and intensity with which garden art has always, and is still being, pursued. Alike in the length of its history, in the vast number of its practitioners, and in the time, energy and resources willingly expended upon it, the fine art of gardening, both in its individual and social appeal, can be seen to take high place among those enduring, creative, rewarding, artistic enterprises characteristic of the age-old pursuit of culture in both private and public life. It will always be honoured as one of the fine products and supports of civilization among all peoples all over the world.

BIBLIOGRAPHY

Vast as the writing about gardens has been, very little of it has been specifically devoted to the relation of garden arts to general cultural and social history or to aesthetic principles of which gardens afford many examples. Of the following, most have been consulted or quoted. Many have bibliographies.

1 Gardens in the Dawn of Civilization

E. Bielsalski, 'Urblumen der Menscheit', *Antike und Abendland* XI (1962) 63

E. Bonavia, *The Flora of the Assyrian Monuments and its Outcome* (Constable, 1894)

J. H. Breasted, *Ancient Records of Egypt* (University of Chicago Press, 1906)

British Museum Guides Egyptian Collections; Assyrian Collections

Sir E. A. Wallis Budge, *The Divine Origin of the Herbalist* (Society of Herbalists, London, 1928)

E. Carter and A. C. Mace, *The Tomb of Tutankhaman* (Cassell, 1923–33)

Grace Crowfoot and Louise Baldensperger, *From Cedar to Hyssop. A Study of Folklore of Plants in Palestine* (Sheldon Press, 1932)

Egyptian Exploration Society: Reports on Excavations in Egypt

A. Erman, *Literature of the Ancient Egyptians*, trs. A. M. Blackman (Methuen, 1927)

E. Frankfort, 'On Egyptian Art', *Journal of Egyptian Archaeology* XVIII (1932) 39–41; *Birth of Civilisation in the Near East* (Williams and Norgate, 1951); *Art and Architecture of the Ancient Orient* (Penguin, 1954)

H. R. H. Hall, *Babylonian and Assyrian Sculpture in the British Museum* (G. van Oest, Paris, 1928)

W. C. Hayes, *The Scepter of Egypt* (Harper & the Metropolitan Museum, New York, 1953)

C. H. W. Johns, *Babylonian and Assyrian Laws. Contracts and Letters* (Clark, 1904)

C. Joret, 'Les Plantes dans l'Antiquité et au Moyen Age' (1904) *Journal of Egyptian Archaeology*

L. Keimer, *Die Gartenpflanzen im alten Agyptes* (Hoffmann und Campe, 1924)

Luise Klebs, *Die Reliefs und Malereien des mittleren Reiches VII–XVII Dyn.* (1922); *Die Reliefs und Malereien des neuen Reiches* (1934); Heidelberger Akad. d. Wissenschaften Phil. Hist. Kl. 6. 9.

K. Lange and M. Hirmer, *Egyptian Architecture, Sculpture, Painting* (Phaidon, 1956)

Laurent-Tackholm, *Faraos Blomster* (Natur och Kultur, Stockholm, 1951)

I. Löw, *Die Flora der Juden* (R. Löwit, Vienna, 1928–34)

A. Lucas, *Ancient Egyptian Materials & Industries* (Arnold, 1962)

G. Maspero, *The Dawn of Civilization* ed A. H. Sayce (SPCK, 1894); *The Struggle of the Nations* (SPCK, 1896); *The Passing of Empires* (SPCK, 1900)

Metropolitan Museum, New York, *Reports* and *Bulletin*

H. N. and Anna L. Moldenke, *Plants of the Bible* (Chronica Botanica Co., Mass., 1952)

A. Parrot, *Sumer* (Thames & Hudson, 1960); *Nineveh and Babylon* (Thames & Hudson, 1961)

M. Pearlman, *Adam to Daniel. Historic Sites in Israel* (Macmillan, New York, 1962)

G. E. Post and J. E. Dinsmore, *Flora of Syria, Palestine and Sinai* (American University Press, Beirut 1933)

J. B. Pritchard, *Ancient Near Eastern Texts* (Princetown University Press, 1955)

R. W. Rogers, *Cuneiform Parallels to the Old Testament* (Eaton & Mains, New York, 1912)

A. E. Rüthy, *Die Pflanzen und ihre Teile in bibischerhebräischen Sprachgebrauch* (Berne, 1942)

R. C. Thompson, *Dictionary of Assyrian Botany* (British Academy, 1949); *Monograph on Assyrian Vegetable Drugs* (Luzac, 1924)

F. Woenig, *Pflanzen im alten Ägypten* (A. Heitz, Leipzig, 1897)

Sir C. L. Woolley, *Excavations at Ur* (Benn, 1954)

2 The Creators of Western Culture

Sir C. Allbutt, *Greek Medicine in Rome* (Macmillan, 1921)

J. André, *Lexique des Termes de Botanique en Latin* (Klincksieck, 1956); *Notes de Lexicographie Botanique Grecque* (Champion, 1958)

S. C. Atchley, *Wild Flowers of Attica* (Oxford University Press, 1929)

A. L. P. de Candolle, *Origin of Cultivated Plants* (Routledge, 1886)

W. Capelle, 'Der Garten der Theophrast' in *Festschrift für Friedrich Zucker* (1954)

A. Carnoy, *Dictionnaire Etymologique des Noms Grecs de Plantes* (Louvain, Publications Universitaires, 1959)

R. Carpenter, *The Aesthetic Basis of Greek Art* (Indiana University Press, 1959)

Sir A. Evans, *The Palace of Minos* Macmillan, 1928–36)

L. R. Farnell, *The Cults of the Greek States* (Oxford University Press, 1896)

E. S. Foster, 'Trees and Plants in Homer' *Classical Review* L (1936) 97–104

V. Hehn, *The Wandering of Plants and Animals*, trs. J. C. Stallybrass (Sonnenschein, 1888)

B. Laufer, *Sino-Iranica, Chinese Contributions to the History of Civilization in Ancient Iran with special reference to the History of cultivated Plants and Products*, Chicago Field Museum of Natural History Publn 201

S. Marinatos, *Crete and Mycenae* (Thames & Hudson, 1960)

M. Möbius, 'Pflanzenbilder der Minoischen Kunst in botan-Betrachtung', *Jahrb. Deutsch. Archäol. Inst.* (1933) 48

J. Murr, *Die Pflanzenwelt in der Griecheschen Mythologie* (Innsbruck, 1890)

Olck, 'Gartenbau' in Pauly-Wissowa, *Real-Enzyk d. klassichen Altertunswissenschaft* VII I

R. Strömberg, *Griechische Pflanzennamen* (Elander, Göteborg, 1940)

Sir W. Thistleton-Dyer, 'Index of Plants' in *History of Plants* by Theophrastus, trs. Sir A. Hort (Loeb Library)

Dorothy Thompson and R. E. Griswold, *Garden Lore of Ancient Athens* (American School of Classical Studies, Princeton NJ, 1963)

W. R. Turrill, *Plant Life in the Balkan Peninsula* (Oxford University Press, 1938)

Roman writings on agricultural and horticultural subjects are available with English translations in the Loeb Classical Library which has editions of Cato, Cicero's *Letters*, Varro, Columella, Pliny's *Natural History*, Pliny's *Letters*, Vitruvius.

B. Cunliffe, *Fishbourne: A Roman Palace and its Garden* (Thames & Hudson, 1971)

S. Dill, *Roman Society from Nero to Marcus Aurelius* (Macmillan, 1905); *Roman Society in the Last Century of the Western Empire* (Macmillan, 1925)

L. Friedländer, *Roman Life and Manners under the Early Empire* (Routledge, 1940)

Sir. A. Geikie, *The Love of Nature among the Romans* (Murray, 1912)

P. Grimal, *Les Jardins Romains* (Boccard, 1943)

T. J. Haarhoff, 'Virgil's Garden of Flowers', *Greece and Rome* v (1958) 67–8

A. H. M. Jones, *The Later Roman Empire* (Blackwell, 1964)

J. Levy, 'Contributions to the Identification of some Trees and Shrubs in Classical Literature', *Isis* 52 (1961) 78–86

J. Lindsay, *Leisure and Pleasure in Roman Egypt* (Muller, 1965)

G. Nash, *Pictorial Dictionary of Ancient Rome* (Zwemmer, 1961/2)

Palladius, *Opus Agriculturae* (Teubner, 1898)

S. B. Platner and T. Ashby, *Topographical Dictionary of Ancient Rome* (Oxford University Press, 1929)

M. Rostovtzeff, *Social and Economic History of the Roman Empire* (Oxford University Press, 1926); *Social and Economic History of the Hellenistic World* (Oxford University Press, 1953)

J. Stannard, 'Pliny and Roman Botany', *Isis* 56 (1965) 420–5

S. Tolkowsky, *Hesperides: A Study in the Culture and Use of Citrus Fruits* (Bale Sons & Curnow, 1938)

3 Gardens and the Great Religions

BYZANTIUM

D. V. Ainalov, *The Hellenic Origins of Byzantine Art* (Rutgers University Press, 1961)

K. J. Basmadjian, 'L'Identification des Noms de Plantes du Codex Constantinopolitanus de Discoride', *Journal Asiatique* (1938) 577–621

N. H. Baynes and H. St L. B. Moss, eds, *Byzantium* (Clarendon Press, 1948)

J. Beckwith, *The Art of Constantinople* (Phaidon, 1968)

L. Brehier, *Le Monde Byzantine* (Albin Michel, 1948–50)

C. Diehl, *Manuel d'art byzantin* (Picard, 1925–6); *Byzantium Greatness and Decline*, trs. Walford (Rutgers University Press, 1957)

Cambridge Medieval History iv part ii 'The Byzantine Empire' (Cambridge University Press, 1967)

Dioscorides, *The Great Herbal of Dioscorides*, trs. J. Goodyer, ed R. T. Gunter (Oxford University Press, 1934)

'Geoponica', Cassianus Bassus, *Geoponicorum sive de Re Rustica libri* xx, eds P. Needham and I. N. Niclas (Leipzig, 1781) also ed. H. Beckh (Leipzig, 1895)

G. Mathew, *Byzantine Aesthetics* (Murray, 1963)

P. A. Michelis, 'Comments on Gervase Mathew's "Byzantine Aesthetics"', *Brit. Jnl of Aesthetics* 4 (1964) 253–262

D. Talbot Rice, *The Art of the Byzantine Era* (Thames & Hudson, 1964)

MEDIEVAL EUROPE

Alicia Amherst, *History of Gardening in England* (1910)

G. Baskerville, *English Monks and the Suppression of the Monasteries* (Cape, 1937)

H. S. Bennett, *Life on the English Manor 1150–1400* (Cambridge University Press)

Cambridge Medieval History, Cambridge Economic History. Both series contain full bibliographies

Sir Frank Crisp, *Medieval Gardens* (Lane, 1924)

A. Dopsch, *Die Wirtschaftsentwicklung der Karolingerzeit* (1921)

H. Fischer, *Mittelalterliche Pflanzenkunde* (Münchnerdrucke, 1929)

Glanzenmüller, *Das Naturgefühl im Mittelalter* (Teubner, 1914)

C. Joret, *La Rose dans l'Antiquité et au Moyen Age* (Paris, 1892); *Les Plantes dans l'Antiquité et au Moyen Age* (Bouillon, 1904)

E. Martin Saint-Léon, *Histoire des Corporations de Métiers* (1941) 200n, 240, 245, 402, 438, 499, 530

B. H. Schlicher van Bath, *The Agrarian History of Western Europe AD 500–1850* (Arnold, 1963)

Smith Toulmin, ed. *English Guilds*, Early English Text Society (1870)

Thos. Tusser, *His Good Points of Husbandry*, ed Dorothy Hartley (Country Life, n.d.)

P. Vallet, *L'Idée du Beau dans la Philosophie de Saint Thomas d'Aquin* (1887)

Strabo Walahfrid, *Hortulus*, trs. R. Payne (Hunt Botanical Library, Pittsburgh, 1966)

C. Welch, *History of the Worshipful Company of Gardeners* (1900)

PERSIAN AND MOHAMMEDAN

K. A. C. Cresswell, *A Bibliography of the Architecture, Arts and Crafts of Islam* (American University at Cairo Press, 1961)

J. Dickie, 'The Hispano-Arab Garden, its Philosophy and Function', *Bulletin of the School of Oriental Studies* xxxi (1968) 237–248

I. C. N. Forrestier, 'Jardins Arabes', *France-Maroc* ii 69–77

Hitti, *History of the Arabs* (Macmillan, 1956)

B. Laufer, 'Sino-Iranica: Chinese contributions to the History of Civilization in Ancient Iran with Special Reference to the History of Cultivated Plants and Products', *Field Museum of Natural History*, Anthropological Series vol. xv no. 3 (Chicago, 1919)

Bibliography

A. U. Pope, *A Survey of Persian Art* (Oxford University Press 1938–9)

D. N. Wilber, *Persian Gardens and Garden Pavilions* (Tuttle, 1962)

INDIA

Mildred Archer, 'Gardens of Delight', *Apollo* (Sept. 1968) 172–84 *British Drawings in the India Office Library* (HMSO 1967)

Jeannine Auboyer, *Daily Life in Ancient India 200 BC–AD 700* (Weidenfeld & Nicolson, 1965)

Sri Aurobindo, *Eight Upanishads* (Ashram Pondicherry, 1960)

Babur, *Memoirs of Zehir-ed-Din Muhammed Babur*, trs. J. Leyden and W. Erskine, rev. by Sir Lucas King (Oxford University Press, 1921)

Bhagavad Gita or *The Lord's Song*, trs. L. D. Barnett (Dent, 1905)

Cambridge History of India vols I–IV

O. Caroe, *The Pathans 550 BC–AD 1957* (Macmillan, 1965)

J. R. Chethimattam, 'Rasa, the Soul of Indian Art', *International Philosophical Quarterly* vol. V (1970) 44–62

Ann Hibbert, 'Collecting Wild Flowers at Ulan Bator', *Royal Central Asian Society Journal* vol. LIV (1967) 63–5

E. A. Langley, *Narrative of a Residence at the Court of Meer Ali Moorad* (London, 1860)

Yutang Lin, ed. *The Wisdom of India* (Michael Joseph, 1949)

R. C. Majumdar, *Outline of Ancient Indian History and Civilisation* (Calcutta, 1927)

J. W. McCrindle, *The Invasion of India by Alexander the Great* (London, 1893); *Ancient India described by Ptolemy* (Calcutta, Thacker Spink, 1885); *Ancient India described by Megasthenes and Arrian* (Calcutta, Thacker Spink, 1877)

R. Mookerjii, *Local Government in Ancient India* (Clarendon Press, 1919)

F. Moussa-Mahmoud, *Sir William Jones and the Romantics* (Cairo, 1962)

G. Patterson, *The Gardens of the Great Moghuls* (Thames & Hudson, 1972)

S. Percy-Lancaster, *An Amateur in an Indian Garden* (Alipur, n.d.)

R. W. Pickford, 'The Psychology of Cultural Change in Painting', *Brit. Jnl of Psychology Monograph Supplements* XXVI (1943) 24–8

J. Postans, *Personal Observations on Sindh* (London, 1843)

P. Rawson, 'An Exalted Theory of Ornament. A Study in Indian Aesthetics', *Brit. Jnl of Aesthetics* vol. VII (1967) 31–46

L. Renou and J. Fillozat, *L'Inde Classique* (Payot, Paris, 1953)

Sir Thomas Roe, *Embassy to the Court of the Great Mogul 1615–1619*, ed. W. Foster, Hakluyt Soc. 2nd series no. 2 (1899)

G. Slater, *The Dravidian Element in Indian Culture* (Benn, 1924)

V. A. Smith, *Akbar the Great Mogul 1542–1605* (Oxford University Press, 1927)

Bhattcharyya Tarapada, *The Canons of Indian Art* (Kl. Mukhopadhyay, Calcutta, 1963)

The Tuzuk-i-Jahāngirī, *Memoirs of Jahangir*, trs. A. Rogers (Munshiram Manoharal, Delhi, 1968)

G. T. Vigne, *Travels in Kashmir, Ladak, Iskardo* (Colbourn, 1844)

Mrs C. M. Villiers-Stuart, *Gardens of the Great Moghals* (A. & C. Black, 1913)

Sir Francis Younghusband, *Kashmir* (A. &. C. Black, 1911)

R. C. Zaehner, *Mysticism Sacred and Profane* (Oxford University Press.)

4 Garden Arts of the Far East

Yee Chiang, *The Chinese Eye* (Methuen, 1960)

J. Conder, *Landscape Gardening in Japan* (1898, Dover, 1964)

Deutsche Ikebana Schule, *Ikebana Almanach* (Ostasiatischer Kunstverlag, Köln, 1969)

A. Ehner, *Bäume sind zu Gott die Stufen* (Japanese forestry and attitudes to Nature, gardens and flowers), (Hellmut Neureuter Wolfratshausen, 1966)

J. Harada, *The Gardens of Japan* (Studio, 1908)

H. Inn, *Chinese Houses and Gardens*, ed. Shao Chang Lee (Bonanza Books, 1950)

T. Ishimoto, *Treasury of Japanese Flower Arrangements* (Crown, 1959)

E. Kaempfer, *History of Japan*, 3 vols (Maclehose, 1906)

N. Kobayashi, *Bonsai* (Japan Travel Bureau, 1951)

N. Kudo, *Chinese Landscape Painting and Nature Poetry* (Waseda University Law Association, n.d.)

J. Needham, *Science and Civilisation in China* vol. 1 (Cambridge University Press, 1954)

D. Riesman, *Conversations in Japan* (Allen Lane, 1967)

O. Siren, *Gardens of China* (Ronald Press, 1949); *China and the Gardens of Europe of the Eighteenth Century* (Ronald Press, 1950)

Sacheverell Sitwell, *Brigade of the Brocade Sash* (Weidenfeld & Nicolson, 1959)

Ito Teiji, *The Japanese Garden: An Approach to Nature* (Yale University Press, 1972)

5 The Rule of Reason

D. R. Coffin, ed. *The Italian Garden* (Dumbarton Oaks, Washington DC, 1972)

Commissariat Général au Tourisme, *Parks and Châteaux of France* (Paris, 1960)

Commune di Firenze, *Mostra del Giardino Italiano* (1931)

M. Fouquier, *De l'Art des Jardins* (E. Paul, 1911)

Helen M. Fox, *André le Nôtre* (Batsford, 1962)

E. de Ganay, *Beaux Jardins de France* (Plon, 1950)

E. H. Combrich, *Norm and Form*, 107–121 (Phaidon, 1966)

W. L. Grant, *Neo-Latin Literature and the Pastoral* (University of North Carolina Press, 1965)

Le Nôtre et l'Art des Jardins, Catalogue de l'Exposition Bibliothèque Nationale (Paris, 1964)

A. Marie, *Jardins Français Classiques des XVII et XVIII Siècles* (Fréal, 1909)

'David Marot', *Connoisseur* (March 1949)

Georgina Masson, *Italian Gardens* (Thames & Hudson)

J. Parkinson, *Paradisi in Sole Paradisus Terrestris* (1629)

W. Robinson, *Parks and Gardens of Paris* (Murray, 1883)

J. C. Shepherd and G. A. Jellicoe, *Italian Gardens of the Renaissance* (Benn, 1925, Tiranti, 1931)

C. Th. Sørensen, *The Origin of Landscape Art* (Danish Architectural Press, 1963)

H. I. Triggs, *The Art of Garden Design in Italy* (Longmans, 1906)

6 The English Revolt

Mea Allan, *The Tradescants* (Joseph, 1964)

R. L. Arkell, *Caroline of Ansbach* (Oxford University Press, 1939)

Sir J. Banks, *Catalogus Bibliothecae historico-naturalis* (Johnson Reprint, 1965)

C. P. Barbier, *William Gilpin* (Clarendon Press, 1963)

Daines Barrington, 'On the Progress of Gardening', *Archaeologia* v (1782) 113–130

T. Blaikie, *Diary of a Scottish Gardener at the French Court at the end of the 18th Century* (Routledge, 1931)

Hon. Mrs. Evelyn Cecil (Alicia Amherst, Lady Roxley), *A History of Gardening in England*, 3rd ed. (Murray, 1910) reviewed in *Economic Review* (1896) 151–63

Sir W. Chambers, *Dissertation on Oriental Gardening* (1773)

G. Charlier, *Le Sentiment de la Nature chez les Romantiques Français 1762–1830* (Brussels, 1914)

G. Clarke, 'The Gardens of Stowe' *Apollo* xcvii (1973) 558–65

H. Colvin and J. Harris *The Country Seat* (Penguin, 1970)

E. H. M. Cox, *History of Gardening in Scotland* (Chatto, 1935)

R. Desmond and W. T. Stearn, *Dictionary of British and Irish Botanists and Horticulturists* (Taylor & Francis, 1977)

J. Gibson, 'A Short Account of Several (28) Gardens near London' in 1691, *Archaeologia* xii (1796) 181

C. J. Glacken, *Traces on the Rhodian Shore* (University of California Press, 1967)

M. Hadfield, *Gardening in Britain* (Hutchinson, 1960)

Elizabeth S. Haldane, *Scots Gardens in Olden Times 1200–1800* (Maclehose, 1931)

W. J. Hipple, *The Beautiful, the Sublime and the Picturesque in Eighteenth century British Aesthetic Theory* (Southern Illinois Press, 1957)

C. Hussey, *English Gardens and Landscape 1700–1750* (Country Life, 1967)

E. Hyams, *English Gardens* (Thames & Hudson, 1964); *'Capability' Brown and Humphry Repton* (Dent, 1971)

Gertrude Jekyll and Sir L. Weaver, *Gardens for Small Country Houses*, 6th ed. (Country Life, 1927)

Susan Lang and M. Pevsner, 'Sir William Temple and Sharawaggi', *Architectural Review* (1949) 391–3

J. C. Loudon, *An Encyclopedia of Gardening* (Longmans, 1834, 1850); *The Suburban Garden* (Longmans, 1838)

E. Malins, *English Landscaping & Literature* (Oxford University Press, 1966)

P. Miller, *The Gardener's Kalender*, 4th ed. (London, 1737)

Sir U. Price, *On the Picturesque*, ed. Sir T. D. Lauder (1842)

C. E. Raven, *English Naturalists from Neckham to Ray* (Cambridge University Press, 1947)

H. Repton, *The Landscape Gardening of H. Repton*, ed. J. C. Loudon (1840)

Eleanour S. Rhode, *The Story of the Garden* (Medici, 1932); *Oxford's College Gardens* (Jenkins, 1932); *Old English Garden Books* (Hopkinson, 1924)

Royal Horticultural Society Journals and Lindley Library

G. E. Rumphius, (nomine Plinii Indici celebris), *Herbarium Amboinense*, 6 vols (1750)

E. Smith, *The Life of Sir Joseph Banks* (Lane, 1910)

Dorothy Stroud, *Capability Brown* (Country Life, 1957); *Humphrey Repton* (Country Life, 1962)

S. Switzer, *Ichnographia Rustica or the Nobleman, Gentleman and Gardener's Recreation* (1742)

F. Thompson, *History of Chatsworth* (Country Life, 1949)

G. Thouin, *Plans raisonnés de toutes les espèces de Jardins* (1819)

H. I. Trigg, *Formal Gardens in England and Scotland* (Batsford, 1902)

H. Walpole, *Essay on Modern Gardening* (1770); *Letters*, ed. Mrs P. Toynbee (Oxford University Press, 1903, 1918)

D. Watkin, *Thomas Hope and the Neo-Classical Idea* (Murray, 1968)

T. Whately, *Observations on Modern Gardening* (1770)

K. Woodbridge, *Landscape and Antiquity: Aspects of English Culture at Stourhead 1718–1838* (Oxford University Press, 1970)

7 Gardens in Modern Times

Mea Allen, *The Hookers of Kew* (Joseph, 1967)

Sir R. Blomfield, *The Formal Garden in England* (Macmillan, 1901)

E. Bretschneider, *History of European Botanical Discoveries in China* (Samson Low, 1898; Koehler, 1935)

E. M. Butler, *The Tempestuous Prince Hermann Pückler-Muskau* (Longmans, 1929)

Marquesa de Casa Valdés, *Jardines de España* (Madrid, 1973)

Hon. Mrs Evelyn Cecil (Alicia Amherst, Lady Roxley), *London Parks and Gardens* (Constable, 1907)

Marion Cran, *Gardens in America* (Jenkins, 1933)

Joan P. Dutton, *Exploring America's Gardens* (Secker & Warburg 1959)

P. Edwards, *Trees and English Landscape* (Bell, 1962)

H. R. Fletcher, *The Story of the Royal Horticultural Society 1804–1968* (Oxford University Press, 1969)

K. Foerster, *Garten als Zauberschlüssel* (Rowohlt, 1934); *Vom grossen Welt- und Gartenspiel* (Schwinn u. Helène, 1950)

P. Geddes, *Cities in Evolution* (Williams & Norgate, 1915)

G. F. Hartlaub, *Der Gartenzwerg und seine Ahnen* (Heinz Moos, Heidelberg, 1962)

T. G. Henslow, *Suburban Gardens* (Rich & Cowan, 1934)

H. N. Hubbard and Theodora Kimball, *An Introduction to the Study of Landscape Design* (Macmillan, NY 1917)

Gertrude Jekyll, *Home and Garden* (Longman, 1900)

M. Iljin, 'Russian Parks of the Eighteenth Century', *Architectural Review* vol. 135 (1964) 101–11

Landscape Architecture, Journal of the American Society of Landscape Artists (Cambridge, Mass., 1910)

Landscape and Garden, Journal of the Institute of Landscape Artists (1934)

W. Lange, *Der Garten und seine Bepflanzung* (Kosmos, 1913)

W. H. Matthews, *Mazes and Labyrinths* (Longmans, 1922)

Max Nicholson, *The Environmental Revolution* (McGraw-Hill, 1970)

Pückler-Muskau, *Hints on Landscape Gardening*, ed. S. Parsons (Houghton Mifflin, 1917)

Bibliography

Gustav Rohlfs, *Die schönsten Garten deutschlands* (Ulmer, Stuttgart, 1967)

J. J. Sexby, *Municipal Parks, Gardens and Open Spaces of London* (Elliot Stock, 1915)

Sir G. Sitwell, *Of the Making of Gardens* (Duckworth, 1904)

J. W. Stevenson, *The Gardener's Directory* (Hanover House Garden City, New York, 1960)

Tamara Talbot Rice, *Concise History of Russian Art* (Thames & Hudson, 1963)

G. Taylor, *The Victorian Flower Garden* (Skeffington, 1952)

C. Tunnard, *Gardens in the Modern Landscape* (Architectural Press, 1938)

R. Webber, *The Early Horticulturists* (David & Charles, 1968)

W. Wroth, *London Pleasure Gardens of the Eighteenth Century* (Macmillan, 1896)

Agnes Arber, *Herbals 1470–1670* (Cambridge University Press, 1938)

Elizabeth Barlow, *Frederick Law Olmsted's New York* (Praeger, 1972)

British Journal of Aesthetics

F. W. Burbidge, *The Book of the Scented Garden* (John Lane, 1905)

W. H. Camp, V. H. Boswell and J. H. Magness, *The World in Your Garden* (National Geographic Society, USA, 1957)

Sir K. Clark, (Lord Clark) *Landscape into Art* (Murray, 1949); *Civilisation* (Murray, 1969)

D. Clifford, *A History of Garden Design* (Faber, 1962)

E. H. M. Cox, *Plant Hunting in China* (Collins, 1945, Oldbourne, 1961)

F. Crace, *A Catalogue of Maps Plans and Views of London* (1878)

Aytoun Ellis, *The Essence of Beauty: A History of Perfume and Cosmetics* (Secker & Warburg, 1960)

Nan Fairbrother, *The Nature of Landscape Design* (Architectural Press, 1974)

H. F. Felton, *British Floral Decoration* (Black, 1910)

H. R. Fletcher, *The Story of the Royal Horticultural Society 1804–1968* (Oxford University Press, 1969)

Maria L. Gothein, *A History of Garden Art*, trs. Mrs Archer-Hind (Dent, 1928)

M. Hadfield, *The Art of the Garden* (Studio Vista, 1965)

Duc d'Harcourt, *Des Jardins Heureux* (Laffont, 1969)

R. G. Hatton, *Handbook of Plant and Floral Ornament* (Dover, 1960)

T. G. W. Henslow, *Garden Architecture* (Dean & Son, 1926)

P. Hunt, ed. *The Book of Garden Ornament* (Dent, 1974)

G. A. Jellicoe, *Gardens of Europe* (Blackie, 1937); *Studies in Landscape Design* (Oxford University Press, 1960)

G. A. and S. Jellicoe, *Water: Use of Water in Landscape Architecture* (Black, 1971)

C. Millet-Robinett, *Le Jardinier des Fenêtres et des Appartements et des Petits Jardins* (Paris, 1860)

May, Morris, *William Morris: Artist, Writer, Socialist*, 2 vols (Blackwell 1926)

E. Newton, *The Meaning of Beauty* (Longmans, 1950); *The Romantic Rebellion* (Longmans, 1950)

F. L. Olmsted, Library of Congress Information Bulletin vol. 31 (1972) 221–2

H. Osborne, *Theory of Beauty* (Routledge, 1952)

Laura W. Roper, *FLO: A Biography of Frederick Law Olmsted* (Johns Hopkins, 1974)

Royal Horticultural Society Dictionary of Gardening (Oxford University Press, 1956)

F. Schnack, *Traum vom Paradies* (Rütten und Loening, 1962)

R. E. Shepherd, *History of the Rose* (Macmillan, NY, 1954)

A. Simmonds, *A Horticultural Who's Who* (Royal Horticultural Society, 1948)

P. A. Sorokin, *Social and Cultural Dynamics* vol. 1 (Allen & Unwin, 1937)

G. B. Tobey, *History of Landscape Architecture: Relationships of People to Environment* (Elsevier, 1973)

A. E. Weddle, ed. *Techniques of Landscape Architecture* (Heinemann, 1967)

H. Wölfflin, *Renaissance and Baroque*, trs. Kathrin Simon (Collins, 1964)

Viscountess Wolseley, *Gardens their Form and Design* (Arnold, 1919)

INDEX

Index